D1190349

Wolfson of Harvard

PORTRAIT OF A SCHOLAR

ALSO BY LEO W. SCHWARZ

The Best Fruits: Three Translations (1934)

The Jewish Caravan:
Great Stories of Twenty-Five Centuries (1935)

A Golden Treasury of Jewish Literature (1937)

Where Hope Lies (1940)

Memoirs of My People Through a Thousand Years (1943)

The Root and the Bough: The Epic of an Enduring People (1949)

The Redeemers: A Saga of the Years 1945–1952 (1953)

Feast of Leviathan:
Tales of Adventure, Faith and Love from Jewish Literature (1956)

Great Ages and Ideas of the Jewish People (1956)

Refugees in Germany Today (1957)

The Menorah Treasury: Harvest of Half a Century (1964)

PUBLISHER'S NOTE

Leo W. Schwarz completed this biography of Harry Austryn Wolfson in January 1965, when Wolfson was seventy-seven years old. The author had looked forward to early publication of his work, but it was not to be. Wolfson, the most reticent and private of men, was reluctant to see a biography of himself published during his lifetime. Schwarz, whose own association with Wolfson extended over a period of four decades, respected the wishes of his friend and mentor, although he continued to hope that Wolfson would reconsider. On December 1, 1967, after a lingering illness, Leo Schwarz died. Harry Wolfson was among the chief mourners. Seven years later, on September 19, 1974, Harry Wolfson died at the age of eighty-seven. Wolfson of Harvard by Leo W. Schwarz, now at last being published, stands as a memorial to both men.

Wolfson of Harvard
PORTRAIT OF A SCHOLAR

LEO W. SCHWARZ

With appreciations by Charles Angoff and Isadore Twersky
and an epilogue by Lewis H. Weinstein

Philadelphia   5738–1978
THE JEWISH PUBLICATION SOCIETY OF AMERICA

Designed by ADRIANNE ONDERDONK DUDDEN

Acknowledgment is gratefully extended to the Harvard University Press for permission to quote from Harry Austryn Wolfson's published books; to the American Jewish Committee for permission to reprint (in slightly different form) the essay by Isadore Twersky in American Jewish Year Book, Volume 76, "Harry Austryn Wolfson (1887–1974)," here titled "Harry Austryn Wolfson, in Appreciation"; and to the American Academy for Jewish Research for permission to reprint the bibliography of Wolfson's principal writings (1912 through January 1963), prepared by Leo W. Schwarz and published in Harry Austryn Wolfson Jubilee Volumes (1965).

Frontispiece: Professor Wolfson passes in front of the statue of John Harvard in the Harvard Yard, May 1956   *(Courtesy of Widener Library)*

Leo W. Schwarz, in Appreciation

CHARLES ANGOFF

Leo W. Schwarz belonged to a small group of American Jewish intellectuals who had an abiding feeling for the lovely echoes of individual words and combinations of them. He was an *homme des lettres* in the European sense. Some of his colleagues in that small group were Marvin Lowenthal, Maurice Samuel, Horace M. Kallen, and of course Harry Wolfson. Indeed, one may argue plausibly that perhaps the thing that first appealed to Leo Schwarz in Wolfson's writings was his style, the careful orchestration of the tonalities of words for the purpose not merely of sculpturing precise epistemological, historical, and metaphysical meanings but also releasing the innermost melodies in them. To Schwarz, as to Wolfson, words were to be heard as well as understood, and part of their meaning was the silent song that rose from them.

Among that group of Jewish intellectuals, it was Leo Schwarz and Harry Wolfson who had the fullest appreciation of what a miraculous thing Judaism is. Wolfson called himself a non-observant Orthodox Jew. Schwarz liked that phrase, but he was less interested in denominationalism. Time and again he declared simply that without Judaism and its multifarious emanations in every area of being, life would be intolerable, certainly much duller. Sometimes, in a playful mood, he would say that the real trouble with the world—"and the goyim are afraid to admit it"—is that "there are not enough Jews to go around."

Many people knew Leo Schwarz best as an anthologist, but few recognized the high quality of his anthologies, each of which was an act of literary creativity. He did not throw his collections together (alas, a common practice in the trade); he molded them, sought meanings in them, always wanted to make sure that they had the unity of a mirror held up to a people or an era. Of course, the people who were closest to him were the Jews, and every period in Jewish history had a special flavor to him—a peculiar combination of *tsores, naches,* and bewildered bedazzlement.

Leo Schwarz's knowledge of Jewish history—political, sociological, literary, theological, folkloric—was truly phenomenal. Moreover, that knowledge was never merely journalistic, or even scholarly in the narrow sense. It was a fund of information that his mind had distilled, bringing forth innumerable nuances, and that his heart had caressed tenderly, for to him Jewish history was a sacred thing. Here is what he says in his introduction to *The Jewish Caravan: Great Stories of Twenty-five Centuries:*

Out of the pages of the Talmud and the Midrash shines the word Torah. It is a comprehensive expression for a whole social organization based on the regimen of the law (Halakah). It implies a society in which institutions and social relations, not verbal ideals or theological dogmas, are the quintessence of religion, in which the pragmatic and the ideal, the desirable and the actual are completely fused. Every detail of life, every aspect of the workaday world, is the concern of Torah. The supreme values which it nurtured, as illustrated in the moral myth of the Agada, are justice, wisdom, independence, and goodness; the supreme personality is the *Talmid Hakam,* the practical scholar; the ultimate goal of human life is a messianic Here and Now.

Here Schwarz distills the essence of the Jewish *Weltanschauung* as seen through the Torah and the monumental commentaries on it. In another part of the same introduction—indeed, at the very beginning—he gives us a sharp portrait of Jewish peoplehood through the centuries of time:

This book is more than a compilation of stories; it is a collective portrait of the Jewish people, and reflects, insofar as literature is a reflection of life, the social development of this unique people over a period of almost three thousand years. It is also an effective demonstration of the fact that the Jews, despite a comparatively tragic history and matchless loyalty to religious tradition, have been many-sided human beings living in a real flesh-and-blood world, a world always tempered by the social and cultural climate of each age and of the people among whom they lived.

L'hayim, to life, was to Leo Schwarz the dominant philosophy of the Jews. Indeed, though the Holocaust was surely the worst disaster in all the annals of Jewry, Hitler's Final Solution did not destroy these people. As testament Schwarz collected reports of a number of first-hand experiences by Jews who somehow managed to evade the gas chambers and survive the concentration camps, bringing them together in a book entitled *The Root and the Bough: The Epic of an Enduring People.* But here, as in all his anthologies, he did more than bring articles or stories together. Even beyond plumbing "the sources of endurance that seemed to govern the lives of the remarkable survivors of the tornado of wrath," he made them parts of a philosophy, another confirmation of his conviction that the Jews are eternal. He saw in the tales of these survivors a "clue to the ultimate hidden resources in humankind . . . a grand testament to human valor and endurance." He perceived that the escapees did not merely endure—they maintained their shining humanity at all times: "They bear witness that hatred is human but its works are short-lived; that one can bear the yellow patch with pride, knowing that it is a badge of human dignity; that even in darkness, the heart and the mind contain the seed of all that is gracious and radiant."

Leo Schwarz's scholarship was deep and extensive, so that he was entirely at home in the most wide-ranging and intricate discussions of philosophical and religious matters. This is revealed in his book *Great Ages and Ideas of the Jewish People,* a compilation of papers on the whole sweep of Jewish history by Salo W. Baron, Gerson D. Cohen, Abraham S. Halkin, Yehezkel Kaufmann, Ralph Marcus, and Cecil Roth. One must also mention another valuable aspect of the book, his own "Introduction: Historians to the Reader." There he does nothing less than to present, *in petto,* a poetical-metaphysical overview of the essence of Jewishness and its place in world history. He begins by stating, in fresh terms, the uses of knowledge of the past. It "may not prevent the repetition of error or erase human fallibility. But ignorance of the past is a certain road to the reenactment of the tragedy and folly which glut the pages of man's past record. . . . History has made man but has also been made by him. That is our conviction. We deny the doctrine of historical inevitability. Nothing is inevitable until after it happens."

Jewish history, he continues, is like no other history, as the Jews are like no other people. First, the Jews "have an endurance record in the arena of history." Jewish history must be studied not in terms of decades or generations but in terms of centuries and millennia, and it is very much still in the process of being. Then there is "the geographical span." Unlike any other history, Jewish history is not rooted in any one place, as are even Chinese and Hindu histories. Jewish history "touches and is intermingled with almost every part of the earth." Political misfortune has dogged the Jews from Exile to Exile, but it has not materially stunted their growth. There is also the complexity of Jewish culture. The English people can be studied effectively in one language, the French can also be studied in one language, and so with other peoples, "but the man has not yet been born who could master all the languages and literatures in which the cultures of the Jewish people are expressed." All of which leads to this conclusion: "No other culture has produced a greater faith in the goodness of human nature and in the efficiency of human institutions."

Even in so brief a tribute to Leo Schwarz, one must say something about his stature as a literary critic and historian. While others may have written more in these areas, none has surpassed him in acuity of perception. His major virtues as critic-historian stand out in "Mutations of Jewish Values in Contemporary American Fiction," a paper he delivered in the series of B.G. Rudolph Lectures in Judaic Studies at Syracuse University in 1965. He was his own man, uninfluenced by shifting fashions in literary taste. He knew that often in literary history the immortals of one day become the footnotes of another. Thus, of the popular Broadway musical *Fiddler on the Roof*, he spoke with profound truth. While he admitted that it was "certainly an amusing, successful musical," he recognized that it nevertheless was "false to Sholom Aleichem's Tevye the Milkman." The Broadway Tevye more or less condones the marriage of his daughter to an apostate. "The original Tevye would never have blessed nor condoned the marriage, no matter how painful the decision." The Broadway Tevye "is a purveyor of wisecracks rather than sober wisdom. The original Tevye is a spiritual descendant of the Biblical Job, protesting life's injustice and affirming man's moral integrity—an affirmation enshrined in Jewish tradition and traceable to Mt. Sinai, as Tevye knows—and his bellowing Broadway counterpart does not."

Leo Schwarz was the conscience of the Jewish-American literary scene of his time. He was a most dedicated cultural *maggid*. His place in Jewish-American literary history is secure.

Harry Austryn Wolfson, in Appreciation
ISADORE TWERSKY

The public academic career and impressive scholarly achievement of Harry Austryn Wolfson, Nathan Littauer Professor of Hebrew Literature and Philosophy at Harvard since 1925, are relatively well known. However, in addition to this Wolfson *revelatus*—the straightforward success story of a talented, industrious young immigrant and his rise to scholarly fame—there is a Wolfson *absconditus* —a story, for the most part unknown, of a shy, introspective, sometimes melancholy, former yeshiva student and eminent professor, candidly assessing his own achievement in historical-typological terms, soberly pondering the state of Jewish scholarship and sensitively, sometimes agonizingly, reflecting upon contemporary history and the destiny of Judaism and the Jewish people.

Wolfson was clearly one of this century's great humanists, a prolific and creative scholar in the history of philosophy. The quintessential

Wolfson was pointedly described in the citation accompanying the honorary degree (Litt.D.) which Harvard conferred upon him in 1956: "From enormous knowledge he graciously illumines the major problems of religious philosophy and their relation to revealed truth."

In many respects he resembled an uncrowned and unwreathed scholar laureate, widely acclaimed and admired, respected and honored. Even a partial list of honorary degrees which were bestowed upon him, and organizational affiliations which he maintained, and awards which he received is a suggestive, although very formal, index of the esteem he enjoyed in this country. His honorary degrees came from the Jewish Institute of Religion (1935), the Jewish Theological Seminary of America (1937), Hebrew Union College (1945), Yeshiva University (1950), and Dropsie College (1952), as well as from the University of Chicago (1953), Harvard University (1956), Brandeis University (1958), Columbia University (1970), and Stonehill College (1973). He was a founding member, fellow, and past president of the American Academy for Jewish Research; honorary member of the American Jewish Historical Society; fellow of the Mediaeval Academy of America, American Philosophical Society, and American Academy of Arts and Sciences; and past president of the American Oriental Society. He received the American Council of Learned Societies award for distinguished scholarship in the humanities and the Kaplun prize, awarded by the Hebrew University, for distinguished research and scholarship in Judaica.

Wolfson's trail-blazing study and interpretation of the unpublished commentaries (originals as well as translations) of Averroes and his systematic integration of the study of Jewish and Islamic—and Christian—philosophy (in other words, the philosophical literature written in Hebrew, Arabic, and Latin) attracted wide, even international, attention. His arduous and meticulous investigation of Averroes, in a pre-Xerox, almost pre-technological academic age, without staff or secretariat, led to the preparation of a "Plan for the Publication of a *Corpus Commentariorum Averrois in Aristotelem*," which, in turn, goaded and guided other scholars—students and colleagues in the United States and abroad—to edit the long, intermediate, and short commentaries of Averroes, the great twelfth-century Islamic philosopher whom Wolfson dubbed "a naturalized Hebrew and Latin author." This Averroes project, an academic milestone, may be seen as an Archimedean fulcrum for the originality and scope of his work, and its resonance in the international scholarly community. It may be noted that soon after his death the Mediaeval Academy of America, which sponsored the project, despaired of continuing it without the editorial direction, scholarly supervision, and personal dedication of Wolfson.

Totally un-Aristotelian, shunning moderation in his extreme, all-consuming devotion to learning, Wolfson converted his life into an *itinerarium mentis,* an adventurous journey and colorful odyssey of the mind. He transcended all formal requirements and academic norms, pursuing his scholarly enterprises—truly his calling—with zest and love. Indeed, his prodigious scholarly output is comprehensible only if we see it emerging from a matrix of singleness of purpose, intensity of commitment, consistency of method, and clarity of destination. I may testify that to the very end of his life, when he was lean and wizened, his eyes dim and tired, his body racked with disease, he continued to be preoccupied with scholarly matters.

Wolfson's intense, unqualified commitment to scholarship—there was something fervent about it—bore ripe fruit. His many well-known and justly celebrated volumes are monuments to the pertinacity, perspicacity, and profundity of his life's work: *Crescas' Critique of Aristotle: Problems of Aristotle's* Physics *in Jewish and Arabic Philosophy* (1929); *The Philosophy of Spinoza: Unfolding the Latent Processes of His Reasoning,* 2 vols. (1934); *Philo: Foundations of Religious Philosophy in Judaism, Christianity, and Islam,* 2 vols. (1947); *The Philosophy of the Church Fathers: Faith, Trinity, Incarnation* (1956); *The Philosophy of the Kalam* (1976); and *Kalam Repercussions in Jewish Philosophy* (forthcoming). There are, in addition, three collections of papers and articles, some of which are full-fledged monographs of high quality and wide scope: *Religious Philosophy: A Group of Essays* (1961); *Studies in the History of Philosophy and Religion,* vol. 1 (1973), vol. 2 (1977). Each one of these large tomes in its own right could and would be a scholar's pride; each one would amply justify a lifetime devoted exclusively to Hellenistic, *or* to patristic, *or* to Islamic, *or* to scholastic, *or* to Jewish scholarship.

This is the real measure of Harry Wolfson, of his intellectual daring and imaginativeness; starting as a student of medieval Jewish philosophy (his first published article, growing out of an undergraduate paper written at Harvard for Santayana, was "Maimonides and Halevi: A Study in Typical Jewish Attitudes towards Greek Philosophy in the Middle Ages," *Jewish Quarterly Review*, n.s. 2 [1911], 297–337), he burst the recognized bounds and bonds of specialized, sometimes provincial scholarship and then patiently but vigorously brought within his purview the entire history of philosophy, moving with verve and aplomb and delicacy from pre-Socratics to neo-Kantians, from Greek atomists to American pragmatists. In the process he sought unsolved problems, unexplored sources, unperceived relationships, and uncharted lanes of philosophy. The challenge of understanding and unraveling the origin, structure, and diversity of philosophic systems fascinated and stimulated him; his sustained, simultaneously erudite and imaginative, response to the challenge produced the pageantry and vitality of his wide-ranging scholarship.

This achievement is notable for its happy marriage of philosophical perceptivity and philological precision, its unusual combination of powers of dissection and integration, its fastidious argumentation and felicitous formulation. This tireless scholar, cloistered most of his life in Widener Library, was able to combine unflagging attention to detail—stylistic, structural, or substantive—with powerful skills of original synthesis. While elucidating difficult texts and knotty passages in Averroes or Gersonides, Aquinas or Falaquera, Pico della Mirandola or Abarbanel, he also clearly formulated a new anti-Hegelian scheme for the periodization of the history of philosophy—in which Jewish philosophy from Philo to Spinoza was central —and expounded, more allusively, a philosophy of the history of philosophy—in which religious thought played a major role. Both of these are reflected in the subtitle of his study on Philo: "Foundations of Religious Philosophy in Judaism, Christianity, and Islam." Wolfson depicts Philo as the founder of a new philosophic trend which was continued not only by his immediate chronological successors, the Church Fathers, but also by his indirect disciples, the Muslim, Jewish, and Christian medieval philosophers until the time of Spinoza. The distinctive-innovative feature of Philonic teachings— and that which was to be a dominant influence, latent or visible, indirect or direct, in European philosophic thought for seventeen centuries—was a well-integrated interpretation of Scripture in terms of philosophy and a balanced critique (and, concomitantly, radical revision) of philosophy in light of scriptural principles of belief. It is this *type* of religious philosophy which was new and influential— and which was so fully and sympathetically and imaginatively re-structured by Professor Wolfson.

This central conception concerning the history of philosophy— which positioned Philo, the first-century Jew of Alexandria, and Spinoza, the seventeenth-century Jew of Amsterdam, as the pivots of "medieval" philosophy—was very dear to him; it was, in many respects, the core and catalyst of his life's work. The fact that this conceptual scheme of periodization did not become widely influential was consequently a major disappointment for him.

Furthermore, while developing and sustaining his conception of the history of philosophy, he also provided an unequivocally affirmative answer to the question whether or not there is such a creature as Jewish philosophy, a question which had been answered negatively by many serious scholars. It was Wolfson's contention that not only is there such an intellectual entity as Jewish philosophy but that it is the very core, the essence, of all religious philosophy for seventeen centuries—and indeed, in residual form or unacknowledged guise, down to our own time.

The literary quality of his work, his lucidity of style and precision of expression, should also be underscored. He was as concerned with form as with content. The same patience and exhaustiveness which characterized his approach to research determined his style, which became an integral, not merely ornamental, part of his work. The presentation had to conform with the analysis. He would not consciously settle for "good enough" or "second best," regardless of the requisite expenditure of time and energy. A reader need only turn to one of the collections of Wolfson's essays in order to encounter directly the elegance of style, flow of wit, and effusion of charm; the vigorous prologue, the animated epilogue, the exhilarating character- ization, the intricately-textured and carefully-cadenced generaliza- tion, and the resonant allusion provide a light, soothing ambiance for his philosophic explorations. The fusion of these aspects is seen very clearly in the volume on Crescas, where felicitous translation, exhaustive explication, and enticing conceptualization are com- bined.

The methodological foundation for this literary-philosophic and historiographical achievement is a mode of minute textual-philologi- cal study which Wolfson labeled the "hypothetico-deductive method" or the method of conjecture and verification, but which was in essence the traditional method of studying talmudic texts. Wolfson applied it purely and consistently, free of sociological gen- eralizations, metahistorical hypotheses, and other popular forms of conjecture. He was particularly wary of sociological explanations which often claimed to supplant rather than supplement historical- philological analysis and then ended up as smokescreens for lack of precision. His conjecture was philological, which he always tried to verify by adducing direct, or at least indirect, textual evidence; he developed an interpretation and then proceeded to anchor it textu- ally; he traced abstract problems through their terminological foot- prints, guided all along, to be sure, by his own conception of the history of philosophy, its major trends and traits. There was, in short, constant interplay between the *a priori*-conceptual and the empiri- cal-textual. While his critics sometimes found him to be too specula- tive in his unfolding of latent processes of philosophic reasoning, ready to build upon soaring conjecture without sufficient, self-evi- dent textual verification (his lucid expositions of complex problems and ingenious interpretations of intractable texts are punctuated by such phrases as "it may be reasonably assumed," "from all this we may gather," "his [Ghazali's] explanation may be taken to reflect Aristotle's . . . ," etc.)—and it is precisely the daring of his method which contributes both to the solidity as well as the vulnerability of his achievement—he could only retort that the alternative was deadly, stultifying, or prosaic. The following conclusion of an article —a rejoinder to some critical comments on his explication of "four Arabic terms"—is typical: "But all this is based, of course, only upon circumstantial evidence; we have no direct testimony of either al-Kindi or Israeli that this is exactly how their minds worked; bread-and-butter scholarship may, therefore, brush it all aside and dismiss it as unconvincing." His own erudition and ingenuity (rich but not extravagant) prevented him from being prosaic or timid.

While there is not much material connection between talmudic study and philosophic research—and Wolfson was totally engrossed in the latter—he did try to sustain and benefit from a methodological affinity between them, and in many respects this affinity—natural or contrived, real or imaginary—is the cornerstone of his life. Harry Austryn Wolfson was born November 2, 1887, in Ostrin, Lithuania, and died on September 19, 1974 (4 Tishri, 5735), in Cambridge, Massachusetts. His life—its heterogeneity and creativity as well as its tensions and increasing loneliness of his later years—is symbolized by his odyssey from Ostrin through Grodno, Slonim, Bialystok, Kovno, Slobodka, and Vilna, a roster of place names which throbs with Jewish history and learning, joy and suffering, to Cambridge. Upon his arrival with his family in New York (September 1903) he continued his Jewish studies and shortly thereafter (1905) settled in Scranton, Pennsylvania, where, at the age of eighteen, he enrolled in the Central High School and graduated three years later, supporting himself during this period by part-time Hebrew teaching. A $250 scholarship, awarded on the basis of competitive exams, enabled him to come to Harvard, from which he received his B.A. (1911) and Ph.D. (1915) with two years in Europe as a Sheldon Traveling Fellow; typically enough, he spent most of this time working independently in the great libraries of London, Paris, Berlin, and Munich, rather than in the lecture hall or seminar room. In 1915 he began teaching at Harvard, and, in 1925, after a series of term appointments during which he was also for a few years part-time professor of Jewish history at the recently established Jewish Institute of Religion, he became the first Littauer Professor of Hebrew Literature and Jewish Philosophy.

This student of Santayana—Wolfson came to Harvard toward the end of the university's so-called golden age in philosophy (Josiah Royce, William James, George Santayana)—had attended the last *musar* lecture* delivered by the famous Rabbi Yitzhak (Itzele) Blazer at the yeshiva of Slobodka prior to his becoming the rabbi of Petersburg. We have here in this juxtaposition an effective symbol of the two worlds which constituted Professor Wolfson's universe. His early Lithuanian years left their mark on all the later decades at Harvard. All indications suggest that he was a serious undergraduate, hard-working doctoral student, and imaginative junior faculty member, overflowing with remembrances of things past (particularly his formal educational experiences supplemented by his extracurricular Haskalah reading) and hopes for things future (particularly a career as a freelance Hebrew writer and novelist, a goal he gradually abandoned in favor of academic scholarship). Even in his later years, these experiences continued to reverberate.

The intense education of Harry Wolfson and his Americanization notwithstanding, he could never be singled out as the typical Harvard scholar, even though he spent over sixty-five years of his life at Harvard and became not only one of Harvard's most illustrious but also one of its most loyal and loving sons. There was something different about him—not only because of the accent which stayed with him throughout his life even after he became an eloquent master of English prose. He was reminiscent of an old-fashioned *gaon* transposed into a secular university setting, studying day and night, resisting presumptive attractions and distractions with a tenacity which sometimes seemed awkward and antisocial. Bialik's description of the *matmid*, the paradigm of an assiduous scholar, the classical student of Jewish lore, comes to mind:

> A *matmid*, in his prison-house
> A prisoner, self-guarded, self condemned,
> Self-sacrificed to the study of the Law . . .
>
> Earth and her fullness are concentrated here,
> A thousand suns blaze in the gloomy corner.
> Like vehement coals, his eyes give answering fire
> While, lore-impassioned, back and forth he sways . . .

*A discourse combining homiletics, exegesis, and theology, geared to stimulating or sustaining the individual's quest for ethical perfection.

Day after day firm stands the sentinel
From noon to night, from darkness to darkness.

All you have to do is remove the swaying posture, change the subject matter, and substitute one of the studies in massive Widener Library for the gloomy corner of the modest *beth midrash*—both prison houses—and you have the scenario for Wolfson's scholarly career. A dramatic change, and yet . . . !

The impact and imprint are manifest in many scholarly, as well as personal, ways.

In 1921, at the dawn of his scholarly career, he penned the following lines:

Once, in a great library, I was walking through the narrow aisles between long rows of book-shelves stocked with the works of the church writers. Every great thinker of the church whose teachings helped to mold Christian thought and tradition was represented there by his writings. There were the old Church Fathers, both those who wrote in Greek and those who wrote in Latin; there also were Augustine the saint and Abelard the erratic, the great Albertus and Thomas, he of Aquino. Hundreds upon hundreds of volumes, the choicest products of the printer's art of Venice, Basel, Leipzig, Paris, and Rome, bound in pigskin and in morocco leather, with gilded back and bronzed corners, all were gathered together, standing there in the open shelves, offering themselves for use and for study. And looking at that wealth of magnificent volumes, I thought of those shabby tomes which incarnate the spirit of Saadia, Halevi and Maimonides, of those unpublished works of Gersonides, Narboni and Shem-tobs, scattered all over the world and rotting in the holds of libraries; and I was overcome by that feeling of sadness and sorrow which to our forefathers was ever present throughout their exiled life amid the foreign splendor of European cities, a feeling so well expressed in the touching prayer:

"Lord, I remember, and am sore amazed
To see each city standing in her state,
And God's city to low grave razed."

I see in these words more than just the stirrings of a scholarly consciousness. His citing the words of Amittai ben Shephatiah's penitential hymn—which is recited during the Ten Days of Repentance and repeated at the Ne'ilah service concluding the prayers of the Day of Atonement—is not, in my opinion, merely an academic secularization of a religious motif, but rises from deep emotional wellsprings. His knowledge of this poem came from the prayer book and not from an anthology of Hebrew poetry. His abiding appreciation of traditional Judaism was a formative and pervasive—and sometimes enigmatic and unsettling—influence.

As first incumbent of the first chair in an American university completely devoted to Jewish studies, Wolfson played an important role in the institutionalization and professionalization of Jewish studies and their spread across the American campus. Actually Wolfson's life work at Harvard marks the emergence of Judaica in great universities as a respectable, self-sufficient discipline with its own integrity, autonomy, and comprehensiveness. In the past—and that means up to very recent times—the study of Judaica was ancillary, secondary, fragmentary, or derivative. Jewish studies were sometimes referred to as service departments whose task was to help illumine an obscurity in Tacitus or Posidonius, a midrash in Jerome, a Hebrew allusion in Dante, or an exegetical turn in Nicholas of Lyra, a kabbalistic topos in Pico or a Jewish notion in Ibn Khaldun, a rabbinic metaphor in Milton, a talmudic citation in John Selden, a fact in the biography of Walter Rathenau or Emile Durkheim or Hans Kelsen, a symbol in Franz Kafka, or even a Yiddishism in the memoirs of Bernard Berenson. The establishment of the Littauer chair at Harvard for Harry Wolfson gave Judaica its own station on the frontiers of knowledge and pursuit of truth, and began to redress the lopsidedness or imbalance of quasi-Jewish studies.

Wolfson's impact was great not only because of institutional leverage, but also because of the broad range of his own creative scholarship as well as the even wider range of his literary interests. Personal, professional, and institutional preeminence—happily joined, at some point, by growing seniority and increasing venerability—carved out a central niche for Harry Wolfson in the development of Jewish scholarship in America. He was, really, in his own humble, retiring way, a one-man scholarly establishment, commodious and capacious, a respected symbol of the entire range of twentieth-century Jewish scholarship, a senior scholar-statesman in Judaica, whose learning or intuition made his opinions relevant. Cuneiformists and Americanists, medievalists and modernists, students of belles-lettres as well as philosophy frequented his Widener study, requesting and receiving advice and encouragement. His work provided a general paradigm of thoroughness and originality, his personal involvement and interest in many scholarly fields encouraged scholars to devote their energies to them, and his generally sage and subtle (sometimes apparently innocent) comments on virtually all facets of Jewish learning led different individuals and organizations to seek his support or participation. He revealed great understanding and appreciation of fields in which he was not, but would have liked to be, involved. Rabbinic scholarship in the broadest sense was clearly the most important of these fields, one which attracted him irresistibly and which he respected unboundedly. His acknowledgement of the centrality of talmudic learning in Judaism and Jewish scholarship never wavered, and his respect for talmudists—traditional *talmide hakhamim* or modern talmudic scholars—was steadfast. Early in his career he wrote—and repeated this sentiment throughout his life—that "the Talmud with its literature is the most promising field of study, the most fertile field of original research and investigation." If he had had his way, he would have made a traditional talmudic education a firm prerequisite for any area of Jewish scholarly expertise; he was uncomfortable with academic upstarts and "nouveaux riches" who lacked such Jewish education and pretended to be authorities in Judaica.

All his commitment to detached, humanistic scholarship, his personal shyness, and his rigid sense of discipline notwithstanding, Wolfson was not indifferent to or unconcerned with contemporary realities. He shied away from discussing *his* epistemology and ontology, he did not even formulate his "philosophy of life." He was not a "public" figure in the conventional sense; he did not address large popular gatherings or plenary sessions of philanthropic or cultural organizations and never issued pronouncements concerning the burning issues of the day. Perhaps he was afraid of compromising

—even obliquely—his scholarly objectivity. Nevertheless, his writing is seasoned with relevance and insight, all the more forceful and attractive by virtue of its subtlety and unobstrusiveness, and studded with critical commentary on the contemporary scene. He remained a child of his times: he lived with the complexities, ambiguities, continuities, and discontinuities that characterize a *matmid-maskil* who remained rooted in, and loyal to, his past, who refused to join the ranks of the alienated intellectuals (whom he described so poignantly at the beginning of his study on Philo). The problems of tradition and modernity, faith and enlightenment, religious observance and acculturation, evoked concerned, unsettling, and often paradoxical or apparently inconsistent responses from him. He was particularly agitated by much of the intentional obfuscation or unintentional ignorance which characterized discussion of religious philosophy. Just as he approached those addicted to fashionable jargon or scholarly faddishness with benign but trenchant criticism, he looked with wry humor and suspicion at many aspects of modern Jewish life. He approached the presumptive modernity of certain nineteenth- and twentieth-century philosophers with scholarly reserve and critical insight. He was guided by the discipline of medieval Jewish philosophy; modern distortions or tendentious interpretations of classical Jewish thought were, therefore, distasteful to him.

One could easily compile a collection of Wolfsonian observations —culled from his writings, particularly his occasional pieces and the early articles in the *Menorah Journal,* and the memories of friends and colleagues—which would illustrate his concern with, and attitude to, such specific issues as the relationship of Christianity to Judaism (as broached, for example, by Ahad Ha-am) and Jewish-Christian relations, ecumenicism and goodwill ("bury the hatchet, not the differences"), study of Judaism and the Western humanistic tradition, varieties of scholarship (good and bad), renaissance of Hebrew literature and formation of modern Hebrew style, the danger of Yiddishism and the promise of Hebraism, optimistic and pessimistic appraisals of the prospects for Jewish survival in face of assimilation, Zionism and the varieties of anti-Zionism, religious reform and cultural enlightenment. He tended to view such problems and phenomena from a historical perspective and to form a judgment about them in light of traditional patterns and conceptions.

While many writers were apparently agitated about the tyranny of the past and its stultifying effects—i.e., varieties of traditionalism —Wolfson, despite his settling into an academic routine which appeared to be almost clinically, antiseptically detached from contemporary contingencies and time-bound concerns, was worried about the tyranny of the present—i.e., varieties of conformism, amorphous existentialism, and facile acculturation. He was an unrelenting critic of the "disintegrated consciousness" of modern Judaism. The following words, first published in 1925 and frequently reprinted (most recently in a Hebrew translation as well) are revealing:

Throughout the history of religious controversies between Christians and Jews in the Middle Ages, Christianity was on the defensive. The Christians considered themselves called upon to prove the claims they made on behalf of Jesus by endeavoring to show that the vague prophetic promises were all fulfilled in Christ. The Jews had no counterclaims to make; they simply refused to be impressed. As the historical custodians of the Bible texts as well as of its manifold interpretations, the Jews were rather amazed and at times even amused by the confidence with which the erstwhile heathen interpreted at their own pleasure the mistaken Scriptures quoted from the Vulgate. This attitude of aloofness and incredulity was sufficient to enrage even saints among Christians, for it gave them an uneasiness of feeling, deepening into fear and doubt and a general sense of discomfort, which explains much of the Christian intolerance of the Jews. The great victories achieved by Christianity, its conquest of many youthful barbarian races and its destruction of many effete civilizations—all this did not compensate its adherents for their failure to win over the handful of survivors of the race that had witnessed the birth of Christianity. And so the Jews were dragged to churches and to royal courts to listen to sermons and to partake in disputations in order to be impressed and become convinced.

Today many of us Jews have taken the burden of proof upon ourselves. A century of infiltration of Christian ideas into our life through all the agencies of education has robbed many of us of our essential Jewish character, of our distinctive Jewish philosophy of life, and has left us Jews only in appearance, in occupation, and in the semblance of an external social coherence. In everything that guides our life and determines our view thereof, we have become Christianized.

We may note finally that American Jewish history was also of special interest to Harry Wolfson. Convinced that a historiography of the Jewish experience in America built on sociological platitudes, general political-economic tendencies, impersonal communal and institutional developments, or simplified cultural traits could not be too enlightening, he would urge writers in this field to elaborate case histories of prominent and not so prominent families, to search for the pre-modern and pre-American roots of this experience, to recognize the uniqueness of American Jewish history and yet to relate it to the totality of Jewish history. His articles in the *Menorah Journal* reveal a witty, poignant, and constructive critic of American Judaism. His statement (1922), restrained but firm, concerning the proposed quota for Jewish students at Harvard illustrates how he would invariably—whether addressing himself to Jews or to non-Jews—relate contemporary situations to historical perceptions. All the problems—challenges and frustrations—of modernity could be found in the American Jewish experience. Particularly noteworthy in this context are the notes and observations published under the title "Pomegranates" (*Menorah Journal,* 4 [1918], pp. 16 ff.; 162 ff.). For example:

Today the problem which Judaism has to contend with is indifference. Once it was error. To fight error, be that error superstition or heresy—for superstition is the heresy of the ignorant and heresy is nothing more than the superstition of the educated—implies a certain courage and conviction. Once Judaism had both. It knew its own mind and spoke it. Judaism stood defined, in terms clear and unmistakable, in a cumulative written tradition. Not that the living tradition, the life and institutions of the people, has ever been discounted as a source from which an understanding of Judaism could be derived, but the living tradition was significant only insofar as it had been continuous, pure and unadulterated, guided and controlled by eternal immutable principles. Judaism was then something objectively real and tangible from which it was conceived possible that the entire people could be led astray, and toward which, in that case, it was the duty of those entrusted with its care to lead it back. The nomistic character of Judaism, whatever else it may have meant, surely meant that Judaism was not a mere will-o'-the-wisp. Today a perverted sense of democracy and of a biological nationalism has given rise to a doctrine of the religion of the people corresponding to the old autocratic doctrine of the religion of the king. Judaism is now the changing mood of the Jews. It is no longer an inheritance; it is a set of inherited characteristics. It is no longer a discipline; it is a day-dream. . . . We cannot take Jewish life of today as the source of Judaism, for we are all now in a state of apostasy both in a religious and in a secular cultural sense. To remain as Jews it is not sufficient for us to continue to be what we are, for we are not what we should be. Jewish life of today is indeed peculiar, but it is not peculiarly Jewish.

"Escaping Judaism" (ibid., 7 [1921], pp. 71 ff.), a clever and caustic indictment of that Judaism which "suffers from an excessive craving for modernity, formality, and respectability" and deludes itself into thinking that religion without law is possible, is still timely and refreshing.

Harry Wolfson was a great, laconic, and lonely person; his legacy is rich, colorful, and provocative.

Contents

Author's Preface

The life of Harry Austryn Wolfson is a superlative illustration of the excitements of scholarship. He is revered in the republic of letters, and this veneration invariably takes the form of praise for his learned works. They are his chief monument. But behind the works is a man of rare talent and fascinating personality who is eminently worth examining. Though one cannot escape seeing the events of another man's life through the distorting haze of time, or entirely prevent one's own ego from affecting the view of it, I want to try to reveal something of Wolfson's life and work.

It was at Fort Lee, Virginia, in 1943, while I was serving as a drill corporal, that this portrait had its origin. Perhaps because I was trying to write the introduction to a collection of autobiographies between the "hut-hut" of the drill field and the trivialities of barrack banter, my mind involuntarily turned back to the life and people I had known and loved at Harvard in the twenties: seigneurial President Abbott Lowell and his gifted sister Amy; genial Alfred North Whitehead throwing his philosophic spell over the former domain of William James and George Santayana; Edward Kennard Rand the magnifico, benignly reigning over the Widener Library; the eight Harvard Poets and Baker's "47" Workshop; inimitable "Copey" (Charles Townsend Copeland) reading magnificently to packed lecture halls; the literary spellbinders Bliss Perry and John Livingston Lowes; and the stalwart apostle of an austere kind of humanism, Irving Babbitt.

Most vivid to me, however, were the masters of an autonomous province stretching along a few hundred yards of a "private way" known as Divinity Avenue. The short street and its civilization were *terra incognita* to the visitors who flocked through it to see the glass specimens at the Peabody Museum and even to the denizens of the Germanic Museum and the University Press, which though physically a part of Divinity Avenue were culturally remote from it. While the small population of this province busied itself in only three buildings—the Semitic Museum, Divinity Hall, and the Andover Theological School—their interests encompassed the ancient and modern Near East, the Orient, and the culture of forty centuries. The spirits of Crawford Howell Toy and David Gordon Lyon still hovered over the realm, but the philosopher-king was George Foot Moore, the historian of religion, probably the greatest American scholar of his time. There was also the Egyptologist George Reisner (who returned from Egypt to Divinity Avenue once in five years), short, chunky, and as gritty as the stone of the Sphinx whose mystery he solved. Among Moore's younger colleagues were Robert H. Pfeiffer, later to become outstanding in the biblical field, and Harry A. Wolfson, for whom the Nathan Littauer Chair in Hebrew Literature and Philosophy had recently been established.

Harry Wolfson represented the pinnacle of Harvard scholarship in the humanities. With the exception of two years abroad as a Sheldon Fellow prior to the outbreak of World War I and brief service in the U.S. Army in 1918–19, he lived at Harvard continuously for more than half a century. During those years no Harvard scholar and teacher had been more influential or more beloved. His series of books on philosophic systems from Plato to Spinoza considered the history of religious and philosophic thought in the West in a fresh light.

The story of Wolfson's pursuit of knowledge is full of adventure. "There is sleuthing in scholarship as there is in crime," he wrote, "and it is as full of mystery, danger, intrigue, suspense, and thrills —if only the story were told." It is that story that I have tried to tell in this book. And because the man is as compelling as his work and his personality as many-faceted, I also have attempted to tell the human side of the story. Of course, the principal interest in a pure scholar lies, as Plato suggested, in themes rather than persons. It is primarily his work that best reflects his manner of life and is his best interpreter. Hence I have employed, whenever possible, Wolfson's own words.

Being an original and a "character," Wolfson is the subject of a considerable body of anecdotes. With the exception of one story that is labeled apocryphal, I have used only those for which I could find substantiation. In addition, I have avoided exegesis of his published works; this is subject matter for another book. But if his works are in the main technical, they are also examples of literary craftsmanship; thus I have here and there treated them as such and shown how a man who arrived in the United States as an immigrant boy of sixteen became a master of English prose.

I have tried to study everything written by and about Wolfson. For permission to check records, archives, and correspondence I am indebted to many institutions, particularly Harvard University, the Houghton and Widener Archives, the Central High School of Scranton, Pennsylvania, the Mediaeval Academy of America, the Harvard Divinity School, the Adjutant General's Office of the Army of the United States, the U.S. Department of State, the Archives of the Hebrew University of Jerusalem, the Jewish Theological Seminary of America, the Menorah Association of New York City, and the American Jewish Archives of Cincinnati, Ohio.

I have known Harry Wolfson since I was his student in the twenties, and I have enjoyed his friendship since then. Thus my conversations with him about his work and problems over the years are the basis of much of the narrative. But I am indebted for a good deal of information to members of his family, other former students, his colleagues, and a number of his close friends, none of whom are blameworthy for the use I have made of their information. I should like to record my gratitude for help especially to the following: to Professors Milton V. Anastos, Salo W. Baron, Henry J. Cadbury, Gerson D. Cohen, Lewis S. Feuer, Florence B. Freedman, Eli Ginzberg, Bernard Gould, Horace M. Kallen, Richard P. McKeon, Samuel Eliot Morison, Sayyed Hosein Nasr, Abraham A. Neuman, Arthur Darby Nock, Robert H. Pfeiffer, Leah M. Rich, Morton Smith, Shalom Spiegel, Isadore Twersky; and to Mrs. Carl J. Austrian, Dr. Abraham Berger, McGeorge Bundy, Mrs. Louis Ginzberg, William Gresser, Esq., Dr. Gilbert Klaperman, Dr. Samuel Kurland, Dr. David M. Levy, Anthony Lewis, Marvin Lowenthal, Mrs. Ralph Marcus, Mr. and Mrs. Stuart Marks, Dr. Lawrence Marwick, Mrs. Pearson Neaman, Bernard C. Richards, Dr. Harry A. Savitz, Harry Starr, Esq., Mrs. Leonard Stein, Dr. Norman Survis, Father Michael Urbanowich, Mrs. Benjamin Wolman; and to several persons who prefer to remain anonymous.

For taking the trouble to read the manuscript and give his help and advice, I am grateful to Dr. Leo Roberts, of Cambridge, Massachusetts. His criticism and suggestions were invaluable. Finally, I wish to express my sincere thanks to Dr. Judah Shapiro, Director of the National Foundation of Jewish Culture, and to the Morris L. Shaver Foundation of Detroit, Michigan, for making possible the completion of the book.

Leo W. Schwarz

New York City
January 1965

Wolfson of Harvard
PORTRAIT OF A SCHOLAR

1
The Road to Cambridge

Each one of us has been the Adam of his own soul.

Apocalypse of Baruch

On the afternoon of September 14, 1926, Cambridge was astir. Hundreds of philosophers from many lands had assembled for the first time since World War I and were streaming toward Standish Hall, a modern freshman dormitory facing the Charles River. The air had a winelike, bracing quality, and the autumn sun glistened on the brown and yellow leaves of the trees. Among those crossing Harvard Yard in the direction of the conclave was the spare, short, and energetic figure of Harry A. Wolfson. Having been promoted to a full professorship a year earlier, Wolfson was now almost as much a part of the scene as one of the ancient elms. And on this day he was to make his debut with the renowned philosophic savants of the world at the Sixth International Congress of Philosophy. He had twenty minutes to discuss the theories of the origin of matter in medieval philosophy in a session with such scholars as Étienne Gilson of the Sorbonne and Tjitze de Boer of Amsterdam. If he was at all nervous it was not visible in his face or gait as he walked rapidly over the familiar ground and passed under the Eliot Gate and its legend, "Enter to Grow in Wisdom"—a legend that had impressed him ever since he was an undergraduate. As he took his place at the long table in the Common Room of Standish Hall, he placed the typescript of seven pages on the table in front of him.

The method chosen by Wolfson for the presentation of his subject was analytical rather than purely historical. From the first short paragraph, in which he described the views held by medieval Jewish philosophers regarding the origin of matter, the audience, philosophers and laymen alike, was captivated by his mastery of thought and language. Like a good dramatist, he began *in medias res* and in a single sentence set the theme in perspective: "Of these three views, the first forestalled the problem, the second was merely an evasion of the problem, and the third, emanation, while meant to be a solution of the problem, really became a problem in itself." The effect of this sentence, though spoken without emphasis, was noticeable in a slight movement forward among those in the packed room. Then, in sentences equally clear and incisive, the speaker dissected and reformulated each of the hypotheses with almost mathematical precision. The analysis proceeded on two planes: on the one hand, the specific topic was related to its roots in Greek, Judeo-Christian, and Arab thought and to its consequences in European philosophy; and, on the other hand, the medieval solutions were shown to be analogous to modern philosophic and scientific solutions to the problem of the origin of life. He painted a miniature of a vast theme on a single canvas, a theme ranging from the ancient Platonists to the modern Vitalists. A feat of the sort Wolfson was performing could be achieved only by one possessed of both magisterial knowledge and great artistry. And this was borne out in the discussion following the reading of the paper. His replies to questions, never longer than a minute or two, were meaty, crisp, witty. When Professor de Boer was called upon to make the final comment, he said simply, "I think the subject has been exhausted."

Wolfson blushed within; the praise of his peers brought him pleasure, for his success had been neither quickly nor cheaply won. If his paper was a promise of things to come, it was also a clue to the struggles of the past. A photograph of him in a Boston newspaper, illustrating the report on that conference—and describing Whitehead and Wolfson as the stars—shows a strong, sensitive, pallid face and an abundance of dark, thick hair, and it reveals an intense, intellectual quality; the wise, humorous sparkle in his eyes is obscured by thick horn-rimmed spectacles. Nor can one detect the faint sallow gleam of his skin which, like the ancient books and parchments and their musty repositories where he spent so much of his life, gives a hint of indefatigable intellectual labor.

No more than a hint, however; like the periscope of a submarine, the Wolfson at Standish Hall in 1926 was an indicator of something vast and complex beneath the surface. He was an affectionate, loyal son and brother, but from his boyhood he lived in his own world. Circumstance and endowment forced him to give the whole of himself to learning, and temperament built around him a wall of reserve. The inner discipline characteristic of his adult life was molded in his boyhood years; the storms of emotion that rage in all children were sublimated in the steady conquest of tome after tome, which produced an inner strength that made him a tree deeply rooted, one that neither wind nor storm can wrench from its place. His writings, except for a few excursions into contemporary problems in his youth, sedulously avoid any direct personal reference. From them one can build a picture of an austere intellectual, without private joys or sorrows. Yet for all this he was a man of affection and charm. These facets of his personality revealed themselves on rare occasions—when in the company of a trusted friend he sometimes aired his frustrations, when among his colleagues he laughed and joked, or when he acted as confidant and advisor to his students. These occasions are revelatory, to be sure, and they provide some of the personal elements so elusive in his writings. But to discover more about him we need to retrace the road he traversed, the road that brought him from an obscure village in Eastern Europe to the ivy halls of Cambridge.

The beginnings are in a land swept by the Baltic winds, in a community where intellect and indigence were the staples of existence. In the autumn of 1887—the year that Bernard Berenson, originally also from Lithuania, was graduated from Harvard College—Harry Wolfson was born in Ostrin, a quiet town of about two thousand situated near the border of White Russia and Poland. The town was established in the fifteenth century by Casimir IV, duke of Lithuania and king of Poland, in order to exploit the thick forests of the region. In the late nineteenth century a large part of the forest around Ostrin belonged to the Polish patriot, Prince Drutski Lubetski. Near the center of the town flowed the Ostrinka River; along the bank of a fork of the river was a windmill that was linked to the town by a quaint wooden bridge. A little rural post office near the marketplace was open only three times a week. There was no doctor in the town; one had to travel about 20 miles to the town of Stuchin for medical help. The only means of travel was by horse-drawn wagon: one left daily in the afternoon for Grodno, carrying mainly passengers the 32 miles, and returned to Ostrin the following morning; another wagoner drove 120 miles to Vilna once a week to transport beer, household accessories, and farm implements. The population was about equally divided between Christians and Jews; there was also a sprinkling of Muslim Tartar families.

Wolfson's first published piece, written when he was a high-school student, was a series of sketches of his native place, which opens with the following picture of the town and its inhabitants.

Ostrin is a small town, surrounded by thick forests. In its center is a wide, sandy marketplace which contains the town well. On one side of the marketplace stands the white church building encircled by a stone fence; on the other side stands the black, wooden synagogue with its trebled roof, which is never closed. A number of narrow, unpaved streets, commencing at the marketplace, run in curved lines for about half a mile on each side. The houses around the market and those near it are inhabited by Jews, who are the merchants, the mechanics, and the professional men of the community. These are hewed log houses built at a distance of some yards from each other. Their roofs are shingled, their windows high, and in some cases the frames painted red and white. At the extremities of each street the moujiks live in their humble thatched dwelling places, each of them having in its front a well, a pen, some trees, and a dog lying in wait.

The sketches portray an idyllic rural community knitted together like a single family. The atmosphere was traditionally religious, the church and synagogue being spiritually as well as geographically the homes of the people. Catholic peasants with their products and shepherds trailing their flocks mixed amiably with the Jewish tradesmen on weekdays; business was conducted mainly as barter. Both respected their own Sabbaths; gravely and sedately the folk exchanged greetings on the public square. Life appears to have been free of serious group conflict. The friendliness between the religious groups was due in part to the peasants' pride in their tradition of independence; their forebears had never been serfs but always had been subjects of the king.

Wolfson's family occupied a wooden frame house on the marketplace, facing the entrance to the Orthodox church. It was an excellent vantage point for observing the life of the town, and hardly anything escaped the boy's eyes. During the winter the priests from the church would often drop in at the Wolfson home after mass to warm themselves at the fire and sip glasses of hot tea. On the other side of the marketplace lived his cousins, the Savitsky family, who occupied the only two-story house. It was built of brick and the street floor was used for a *krom*, a hardware and general store. Nearby were the offices of the police and of the lumber companies which engaged in cutting and carting logs from the surrounding wolf-haunted forests.

Wolfson was the second child and oldest son of a family of seven. A daughter, Celia, was age three at the time of his birth. Subsequently there were born in succession, at intervals of a year or two, Mamie, Hyman, Bessie, Morris, and Nathaniel. As a teacher of Russian and Hebrew—and there were no public schools—his father had to scramble for a bare living. Max Wolfson was a dignified, courteous, wisely humorous man who shared with his wife Sarah immense pride in the intellectual prowess that his first-born son began to show very early. The boy performed phenomenally in his biblical and talmudic studies. He had already developed the mental sharpness—the meaning of the root word of Ostrin is "sharp"—which was a characteristic trait of the Lithuanian Jews.

The *starosta* (lay elder) of the church frequently visited the Wolfson house. On Sundays, after mass, he made a ritual of having several glasses of tea there and talking to young Harry. Sometimes, while he was sipping his tea, Harry would sit on a small stool near the stove and relate biblical stories to him. Using the local dialect of Byelorussian, he embellished the biblical text with talmudic legends that he had heard at home or read at school. The *starosta* found these sessions enthralling, remarking to the boy's parents, "Your son is a born storyteller."

The great events in Ostrin, as in all the towns at that time, were fire and famine; as a consequence, births, marriages, and deaths were frequently dated by catastrophes. There was a great fire in 1887, and Wolfson's birth date was spoken of as "six months after the big fire." On the occasion of a fire when the boy was eight years old, everyone ran from the villages to see it. The police corralled all the men to pass the water buckets. When they pulled Wolfson into the line, the *starosta* said to the police, "This boy should be excused. He is a *dachovna*, a spiritual person," and he was excused.

Wolfson drew upon his memory of a fire of another sort in a sketch he wrote as a high-school student, entitled "The House That Jacob Built." It is a story of Jacob who, after many years of labor, built a home in Ostrin and, to the delight of his wife Elka and their children, gradually added a potato cellar, a chicken coop, a tile stove bench ("large enough for half the village to be seated on and discuss the events of the world"), and a double set of windows to protect them from the fierce cold of winter. Jacob took great pride in his house, called it his palace, and enjoyed entertaining his friends. He was sad only because he could not welcome his brother who had disappeared. In the midst of his happiness, he received a notice from the town clerk that either he must pay the government three hundred roubles as a penalty for the failure of his brother to appear for military service or his house would be confiscated. Here, as Wolfson tells it, is the climax of the tale.

"Three hundred roubles," murmured Jacob. "Where shall I get it? I don't believe they will take away my house. There is still justice in St. Petersburg. No! They will not have my house."

The first of October came accompanied by the first snow. Early in the morning, while Jacob was still in the synagogue at the morning service, while Elka was working in the kitchen and the children were still asleep, a gendarme entered the house with several soldiers and said roughly:

"Remove the rubbish, Jews. The house does not belong to you any more."

Without any ceremony, the soldiers began to carry out every movable object from the house. The children woke up and began to cry. A crowd assembled in the street. Old women blew their noses and wiped their eyes with their aprons, and old men shook their gray heads murmuring: "Harsh laws, harsh laws!"

Meanwhile Jacob returned from the synagogue and, seeing the big crowd around his house, his furniture standing on the street and his half-naked children sitting in the snow, he stopped short for a while, but all at once he turned aside and disappeared. The soldiers kept on doing their duty without uttering a word, and, after completing, they shut the door and put a waxen seal on the latch.

"Where is Jacob?" cried Elka.

"Where is Jacob?" the crowd repeated the question to one another. "Why does he not go and find a place for his children?"

Suddenly smoke came out from the cracks of the house.

"Where is Jacob gone?" Elka cried again with a wild voice.

The smoke grew thicker and thicker and a tongue of fire appeared.

"Good people, go and find my Jacob!" shrieked Elka.

The fire increased and now the whole roof was involved in flames, and amidst these flames was a pale and horrid face. Jacob appeared in the attic window, spreading his hands toward heaven.

At this time, too, Wolfson displayed a marked talent for drawing. His Hebrew grammar book, preserved by his grandmother from the Ostrin years, is covered with a gallery of local personages of all types. They show, apart from a natural gift, a keen observation of detail and an interest in the varieties and oddities of nature. Once when his aunt decided to redecorate her house, the boy chose pictures from magazines and arranged them artistically to cover portions of the walls. Whenever he acquired a large piece of paper or cardboard, he used it to draw heads of heroes like Theodor Herzl and of nineteenth-century Hebrew writers like the poet Micah Joseph Lebensohn and the novelist Peretz Smolenskin. So impressed was his aunt by these creations that she made an exhibit of them in her store, and the drawing that attracted most attention was a full-length sketch of a priest.

The wooden synagogue near the marketplace, the hearth and heart of the Jewish community, absorbed the life of the growing boy. The center of worship and study, veiled in a mesh of religious ceremony and custom, it was literally never closed. In one of his written sketches of the town there is a description of shepherds who assemble in the marketplace with their horses at night to sing songs "full of sadness and longing" before departing for their night vigil on the pasture grounds:

While these are thus singing on the street, the Jews, both young and old, are sitting in the synagogue, studying their large thick books, before the light of tallow candles. They find their poetry in solving intricate Talmudical problems and refresh their dry souls after a day's work, with charming Oriental legends. But sometimes the younger ones leave the synagogue silently and, taking position in the same market not far away from the former singers, show that they, too, have music in their hearts. Their songs are of quite a different character. They sing about martyrs who have offered their lives for lofty causes, about an old desolated land beyond the sea which once was flowing with milk and honey, or about a happy future and the final triumph of righteousness. Till late, very late in the night, this mixture of voices rings in that peaceful town.

Except for ice-skating and snowball fights during the winter, there were no other games or sports. Young Harry spent much of his time in the musty *beth ha-midrash*, the communal and study hall of the synagogue. Given to browsing among the books there, he discovered that many of the volumes had come from his great-grandfather's library, stamped as their pages were with the man after whom he had been named. He was fascinated with one set of the Mishnah; it had copious marginal annotations by the then rabbi of Ostrin, Jacob Zvi Shapiro, a cousin of the Hebrew poet Constantine Shapiro, who died in 1900; the notes had been used in his commentary on the Mishnah, *Tifereth Ya'akov*, which was incorporated in the great Vilna edition of the Talmud published by the Romm Brothers. In this manner, Harry accumulated information about the cultural history of Ostrin, which dated back at least to the seventeenth century when, as part of the Grodno region, the community was represented in the Lithuanian Vaad (1623–1764), the Jewish assembly that was also known as the Council of Four Lands. Touching a thread here and catching a thread there, the boy wove them into a mental tapestry that he never forgot.

In his ninth year Harry appears to have exhausted the educational resources of Ostrin. His parents arranged for him to continue his studies in Grodno. In existence since the second half of the four-teenth century, Grodno was an ancient seat of government with one of the oldest Jewish communities in Lithuania. The city was honey-combed with synagogues and the community supported one yeshiva. While attending the yeshiva, Harry lived with his maternal grand-parents, Shmuel Aryeh and Michleh Savitsky, who enjoyed having him in the household. His grandmother's hospitality was proverbial, as was her cooking. Her recipes were much sought after by young matrons: especially admired was her Sabbath *cholent,* a concoction of meat and potatoes mixed with plums and spices which (like old-fashioned Boston baked beans) simmered in an earthen pot for many hours before being served. Equally envied were her confec-tions: *ingberlach,* long, dainty sticks of sugar, ginger, and almonds filtered through honeyed syrup; and *kuchlech,* egg-and-sugar cookies baked to a golden tint. All these culinary delights were in later years often recalled with relish by Wolfson. Harry's grandfather, Rav Shmuel, was the head bookkeeper of Bezalel Yaffe, a manufacturer of vodka and spirits; he was also a leading Zionist as well as a prominent citizen of the Jewish community of Grodno. A kindly, bearded gentleman, he was a keen-witted scholar who took pleasure in sharing his rich store of knowledge with his precocious grandson. The house was stocked with a fine collection of Hebrew books, and Harry could often be seen immersed in the study full of tomes that were stacked taller than he. Whenever an important *maggid,* a kind of itinerant preacher-scholar, came to the city, Rav Shmuel took Harry with him to the synagogue and afterward discussed the topic and explained obscure allusions to rabbinic literature in the dis-course. At the same time Harry advanced so rapidly in his studies at the Grodno yeshiva that the principal advised his transfer to one of the other yeshivas where he could continue his studies under outstanding scholars. The sojourn in Grodno was a happy one for Harry; he later considered that city his second birthplace.

A year later he moved on to a yeshiva in Slonim, and in 1898 he was enrolled in a yeshiva in Bialystok conducted by Rabbi Pinchas Gordon, one of the most learned talmudic scholars of his time. Rabbi Gordon, a bachelor then, conducted a private academy for about forty boys in his own home, a large frame house in the toughest section of the city, a kind of Polish Hell's Kitchen known as "Argentina." Boarded with families in the city, the students were required to be present each morning before daylight and to stay until after dark. The rabbi knew of the boys' fear of the neighborhood roughnecks and helped them overcome it by the time-tried device of an incentive: those students who got there before dawn had letters written to their parents with a gold imprint; the others were sent in plain black. Apparently this method was more effective than the customary use of the ruler. In any case, Wolfson overcame his early fears. Sometimes he slept on a bench in a nearby synagogue, where he could occasionally earn a few pennies by reciting psalms for the dead most of the night. The impression made upon him by Rabbi Gordon was lasting, for Gordon was a born teacher, a compassionate man, and a literary scholar whose writings ultimately won him fame.

When he was thirteen Wolfson returned to Ostrin. Rabbi Shapiro found him ready for advanced study and his parents agreed to send him to Kovno, where one of the best yeshivas in Europe was situated. Armed with a strong written recommendation from Rabbi Shapiro, Wolfson's uncle, Rabbi Isaac Savitsky, accompanied him to Kovno, the third largest city in Lithuania and a center of Hebraic culture. There Rabbi Israel Salanter (1810–83) had inaugurated the Musar conventicle, an institution which stressed morality and the importance of self-perfection; Abraham Mapu, the author of the first historical novels in modern Hebrew and the translator of Eugène Sue's *The Mysteries of Paris* into biblical Hebrew, was born there in 1808 and grew up in the town; and there, at the turn of the century, the influence of Rabbi Isaac Elhanan, known as the Kovno Gaon ("preeminent scholar"), was great.

The yeshiva was situated across the Vilija River in Slobodka, a suburb of Kovno, and was known as the Slobodka yeshiva. It consisted of two separate buildings, the larger one known as the Musar, and the smaller one, founded by Rabbi Isaac Elhanan, called the Knesseth Beth Isaac, or the "old shul." Rabbi Savitsky took Harry to the latter and presented him to the yeshiva head, Rabbi Moses Danishevitz. Small of stature and appearing even younger than he was, the rabbi expressed the thought that the boy seemed too young to be enrolled. Rabbi Savitsky countered with a quotation from the Ethics of the Fathers, "A new flask may be filled with old wine," and after a brief examination Harry became a regular student of the "old shul." He was younger than most of the students, but he readily adjusted himself to the rigorous curriculum of the institution. Not only did he excel in the required *daf yomi*—the daily memorization and explication of a folio of the Talmud—but he pursued the intricacies of the innumerable supercommentaries and codes.

At that time the rationalism of Western culture was making inroads into the thought of the yeshiva students. But all profane activities had to be conducted *sub rosa*. A group of senior students at Slobodka organized a Zionist society, and, although he was younger than the other members, Wolfson became one of the leaders. During those three years he read widely in the works of modern Hebrew writers. In addition, he edited a little mimeographed Hebrew journal called *Ha-Zeman* ("Time"), to which he contributed articles and poems.

What was it that young Harry derived from Slobodka and the other yeshivas? The one subject of study was the Talmud. Only the observance of festivals and holy days interrupted the constant application to folio after folio of talmudic lore and law and the hundreds of codes and commentaries in which the principles laid down by Jewish sages from the second century B.C.E. to the sixth century C.E. were investigated and applied to new conditions in the subsequent centuries. The manner of study had changed little since the Middle Ages: the *yeshiva bocher* studied independently, submitted to a periodical oral examination given by the *rosh yeshiva*, the rector of the academy, and then he continued until he had worked over tractate after tractate and mastered them. The method of study, highly developed since the late Middle Ages and now known as *pilpul*, was dialectical. Every text was studied for its direct meaning *(perush)* and then critically analyzed with parallel texts *(tosaphoth)* in other treatises of the Talmud. The result was a yeshiva frame of mind which at its worst became pointless casuistry and at its best a restless search for logical meaning. Its effects upon the student, apart from intellectual discipline, were habits of frugality and sobriety. Knowledge and personality were inseparably meshed. The student mastered knowledge and knowledge mastered him. One can picture young Harry in this milieu, as he read aloud during the day, his body swaying to the rhythm of his thoughts, and as he studied at night by the light of a tallow candle, whetting his insatiable thirst for knowledge and sharpening his wits anew each day.

When he was almost fifteen Wolfson left the Slobodka yeshiva and lived for six months in Vilna, known as the Jerusalem of Lithuania. He learned something of the revolutionary movements and heard the premonitory rumble of the Russo-Japanese war. But his main interests were centered on the Zionist movement and the renascence of Hebrew literature. He spent long hours reading classical and modern Hebrew literature in the Strashun Library—one of the best Hebrew collections in Europe—which was seized by the Nazis in 1942 during the occupation of Lithuania, was later retrieved by the U.S. Army, and in 1947 was sent to New York, to the YIVO Institute for Jewish Research.

By 1903 the political oppression of the czarist regime and the grinding poverty of the Jews in Russia and her provinces had impelled the Jews to leave their ancestral homes and seek a better future in the Americas. The great migration to the New World was in progress; almost every Jewish family in Lithuania sent one or more of its members abroad as immigrants. Part of the Wolfson family began the trek in the nineties. His mother's sister Zivia and her husband, Shammai Rabinowitz, went to "Far America," New Orleans, where they became founders and pillars of the Orthodox community. An uncle, Bernard Wolfson, settled in Cincinnati, and two others, Bernard Davis and Isaac Savitsky, went to Boston. Wolfson's father made an exploratory trip to Salem, Massachusetts, in 1893, and immigrated alone to Ossining, New York, in 1900.

Wolfson arrived with his sister Mamie in September 1903—the rest of the family arrived four years later—and they joined their father in Ossining a few days before the High Holy Days. The Jews of the city consisted of approximately forty families, half of them recent arrivals from Ostrin; they lived in the Irish section on the hills on Charles and Willen Streets. The reunion of part of the family was joyous, and as it coincided with the New Year there was a deep feeling of thanksgiving. The Wolfsons attended services at a synagogue which was located nearby in the rear of a frame house.

When Harry Wolfson arrived among the steerage passengers in 1903 and passed through New York's immigration offices on Ellis Island, he physically closed the door on a world that would be expunged within his lifetime. But at the turn of the century it was still possible to transfer oneself from the Jewish communities of Eastern Europe to certain enclaves of New York and retain many aspects of one's old life, including poverty. It would not have occurred to Max Wolfson, despite his intense struggle to make ends meet, to put his son to work. Instead he arranged to have him continue his talmudic studies at the Rabbi Isaac Elhanan Yeshiva, at 156 Henry Street, between Pike and Market Streets, on the Lower East Side. There, as an advanced student, he worked independently from 1903 to 1905, piloting himself through all the inlets and bays of the ocean of the Talmud and weathering the dialectical storms of Kabbalah and philosophy. But this devotion to study did not preclude contact with the world about him. For one thing, Israel Bettan, one of the students who had studied at Slobodka, became a close friend. Bettan later distinguished himself as a member of the faculty of the Hebrew Union College. Wolfson also belonged to a small circle of older students who called themselves "The Bunch." They would meet for talk from time to time and occasionally visit the home of the leader, Abraham Neuman. Brought to this country as a boy, Neuman had a knowledge of English and used to act as English secretary to the laymen who administered the institution. Neuman was a born organizer; he put his talent to work and got the whole student body to go on a strike to demand the broadening of the curriculum to include English, study of the Bible, and the classics of Hebrew literature. The students also demanded an increase of allowances: at that time an advanced student received 75 cents weekly for lodging, $1.75 weekly for food, and 25 cents for all other needs; also, a gift of a new suit of clothes annually just before the Passover festival. The strike was an expression of the growing demands of the younger generation for adaptation to American education and life. (In later years Neuman became president of Dropsie College in Philadelphia and had the opportunity to bestow an honorary degree upon Wolfson.)

At that time Wolfson used to take long walks with Bettan all over the East Side, storing away impressions. In a later essay entitled "Escaping Judaism" (published in the *Menorah Journal* in June 1921), he employs one of these early impressions to illustrate the tendency people have to mistake loneliness for religious yearning:

A Jewish boy once lived a lonesome life in a great city, in a city of millions. At every eventide, for many months, he would run off to a street corner in the most congested part of the city where the Salvation Army unfurled its banner and made appeals for the return of the sinners. He would stand there for hours, rooted to his place, eagerly watching militant Christianity in action. He was carried away by the beating of the drum, the blasts of the trombone, the singing of the hymns, the pleadings of the sinners, the frank confessions, the vigorous affirmation of faith, the open welcome, and the triumphant waving of the white kerchiefs. It seemed to him that there must be something wonderful in a religion which takes such a strong hold upon its adherents, brings them out of their churches, and makes them proclaim its truth from the street corners. He thought almost contemptuously of the secretiveness, the hesitancy, the reasonableness, the calculativeness of our religious performances, even of the most orthodox among us today. He took his frequent visits to these meetings on the street corner as the sign of a sudden awakening of a dormant religious feeling within him, of a search for God which the trombone blast of Christianity had succeeded in instigating within him after the Shofar call of Judaism had utterly failed to do so. But when in later years he looked back upon those days from a wider experience and a greater knowledge, he realized that he was utterly mistaken. It was not a search for God, but a search for men, for society, for an escape from loneliness. We often mistake a desire of the body for a yearning of the soul. We suffer the twinge of hunger and think we are weary of the universe; we are in the doldrums and think we have a craving for religion. He knew then that he went to those meetings because he wished to hear the sound of human voices, to be lost in a crowd. For to lose one's self in the multitude, body and soul, is one of the elemental human passions. Man will hug an idol to escape spiritual solitude; he will befriend a dog to escape lonesomeness. [pp. 158–59]

At the same time young Wolfson accumulated information about American life from some of the yeshiva students, particularly from the few who were simultaneously studying at the College of the City of New York. In 1905, when he was eighteen, a decision about his future became necessary. The revolution in Russia had worsened conditions and anxiety for the safety of his family in Ostrin made money for passage imperative. There is a story, probably apocryphal, which suggests that the decision was made for him. He is supposed to have concocted for his own amusement a learned query-and-responsum in which he proved that one should eat on Yom Kippur and fast the day before. It amused his fellow students and added to his growing reputation as a wit, but it fell into the hands of one of the faculty, who was impressed with its logic and learning but shocked by its heretical flippancy. As a result, the principal, an educator in the tradition of Arnold of Rugby, suggested that he exercise his wit elsewhere. In any case, he then spent a few months in a factory owned by an uncle, attempting to learn the manual skills of a cutter of men's suits. But his artistry violated the canons of economy—or so the story goes—so that his first and last venture in industry came to a quick end.

Just then Wolfson saw an advertisement for a teacher at the newly established Montefiore Hebrew School in Scranton, Pennsylvania. Candidates were asked to apply by giving their backgrounds and qualifications in Hebrew; the selection was based only on these letters. Wolfson was given the post. In Scranton during the subsequent three years he first took root in the ways of American life, and his interest in the city and the people he came to know remained unflagging. The story of his life is linked with the lives of the friends he made there.

In the first decade of the century Scranton was a small industrial city in the heart of an anthracite-mining area of the Appalachian mountains. The Jewish community consisted of about four hundred families who were divided between older settlers of German origin, who had organized a Reform congregation in 1860, and those who had immigrated from Eastern Europe since the 1880s. At the time of Wolfson's arrival the latter were more numerous than the former; indeed, the temple was sold to an Orthodox congregation, and this synagogue, known as the Linden Street Shul, became the center of religious and cultural activities, and its rabbi was regarded as head of the city's Orthodox Jewry. The establishment of the Montefiore Talmud Torah was stimulated in large measure by the clubs of Hebraists and Zionists among the immigrants—a fringe of the Hebrew renascence then flourishing in New York and Boston.

Soon after his arrival in March 1905, he found cheap lodgings at the home of a poor milk vendor named Milkman, whose surname made him the subject of local humor. It was near the center of the city, on Adams Street, bordering on the Lackawanna River and a few blocks from the Linden Street Synagogue. Since Milkman was blessed with a large brood of children, the little house was crowded, but two boarders, Wolfson and a rag peddler, helped the family to make ends meet. Wolfson lived in the attic, where he fed himself mainly on tea, bread, and fruit, and occasionally ate with the family. Despite the overcrowding and lack of amenities, the Milkman home provided the semblance of a family atmosphere for the new young teacher.

The Montefiore School was of the old-fashioned variety, with a staff of European-born men of traditional caste who taught by rote. However, Wolfson's predecessor Louis Lichterman, a son-in-law of the Hebrew poet Menahem Mendel Dolitski (1856–1931), had introduced the study of grammar and contemporary Hebrew writers. David M. Levy, one of Lichterman's students who became an eminent New York psychiatrist, recalls that despite the lack of modern educational techniques, the bright boys learned a good deal of Hebrew and that he, at the age of twelve, read a Hebrew rendering of Mark Twain's *Prince and the Pauper*. Wolfson is supposed to have been uninterested in discipline. Absorbed in his own thoughts, he would sometimes pass the principal and some of the lay directors in the halls without recognizing them.

Engaged only from 3:30 to 6:30 P.M. at the Montefiore School, he decided to take advantage of the public schools. He spoke English with difficulty, but he had learned to read it himself in New York. The first books he read were the juveniles then in vogue, Alice Blackwell's *Black Beauty* and G. A. Henty's historical novels. He entered P.S. 36, the Franklin School, in April and received a diploma in June 1905. In the autumn he was admitted as a freshman at the Central High School. Among the students and teachers there he was considered shy but sociable. David Levy was his closest friend. Levy protected him from the taunts and shenanigans of the rowdier students and often came to see Wolfson at the Milkmans' home. When the other Milkman boarder went amok and was placed in the Hillside Home, a mental hospital, David and Harry visited him. As they left Wolfson remarked, "I guess we don't have to worry about him, he's living with such nice people—Abraham Lincoln, George Washington, and Buffalo Bill."

Wolfson, in turn, spent time at his friend's house. He enjoyed talking with Sarah Levy, David's mother, who as a result of typhoid fever had become blind at seventeen and now, a widow, was managing her husband's wholesale hardware and farm-supply store. An accomplished woman, she maintained contact with life and literature by having papers and books read to her, and she was especially fond of the novels of Tolstoi and Turgenev. Wolfson felt that she was a remarkable human being, and since he had not seen his own mother for almost five years, he was especially warmed by her. She encouraged the boys' friendship, certain that both would make their marks as scholars.

Among their adventures was a junket to New York with a group of students from Central High School to attend the young people's meeting of the National Arbitration and Peace Congress, held in Carnegie Hall on April 6, 1907. They had dinner with the Wolfson family—his mother and the other five children had arrived from Ostrin a few months earlier—in a small apartment on Canal Street on the Lower East Side. It was a sizzling hot night, and the boys went up to the roof to sleep. Enthralled by the view of the tenements under a starry sky, they talked far into the night.

Wolfson's record at Central High School—an average of little less than a hundred—is still remembered there. He walked away with the classical honors and was asked to speak at graduation exercises. For a while, because of his heavy accent, he attempted to forgo the honor. But his history teacher, Alice Connor, insisted that he give the address at the graduation exercises. She coached him daily, and for several weeks he paced up and down in a corner of the city park and recited the address aloud. To his delight, he was understood.

Wolfson's social pleasures were few. He was a member of the Adelphia Literary Society, to which he was elected treasurer in 1907. He attended meetings of a Zionist club organized by recent young immigrants who greeted him there and on the streets with the nickname "Pircheh," a word of Yiddish origin, a friendly, affectionate salutation akin to the American use of "Butch."

By a happy coincidence, Wolfson's scholastic feats came to the attention of a local Harvard alumnus, a young attorney who, unlike many college men of his generation, was more interested in brains than brawn. Early in 1908, with graduation approaching, Wolfson had begun thinking about a college, preferably an inexpensive state university or a small private college where he might get a scholarship. Just then Myer Kabatchnick (Harvard '06), who had been the first boy from Scranton to win honors at Harvard and who was secretary to the mayor, made a speech on Disraeli at the Friday assembly at Central High School. Afterward A. H. Wells, the principal, told Kabatchnick about Wolfson and his remarkable record in the difficult classics course. Inviting Wolfson to his office, Kabatchnick discussed college prospects with him. When the alumnus spoke with enthusiasm about Harvard College, Wolfson asked shyly whether it would be wise for a poor boy to attend a "rich man's college." Indicating that his description was only partly true and that in any case a worthy student who distinguished himself in a competitive examination could win a scholarship there, he encouraged him to apply for the Price-Greenleaf aid. Wolfson took the examination in June and received the sum of $250.

Whatever notions he may have harbored for a career, by the time of his admission to Harvard he probably felt that he was a born writer. He had been an ardent member of the literary society at Central High School. During 1907 and 1908 three of his prose pieces—one of them embroidered with poetic quatrains—had appeared in *High School Impressions,* a journal published by the students of Scranton high schools. For a romantic story about a Polish peasant girl whose disappointment in love ended in death he had won a prize of five dollars. He drew his material not from the life about him but from recollections of his native town, Ostrin. At the same time he was experimenting with Hebrew verse. On one occasion Wolfson showed David Levy a Hebrew translation he had made of Longfellow's *Hiawatha.* During the summer before he went to Harvard he sent one of his poems to *Ha-Le'om* ("The Nation"), a Hebrew journal published in New York. Under the title *"Ha-Dima"* ("The Tear") it was published on September 4, 1908. He was evidently still influenced by Longfellow, for this poem was written in the rhythm of "The Arrow and the Song."

Wolfson's intellectual mold had been cast in his boyhood. It remained for him only to deepen and broaden it. He went up to Harvard, poor and devoted to learning, in the manner of a medieval student going up to Oxford.

2
Harvard

Enter to Grow in Wisdom

Eliot Gate, Harvard Yard

Wolfson entered Harvard College in September 1908. He paid little attention to the unaccustomed circumstances in which he found himself on the campus; his immediate problem was financial, for after he deducted $150 for tuition from the Price-Greenleaf aid, he was left with $100 to live on for the rest of the year. His uncle, Bernard Davis, came to his rescue, inviting him to lodge at his home in Roxbury for the year—an act which greatly touched Wolfson. Despite this and other efforts at economy, at midyear he was short $30 for the second-term bill; but the dean of freshmen, William Castle, who had heard from several instructors that Wolfson was one of the most brilliant men in his class, gladly helped with a loan.

That he was a stranger among strangers on the campus was hardly a new experience for him. Aside from the freshmen who were taken from registration at Memorial Hall and brought to "punch" parties at Holworthy or to the plush apartments on the

"Gold Coast," many of the new students were initiated into college life solely in classrooms, laboratories, and libraries. In this regard Wolfson felt at home, for in the early decades after 1900 all the courses were optional and students set their own compasses. He enrolled in six courses—nothing less exacting could have satisfied him—and his half-legendary performance in them made even those classmates who did not know him aware of his presence.

Living off campus afforded an unexpected opportunity to foster his Hebraist and Zionist aspirations. He became a member of Ohavei Sefer ("Book Lovers"), a Hebrew club which held monthly meetings in the Jewish People's Institute at 62 Chambers Street on the North Side. He won the regard of the group by his discussions of literary tropics, and on the occasion of the hundredth anniversary of the birth of Edgar Allan Poe, he read a paper on Poe as a literary artist that was reported in the Hebrew and Yiddish press. There is another incident which has lingered in the memory of his contemporaries. After a lecture by Dr. Shmarya Levin, the eloquent orator of Svislovitz, at a Zionist gathering in Boston, one of the Harvard students, a red-headed, fiery Zionist, took issue with the speaker and attempted to argue his case in Hebrew. His talk was punctuated with grammatical errors, and as each occurred the lecturer caustically corrected it. Wolfson watched this discordant duet with mounting anger, and finally, determined to assuage his fellow student's humiliation, he took the floor and in felicitous Hebrew riddled Levin's rhetoric. Ostrin prevailed over Svislovitz; but, of greater importance, the underdog's dignity had been restored.

Busily occupied with study during the first year, he had little time to indulge in literary undertakings. But the intensely literary atmosphere of Harvard at that time must have touched him. During the first summer vacation he got a job teaching at a Hebrew school in Manchester, New Hampshire. Just at that time the daily Hebrew newspaper *Ha-Yom* ("The Day") began publication in New York, and he was invited to contribute articles. From these writings it is possible to glimpse certain aspects of the intellectual ferment at Harvard which engaged him.

Deeply committed to Hebrew learning, Wolfson found his imagination stirred by the discovery of the Department of Semitic Languages and Literature. It brought him into intimate contact with a group of world-famous scholars: Crawford Howell Toy and George Foot Moore in the history of religions; William R. Arnold in Bible; James Richard Jewett in Arabic; and the Assyriologist David Gordon Lyon, who was chairman. Lyon and Moore were the mentors, and soon became the friends, of the young Wolfson, whose brilliance and industry they admired. It was natural for him, therefore, to devote his first article in *Ha-Yom* to "Hebrew Studies at Harvard" (4 Elul 5669 [Sept. 1909], p. 3). He described concisely the spectrum of courses and the range of the scholars, with a touching reference to Lyon and his efforts to interest the Jewish students—Wolfson puts the number at two hundred—in biblical and Semitic courses. His appeal may have fallen on deaf ears, but on Wolfson this great gentleman and scholar had a strong influence, and his many kindnesses, then and later, always remained green in Wolfson's memory.

A sign of the new spiritual trend which developed toward the end of the first decade of the twentieth century was the appearance in the universities of societies like the Deutscher Verein, the Cercle Français, and the Casa Italiana. These groups were more than dilettantish searchers after continental cultures; they were linked to the effort to bridge the Old World culture and the New. Among these circles, although of a somewhat different character, was the Harvard Menorah Society. It was formed by a small group of Jewish students —all of them either immigrants or the children of immigrants from Eastern Europe—who, calling themselves "Pandemonium," All-Demons, had met periodically to discuss and debate themes of Jewish interest. Two years before Wolfson's arrival on the campus, on October 25, 1906, sixteen students gathered at 44 Grays Hall in Harvard Yard and drew up a constitution for a society, adopting the ancient symbol of the menorah (candelabrum, signifying enlightenment), to unite Jewish students of every background and viewpoint in order to study and promote "Hebraic culture and ideals." Among them were Horace M. Kallen, I. Leo Sharfman, Henry M. Sheffer, who in due course would achieve academic eminence, and Henry Hurwitz, who later became the professional leader of the Menorah movement and served as the editor of the *Menorah Journal* until his death in 1961. The society was welcomed by President Charles W. Eliot, and the meetings were addressed by distinguished scholars and notables. Wolfson attended the Menorah meetings and got to know several of the society's leaders; thus he devoted his second article in *Ha-Yom* to "The Menorah Society at Harvard" (24 Elul 5669 [Sept. 1909], pp. 3–4). He enthusiastically describes the activities of the Society and foresees in this cadre of university intellectuals, which was already spreading its influence to other campuses, the beginnings of an American Hebrew renascence. The article closes with a Hebrew poem by Wolfson which had been adopted as the Menorah Society's song.

How far Wolfson was casting his net is suggested by his comment on an event that was headlined in the newspapers that year. President Charles W. Eliot, then a majestic, venerable figure, had made a controversial speech, "The Future of Religion," which was printed in the *Harvard Theological Review* (2:384–407 [1909]). The great educator's rejection of dogma and authority and espousal of religious modernism must have produced a smile in William James and tears in George Santayana. The optimism and hope which informed everything Eliot said and did was a state of mind which did not appeal to the analytical mind of Wolfson. In a logical and lucid essay he argued that Eliot's "new religion" was not new at all, and to nail down the argument he wittily riddled Eliot's modernism by exposing the antiquity of certain of his views. He had made his bow as a polemicist; but, as the article was printed in a Hebrew daily, it drew the attention only of the Hebraist intellectuals.

Another fruit of his first year at Harvard was a solid piece of literary criticism, "The American Trend in Hebrew Literature" (*Ha-Yom*, 22 Av 5669 [Aug. 1909], p. 3). Here he demonstrated his familiarity with modern Hebrew literature and offered a sound analysis of the underlying influences and trends among living Hebrew writers. Taking a leap into the future, he predicted a shift of the centers of gravity of Hebrew culture to America and Palestine, each center fructifying the other.

In the fall of 1909 Wolfson took rooms, which he shared with a Harvard medical student, on the top floor of College House, now an office building opposite the entrance to the Yard on Harvard Square. Since his roommate, poor like himself, spent the days and evenings at the medical school and the room was heated with coal which cost ten dollars for the year, he could either spend that sum to heat the rooms or join the Harvard Union, which was well-heated and a pleasant place to read and study. He decided to join the Union, and it was in this student recreation center that he pursued his studies in classics, science, literature, philosophy, and Semitics. There he continued his childhood habit, which persisted throughout his life, of studying until the lights went out.

Yet, despite his prodigious application to scholastics, he devoted some time, not to the prevalent tendency at Harvard of cultivating one's "taste," but to the nourishment of his talents. Influential in his development at this time was Horace M. Kallen of the class of 1903, who had recently returned to the Philosophy Department from a two-year appointment as an English instructor at Princeton. Kallen was a favorite of William James and later one of his most perceptive interpreters; besides being Wolfson's instructor in philosophy, he was a founder and stalwart of the Harvard Menorah Society. Indeed, he had composed the motto "for the study of Hebraic learning and ideals." On a number of occasions he persuaded William James and Barrett Wendell to attend Zionist dinners in Boston and paraphrased for them the Hebrew and Yiddish speeches. He shared with Wolfson, who was five years his junior, the intellectual excitement of the Menorah Society and the Hebrew renascence which was blossoming both in Boston and New York in the two decades prior to World War I.

Wolfson was painfully shy. He could not go to people: they had to come to him. The accident of a surname at the end of the alphabet enabled him to sit at the back of lecture halls. When he attended student meetings he would appear a little late so that he could conceal himself at the back of the room or in a corner where he would remain inconspicuous. Yet at times the reserve could be penetrated, as when he undertook to lead the Menorah study groups at Harvard and Radcliffe. One of the students who attended a study circle of the Menorah Society wrote in a report that "our sophomore leader conducted the sessions brilliantly, elucidating Hebrew literature with the aplomb of Kittredge on Shakespeare."

Later, in the spring of 1909, at a Zionist meeting in Tremont Temple, the first great Hebrew meeting of its kind in Boston, Wolfson welcomed the speaker, Reuben Brainin (1862–1939), a distinguished Hebrew editor and biographer who had just settled in New York. Brainin, tall and imposing, with a Vandyke beard and brooding eyes, sought Wolfson out after the meeting and, recognizing his talent, befriended him. The older Hebraist encouraged Wolfson to continue writing in Hebrew.

These little triumphs outside Cambridge supplemented his extracurricular pursuits. On campus he was also receiving honors that rarely come to an undergraduate. In his sophomore year Professor Lyon invited him to read a paper at a meeting of the Semitic Conference, a group of faculty and graduates which met periodically as an informal seminar. He presented a solid exposition, "A Comparative Study of the Structure of Biblical and Modern Hebrew." It was a philological study handled with originality; Lyon encouraged Wolfson to prepare it for publication and offered to edit the English. Twenty years later Lyon recalled this paper and remarked, "In those days Dr. Wolfson was no John L. Sullivan; but his brains and concentration were a rarity here." Busy with study and papers for regular courses and pressed by financial needs, he did not get around to readying the study for publication, and, unfortunately, the manuscript has not survived.

Wolfson's only other literary production of that term was a Hebrew poem read at the annual Menorah dinner held in Boston. Rendered into English by Kallen, from a literal translation by Wolfson, "The Arch of Titus" still betrays the influence of Longfellow, though the Hebrew original is more metrical and less mimetic than the translation.

> Crumbling, age-worn, in Rome the eternal
> Stands the arch of Titus's triumph,
> With its carven Jewish captives
> Stooped before the holy Menorah.

And each nightfall, when the turmoil
Of the Petrine clangor ceaseth,
Seven flames the arch illumine,
Mystic burnings, glowing strangely.

They cast off their graven shackles
Judah's sons of beaten marble;
Living step they from the ruin
Living strike they to the Jordan.

They are healed in its waters,
Till the freshness of each dawning;
They resume their ancient sorrow,
Perfect marble, whole and holy.

Dust of dust the wheeling seasons,
Grind that mighty archèd splendor,
Raze the Gaul and raze the Roman,
Grind away their fame and glory,
The shackled Jews alone withstand them,
Stooped before the holy Menorah.

Louis D. Brandeis, who had then become interested in Zionism and attended the Menorah dinner, was reported to have been moved by the poem, which was read both in English and Hebrew.

During the summer of 1911, poverty seems to have been a stimulus rather than a deterrent for Wolfson. In any case, worry seems to have fired his smoldering passion to write, and during that summer Wolfson wrote two long essays for *Ha-Dror* ("Freedom"), a new Hebrew literary monthly which had just been launched in New York by Reuben Brainin. One of the essays was a critique of the newly published edition of the *Encyclopaedia Britannica.* He criticized the editors and contributors for perpetuating certain stereotypes of Jewish life and culture. Equally perceptive, and even more striking, is the second essay, a piece of literary criticism. Wolfson took as his subject a 1910 book-length epic poem, *Mul Ohel Timmurah* ("Before the Tent of Timmurah"), by Benjamin Nahum Silkiner (1882–1933), the first Hebrew production of importance written in America. The young critic immediately recognized the significance of the poem (which appeared to document the view he had expressed in his essay published a year earlier on the probable trends in contemporary Hebrew literature), and said that it was unique. The poem is named after an American Indian girl whose father relates the ways of the tribe and the wars with other Indian tribes and with the Spaniards. Wolfson contends that even though the language is distinguished, the poem, as an epic, must be judged in the light of both history and poetry. In this regard, he shows how Silkiner has falsified the true American Indian by endowing him with ideas and folkways which are in fact unhistorical. Wolfson's references to Virgil, Shakespeare, Johnson, Hauptmann, and Maeterlinck suggest that he had been immersing himself in ancient and modern literature. And he himself was writing excellent Hebrew prose. Reading these essays now gives fuller meaning to a remark of the late Professor Joseph Klausner of the Hebrew University to the effect that when Wolfson gave up writing in Hebrew the literature lost a potential master. He carried on Hebrew correspondence with Klausner for many years and Klausner made a point of singing his praises to visiting scholars and writers.

In September 1911 Wolfson moved from College Hall to a room at Divinity Hall, where he continued to live, as student and teacher, for thirteen years. As it had been for Ralph Waldo Emerson a half century earlier, Divinity Hall became for Wolfson a refuge and a sanctuary. There was none of the plush of the Gold Coast on Mt. Auburn Street nor the excessive social life of the more democratic dormitories like Holworthy in the Yard. Divinity Hall was isolated, in a pastoral patch at the end of the "private way," and it thus afforded excellent quarters for a serious-minded student. Old and rich in tradition, the rectangular building had three floors, and each floor (until it was somewhat modernized in the postwar years) had one common bathroom and lavatory. Each student had a room to himself, and the rent for these single rooms was the cheapest on the campus, or for that matter in town—ranging from thirty-five to seventy dollars a year. The theological students were in a minority, and Harold E. Stearns, a resident at the time, reported that they barely avoided contamination from the coarse atheism of the nearby law students. That the residents desired privacy was evidenced by the small number—primarily theologues—who used the plain, little common room, which as a consequence was converted to living quarters.

At any rate, for one who ate little and lived with books, as Wolfson did, the room at Divinity Hall was perfect. Nearby were the library of the Theological School and the red-brick Semitic Museum, a gift of the philanthropist Jacob H. Schiff. As an advanced student in Semitics, Wolfson had a key to the well-stocked library at the rear of the first floor, which because of the paucity of students in the department served virtually as a private library.

Another tale begins at Divinity Hall's portals.

On a bright, warm day that September, Wolfson loaded his belongings into a wheelbarrow and pushed it precariously across the streets to Divinity Hall. As he approached the entrance to the building, he was greeted warmly by a student who was coming out. "Rab!" exclaimed Wolfson, running up the steps to welcome Isidor Rabinovitz to Harvard. He helped Wolfson carry the things from the wheelbarrow to Room 1 on the first floor; then they went up to the third floor and looked at Rab's quarters in Room 34, which the eager freshman had already put in order. As they congratulated themselves on being together, Wolfson said, *"Mi millel?* Who would have expected this?" alluding to Abraham's exclamation when Sarah at ninety-nine years of age bore Isaac. In the future, whenever they won honors or enjoyed some triumph, they used the phrase to communicate their mutual delight. Wolfson enjoyed code-using, that allusive elliptical speech that one used only with another of one's kind or profession.

The friendship of Wolfson and Rab became one of the most important friendships of both their lives. They had first met casually at the meetings of the Hebrew Club at the Jewish People's Institute, where Rab was teaching Hebrew. Rab had been brought up in the Russian city of Brisk, where he had received an excellent Hebrew background from private tutors. His father was a manufacturer who wrote learned Hebrew works. At the outbreak of the revolution in 1905, the arrest of Rab's sister as a revolutionary suspect moved his frightened parents to find a way of getting him out of the country and sending him to America. His family, unlike Wolfson's, remained in Russia (indeed, to this day the survivors of his family still live in Soviet Russia), so that he was alone and had to make his own way. He shared Wolfson's interest in Hebrew learning and Zionism as well as his literary leanings; in his senior year at the Roxbury High School he had published an article, "Why I Came to America," in the *Atlantic Monthly.* That he found himself at Harvard and at the same time a neighbor of Wolfson's seemed to him a piece of flawless good fortune.

Rab was a studious, engaging young man. Though somewhat in awe of Wolfson, he could hold his own in literary conversation; he delighted in his friend's accomplishments—in fact, his first inclination was to follow Wolfson's example and become a Hebrew scholar and writer. But it was Wolfson who diverted him from this goal. One evening they began talking of their future: Wolfson used Brainin as an example of a Hebrew writer who had achieved eminence and yet was miserably poor and without influence in the community. He confessed—and Rab was in accord—that the impoverishment of so prominent a figure in Hebrew letters was disillusioning. He wondered whether he ought not give up his own studies and try his luck in New York on Grub Street, or perhaps become a doctor. Mostly, he kept hammering away at Rab, showing how he could carve a niche for himself in the sciences rather than the humanities, above all in chemistry which, he felt, held out undreamed-of possibilities. As dawn broke, Rab was completely convinced; he specialized in the sciences and later pioneered as a consulting chemist in Boston.

Months of increasing friendship revealed to Rab intimacies of Wolfson's life that were sealed off from other acquaintances. He was concerned about Wolfson's frequent colds, his difficulty in digesting the little food he ate, his ineptness with girls, his obsession with study, and the pressure of financial needs at home (Wolfson's maternal grandparents had recently joined the family in New York). He also was fascinated by certain facets of Wolfson's personality. He observed that, like so many other budding writers on the campus, Wolfson dramatized his own eccentricities; for example, by affecting a limp for a while he harbored the illusion that this gave him a secret strength. Rab admired Wolfson's artistic sensibility. Once he found a colored reproduction of "Jesus of the Handkerchief of Cremona" pinned up on the wall of Wolfson's room at Divinity Hall. At first it seemed to him irreverent. Wolfson explained that he was not paying homage to the founder of Christianity; he was fascinated by the power of the eyes, which seemed to open whenever he looked at the picture.

Another neighbor of Wolfson at Divinity Hall in 1912 was another senior, Harold E. Stearns, who was already a practicing journalist. He had occasional chats with Wolfson, at first at odd moments while they shaved together in the bathroom or walked toward Harvard Yard. Later, as Stearns began work on his honors thesis, there were longer conversations, including two autobiographical ones, which provided him a glimpse of Wolfson's character at that time. Stearns refers to Wolfson as a "clean Emersonian soul" who had "a clear, original mind." In one of his articles he describes the six Harvard intellectuals of his time whom he considered outstanding, mentioning Wolfson under the peusdonym "Wilder." The thumbnail description in *The Street I Know,* Stearns' autobiographical work, is especially valuable because it shows that Wolfson had already formulated, to some extent, the original method of research that became the trademark of his life's work. "A brilliant Jewish scholar, named Wolfson," Stearns wrote, "lived next to me, and I found him quiet and interesting—and devastatingly well-informed on almost any subject I brought up, except the subject of girls, or, indeed, of sex in general, about which he appeared to be as innocent as a babe unborn. Yet I learned thoroughness in scholarly details from him—learned to be careful and to be sure of my authorities when I cited them by a random quotation which might temporarily, taken alone and without the context, appear to support my argument. I learned from him to cast all forms of 'bluff' far from me."

The qualities that Stearns discovered—and other qualities that he did not discover—had made a firm impression on Wolfson's teachers, who considered him more of a scholar than a student. Wolfson had great admiration for George Santayana, all of whose courses he took. Santayana, poet as well as philosopher, preferred to describe himself as an "American writer," but his mind was rooted in the European and classical traditions. Like those of William James and Barrett Wendell, his lectures at the recently opened Emerson Hall—still the home of the Department of Philosophy—had immense appeal to mature students. He lectured as he wrote, in cadenced sentences, with every thought and every comma in place. He never used notes; he sat behind a desk and his discourses sounded as relaxed as if he were sitting at home before the fireplace, chatting with friends. Santayana's skepticism, love for Spinoza, and disdain for the facile optimist made a strong impression on Wolfson.

Wolfson, in turn, made an impression on Santayana. Preserved in the archives of the Houghton Library are two of Wolfson's papers for 1910–11, written in bluebooks, together with a plan for a term paper, all of which contain marginal comment by Santayana. On the cover of an examination paper for Philosophy 12, dealing with Greek philosophy and Plato's dialogues particularly, Santayana wrote, "Excellent throughout." And so it is: the answers are all to the point, the exposition precise and lucid. Wolfson has clearly mastered the texts, fathomed their meaning; and in at least one instance—in discussing a dialogue of Parmenides, usually considered to be a denial of the Platonic Idea—he offers an original interpretation, which makes Parmenides' statements consistent with Plato's concept. Turning to Wolfson's paper on Lessing's *Laocoön*, we move to the realm of the philosophy of art. Aside from being an example of the erudition on which Stearns commented, there is in Wolfson's critique on Greek sculpture and painting an astute observation of detail and delicate sensitivity to form and line. Nor does his facility for analysis outrun his sense of style, despite the fact that he occasionally falters in the use of English idioms. Moreover, one can read between the lines attitudes stemming from personal experience, and the psychological observation in such passages is a presentiment of the method Wolfson later applied with unusual results in his work on Spinoza. Here is a representative excerpt from a passage in which he discusses Lessing's view of physical suffering:

The unpleasantness we experience at the sight of ugliness seems to be identical with that we experience at the sight of physical pain. Lessing says that deformity should never be represented in painting because it wounds our sight and feeling. Now why does deformity wound our sight? Is it painful in the same sense as a *pinch* or a blow is painful? Certainly not; for a man cannot get used to pinches and blows so as not to feel their pain, while he may get used to all kinds of deformity so as not to be shocked by them. Ugly persons don't feel the ugliness of their features, while they feel the pain of their own pinches. Deformity, therefore, is repulsive because we are not used to it, because it is out of the ordinary, and we always have antipathy to things we are not accustomed to. And the feeling we experience at the sight of physical pain, that is the fear that we may be deformed in the same manner. This can be shown by the fact that such deformities, the like of which we can easily receive, are more shocking to us than others. Deformities caused by disease, for instance, are more repulsive than those caused by external accidents, and these more than those with which one was born or those caused by nature. The reason is that we feel that we are less secure from disease than from an external accident and that we have no reason at all to be afraid of receiving a natural deformity, after we had been born and passed the age of growing.

But all these deformities seem to lose their unpleasant effect when imitated by an artist, and there is no reason why they should not be allowed to be represented in painting. That imitation does not transmit the unpleasant effect of the original deformity can be shown by the following fact. Almost every man has felt the unpleasant, if not irritating, effect of the bad handwriting of a man who is not used to handle the pen, especially that of the signature of a man who has learned to write but his own name. The crooked, quivering lines, the uneven letters and their wild diffusion over the paper almost irritate us and jar upon the nerves, and it is impossible to look with repose upon the writing. Yet when such a signature is impressed by a rubber stamp or printed from a lithograph, it receives a kind of quieting, calming, and cooling effect. Why is this? Is it not because that signature was only an imitation, and this very awareness of its being an imitation is sufficient to remove the bad effect of the original? Why, then, is it not allowed to paint a physical deformity?

Santayana obviously felt that the paper deserved something more than a brief encomium. "To answer your last question first:" he wrote at the end, "Because Lessing wrote in the eighteenth century, and could not imagine positive religion to be beautiful and spontaneous." The teacher then added the sort of comment for which the exceptional student is grateful. "You have a firm, resolute way of arguing; but I am not so sure that your psychological analysis is adequate or final in every case. It has happened to me to go out of the theatre to avoid represented torments—in *La Tosca*—and probably, in every instance you mention, various natures would be found to act in various ways. However, you have the *power* of analysis if only you can acquire the necessary scope in experience, or by sympathy. Don't let premature certitude prevent you from doing so with an open mind. Your summary is excellent."

For a term paper Wolfson proposed to use as a basis Hegel's *Philosophy of Art.* He divided the outline into four parts, Symbolism, Classicism, Romanticism, and the Future of Art, and suggested a free discussion of the subject rather than of Hegel's work. Apparently the first part, Symbolism, which was in that decade a topic of discussion in art, literature and music, was of primary concern to him, for it was the only part of the essay which he elaborated. "In discussing Symbolism," Wolfson wrote, "I will draw an analogy between the ancient symbolism produced by lack of civilization, and modern forms of symbolism, produced by over-civilization. Hegel points out the fact that Hebrew poetry has not passed through the various stages as the poetry of other nations. Taking up this point, I will discuss at first if it is true that Hebrew poetry contains no traces of symbolism, then, if this will turn out to be true, I will try to explain it by some theory. At last, I will take up the discussion of Symbolism in mediaeval and modern Hebrew poetry."

"Why not limit the subject," suggested Santayana in a marginal note, "to 'The Applicability of Hegel's Philosophy of Art to Hebrew Poetry.' That will be new, interesting and would amount to a valuable test of Hegel's position." Wolfson considered the suggestion, but for lack of time he wrote instead a paper on a purely philosophical theme.

Meanwhile, at Divinity Hall, Wolfson followed his bent under the elective system which allowed him free choice of courses and study.

In 1911 he entered the competition for the Harvard Menorah Society's prize of $100 "for the best essay by an undergraduate on a subject connected with the work and achievements of the Jewish people." An annual grant was provided by Jacob H. Schiff, and the prize was awarded by a faculty committee appointed by President Eliot. Wolfson's essay, "Maimonides and Halevi," dealing with the attitudes of medieval philosophers toward Greek philosophy, won the prize. It was published the following year in the *Jewish Quarterly Review,* during the second year of the publication of that learned journal in America. This essay marks the beginning of Wolfson's career as a student of Jewish philosophy.

If Wolfson succumbed to philosophy it was not because of a feeling that there were laurels to be gathered or because philosophy floated through the Harvard air. It was a natural, perhaps inevitable, consequence of his early education and training. In a 1927 essay retrieving a philosophic excursus from a book on Hebrew synonyms by Solomon Pappenheim (1740–1814), Wolfson's explanation of the predominance of Jews of yeshiva background in the field of philosophy hit the mark:

That philosophy should have been the vehicle through which the first linguistically emancipated Jews should break into the world's literature was only natural, for outside the Bible philosophy was the only field of knowledge which the Jews shared in common with the rest of Europe. It is characteristic of all these early Jewish pioneers in European letters that even in their new state they continued to draw upon their early knowledge and training and to show the unmistakable influence of their early traditions and interests. Mendelssohn wrote a commentary in Hebrew on Maimonides' logic and composed books on psychology and theology which abound in old-time allusions. Solomon Maimon not only borrowed his surname from Maimonides but published a commentary in Hebrew on the latter's *Moreh Nebukim* [*Guide of the Perplexed*] and also discussed Maimonides' philosophy in his German autobiography. Among the kind of Jews to whom these men belonged they marked the transition from mediaeval to modern philosophy, just as in an earlier generation Spinoza performed a similar function among Jews of another kind and Descartes among Christians. By the vicissitudes of life and education they formed a link, as it were, between the Jewish philosophic tradition and the European.

["Solomon Pappenheim on Time and Space and his Relation to Locke and Kant," *Israel Abrahams Memorial Volume,* pp. 426–27]

Yet the decision to pursue an almost virginal field in the humanities was not quite that simple. There was the temptation of literature and writing—and in the intensely literary atmosphere of Harvard at that time he might have succumbed, as did so many other talented Harvard contemporaries. But his ingrained love of Hebrew learning unconsciously exercised the veto. Furthermore, there was the strong influence of his teachers in the Semitics Department, especially that of George Foot Moore.

Moore lived to the rear of Divinity Hall, at 3 Divinity Avenue, in a yellow frame house surrounded by a pleasant garden and a quaint picket fence. He often could be seen walking to the Semitic Museum or along the avenue toward Harvard Yard. He was a giant of a man, always erect, simply dressed, with clear, laughing blue eyes dominating his strong face—a true gentleman and a veritable Georgium Sidus. By the time Wolfson became a resident of Divinity Hall, Moore had established himself as a preeminent biblical scholar and historian of religions. His succinct work *The Literature of the Old Testament* (1913) is the sort of book that could have been written only by a master of the field. His 1895 commentary on the Book of Judges, published as part of the International Critical Commentaries, remains unsurpassed; it was the first book by a modern critical scholar to employ the Hebrew biblical commentaries of medieval scholars. And here we have a clue to the talmudic scholarship that Moore later evidenced in his distinguished work, *Judaism in the First Centuries of the Christian Era* (1927). Early in Moore's career, when he was serving as a minister in Zanesville, Ohio, he had been a friend of a local rabbi with whom he studied rabbinic Hebrew and under whom he laid the foundation of his talmudic learning. "It was an old-fashioned training," Moore once remarked. "Its methods were doubtless of a kind which our pedagogical experts would regard as altogether obsolete; but it accomplished its end, which is, after all, the final test of the efficiency of a method. In one respect it differed widely from that of our schools; unsophisticated by educational psychology, the yeshiva-trained teacher, like his predecessors in the great age of classical learning in Western Europe, naively assumed that the object of studying a subject was to know it, not to acquire a certificate of having been through it. In that antiquated education the memory was systematically trained, not methodically ruined." At the same time Moore learned modern Hebrew.

Moore was a naturally gracious man, and his door was always open to Wolfson, as it was to all of his exceptional students. They always left his study exhilarated, walking out the front door with new paths to tread. At Moore's suggestion, for example, Wolfson contributed a bibliography of Professor Toy's writings to a scholarly volume published in honor of Toy in 1912. The thoroughness with which it was done pleased the professor, who expressed surprise at Wolfson's discovery of things he no longer remembered having written.

One day in March 1912, Wolfson met Professor Lyon on Divinity Avenue, and Lyon asked, "Suppose you were awarded a fellowship, what would you write about?" Unhesitatingly he replied, "A literary essay on Crescas." Wolfson was not able to explain fully what made him answer as he did. Once he had spoken, however, he felt committed. The name of the fourteenth-century philosopher, a Spanish Jew, whose masterwork, *Or Adonai* ("Light of the Lord") is a critique of Maimonides and Aristotle, was probably known to few other scholars at Harvard. Moore, too, saw the possibilities—and the difficulties— of the subject, and he expressed approval. He took Wolfson to the library at Gore Hall, the predecessor of Widener Library, and introduced him to the stacks where there were bibliographies of the manuscript collections of the great libraries of Europe. Wolfson pored over the huge volumes: *Descriptive Catalogue of the Hebrew MSS of the Montefiore Library* (London), *Die Hebräischen Handschriften der Nationalbibliothek in Wien*, and others listing and describing manuscripts in the libraries of Munich, Paris, Rome, Parma, and Berlin. He knew something about the printed copies of Crescas's book; indeed, in the course of his study at the yeshiva in New York, he had read a copy of the Ferrara edition (1555). But the existence of a half dozen or more original manuscripts, one of which purported to be an autograph of Crescas, whetted his appetite. He also saw a manuscript of the same work at Columbia and another at the Jewish Theological Seminary, which was defective because many of the leaves had been burned out. Soon he formulated a plan of study that he discussed with Moore. The dark premonitions that Wolfson had had about his future seemed to have disappeared; he now felt committed to a career in scholarship.

In April 1912, on the eve of his obtaining the M.A. degree, he said to Rab during a visit in Divinity 34, "A man should have a middle name," and thus he chose the name of his birthplace as a *nom d'honneur.* The Anglicized spelling of the town would ordinarily have been "Ostrin." But Wolfson at that time was deep in his study of Greek, so he decided to use "Au" and "y" and thus gave Austryn a Greek flavor. Wolfson took his degree in three years, and in 1912 he also took his M.A. With recommendations from Moore and Santayana, he was awarded the coveted Sheldon Traveling Fellowship, a grant of $1,000 for a year's study abroad. The recipients of the award that year, Harry Austryn Wolfson and Henry Wadsworth Longfellow Dana, were featured on the front page of the *New York Times.*

3
Following the Scent

To follow knowledge like a sinking star,
Beyond the utmost bound of human thought.

Alfred, Lord Tennyson

"Don't work so hard," said Horace M. Kallen to Wolfson on the eve
of his departure for Europe in the summer of 1912. "Go to Paris and
enjoy yourself." But unlike many Harvard graduates of that day who
went abroad either to do the "grand tour" or to become literary
expatriates, Wolfson was a young scholar with a mission. He planned
to travel inexpensively, since the first thing he had done was to
appropriate part of his fellowship funds for his family. However, if
one had no need of luxuries, it was possible just prior to World War
I, by a frugal management of one's money, to stretch it a long way.

Wolfson went from the port of Antwerp to Berlin, than a hub of
European learning. During the first term at the University of Berlin
he listened to lectures by Georg Simmel, Carl Stumpf, the Kantian
expert, and Ernst Cassirer, the exponent of the philosophy of symbolic forms, who spent the last years of his life in the United States.
As always, Wolfson took great interest in the life and attitudes of

the students. He scanned the bulletin boards, which told him the story of all phases of student activities "more fully than the frescoed walls of Dido's temple told their story to pious Aeneas." Visits to the Kneipe of the Sprevia (anti-Zionist) and the Hasmonea (Zionist) organizations at their quarters around Linienstrasse and Charlottenburg gave him ample opportunity to study their opposing views. There he enjoyed good talk, and the meetings made no demands upon his pocketbook. He followed, and was grateful for, the local custom of bringing one or two salami sandwiches in his pocket and slaking his thirst with a large stein of beer at the cost of a few pfennigs.

Nevertheless, despite such pleasant diversions, it was his mission that really counted—the mission that would form a recurrent underlying pattern of his sojourn abroad. For one thing, he immediately located a Crescas manuscript at the Akademie für Wissenschaft des Judentums and made a copy of it. At the same time he delved into the Greek texts of Aristotle and made a critical study of Aristotle's *Physica,* a work to which scholars had paid little attention. The upshot was that he scuttled his preliminary plan for the study of Crescas, which he had prepared in Cambridge before his departure, and outlined a new plan of procedure. By this time the term was near the end and, tired of listening to lectures and argument, he decided to go on the trail of manuscripts. While reading the work of Crescas earlier, he had come across references to "Ibn-Rushd," the great Spanish-Arabian philosopher of the twelfth century who had revived Aristotle and, under the barbarized name of Averroes, was a major influence in medieval religious and philosophic thought. Thus Wolfson chose as his next stop Munich, where the catalogues indicated that many manuscripts of Averroes were available. And for the next eighteen months he stalked medieval manuscripts the way Richard Hannay stalked the man with the hooded eyes in *The Thirty-Nine Steps.*

The manuscript collection at Munich held undreamed riches. Wolfson's original plan had been to read the manuscripts of Averroes and garner passages which would explain the references in Crescas. But he discovered that the writings of Averroes were an essential part of Crescas's intellectual background. Hence he plunged into a minutely detailed study of every manuscript: he read the manuscript copies of Averroes's commentaries on Aristotle, and on paper of every sort and color he kept notes and made outlines and analyses. He also kept in mind phrases which he had come upon in his readings and which reappeared in the manuscripts. These notes, written in a small, clear script, he placed in an oilcloth briefcase that had the appearance of a black folding bag.

With the bag of loot in his valise, he went to Paris and ensconced himself in the manuscript section of the Bibliothèque Nationale, the closest thing in modern times to the Royal Library of ancient Alexandria. That globe-trotting bibliophile Hayyim David Azulai wrote in his diaries in 1778: "There are said to be nearly fifty thousand manuscripts here. . . . This Bibliothèque of Paris is considered the largest and most remarkable in the world." There Wolfson found manuscripts not only of Crescas and Averroes but also of Isaac Albalag, Gersonides, Moses Narboni, Zerahiah Gracian, and Hebrew translations of the medieval Arab and Christian philosophers. He pursued the same method of study and note taking; the briefcase grew heavier.

The pursuit continued in Vienna, Parma, Rome, London, Cambridge, and Oxford, until he had finally hunted every relevant manuscript abroad to its lair. He stayed in Paris from April to July. Since his fellowship provided for one year and time was running out, he made the city his headquarters and began to correspond with librarians and scholars elsewhere about certain passages in manuscripts. In June he received a letter from Harvard, informing him that the fellowship would be extended for another year. The news was exciting, and his work at the Bibliothèque was equally so.

Soon after his arrival in Paris he had found a manuscript copy of a Hebrew supercommentary on Averroes by the fourteenth-century Provençal translator and philosopher, Moses of Narbonne, or Narboni. It was of the greatest importance because it deals with Averroes's *Intermediate Physics* and because Narboni is mentioned and used by Crescas. But the paleography was completely illegible, giving the impression of a series of meaningless dots and dashes, and

Wolfson decided that further efforts to decode it would be idle. Nevertheless, each day he succumbed to the lure of its mystery and examined its leaves until, after months of effort, first words and then phrases became decipherable; then, just after receiving the welcome letter regarding the extension of his fellowship, he was able to read and make a copy of that document. Apart from giving him the pleasure of bagging his quarry, Narboni's work later helped to clear up many Crescan problems.

Another experience should be put on record as an illustration of the rewards Wolfson found in scholarly sleuthing. Toward the end of his stay in Paris, Wolfson one day chanced upon a reference to a manuscript of a supercommentary on Averroes that Moritz Steinschneider, the colossus of Hebrew bibliographers, in his 1,077-page work on Hebrew translations of the Middle Ages, ascribed to the thirteenth-century thinker Isaac Albalag. Having failed to examine this manuscript during his stay in Munich, he returned there en route to Vienna, and found it in the Staatsbibliothek. He read the first half-dozen leaves and stopped short: something was wrong. He reread the pages with the closest attention. Surely this was not Albalag. Could the monumental Steinschneider be wrong? It was not until he reached the university library in Cambridge and found another copy of the same manuscript that he felt certain his suspicion was right. Subsequently he established without doubt that it— and three other commentaries on Averroes's *Intermediate Physics*— were from the hand of Isaac ben Shemtob, a prolific writer of a family which for three generations had a tradition of specializing in the works of Aristotle and Averroes.

The prospect of Vienna, to which he now journeyed by train, was inviting. The Hofbibliothek was closed for the summer, but, locating an official and presenting his credentials from Harvard, he was permitted to work in the library during the mornings. (A half-century earlier Steinschneider had been denied this privilege because he was a Jew.) He copied another manuscript of Crescas's *Light of the Lord* as well as manuscripts of Narboni's commentary on Maimonides's twenty-five propositions. He saw little of the Vienna of lebkuchen and marzipan, of Strauss waltzes and Hansel and Gretel, of the Opera and the Dom. What absorbed his free time were the sessions of the Eleventh Zionist Congress, then in progress. There he met many friends from New York and Boston—he was elected secretary of the Boston delegation—and students he had encountered in Berlin and Paris. It was especially pleasant to see again Reuben Brainin, with whom he passed many hours of talk on literary topics. Of the dignitaries he greatly admired was the veteran leader of the Zionist movement, Nahum Sokolow. He was impressed with his urbanity and intellectual poise. His respect for Sokolow was enhanced when one morning he saw this political leader walking alone in the library, deep in thought as he paced back and forth among the bookshelves. At the close of the Congress many of the delegates went to Palestine by way of Italy, and Brainin tried to persuade Wolfson to accompany them. He was tempted, but his responsibility to his mission kept him from giving in. This was the closest he ever came to visiting the Holy Land.

Wolfson stopped in Venice and Bologna en route to Rome, where he again met some of the people who had attended the Congress in Vienna. But his goal was the Vatican Library, a great repository of medieval manuscripts and incunabula. Here too his Harvard credentials won him admission to the library for a few hours a day, allowing free time to visit places in Rome and its environs and to make short trips to nearby cities like Naples. His findings held no surprises: he copied a manuscript of Crescas's work which had many readings in common with the Paris manuscript. Then to Parma by way of Milan and Turin, with another haul in his briefcase, and by the late fall he reached London. There he made the British Museum his headquarters, and, after intermittent trips to the collections at Oxford and Cambridge, he left for America before the outbreak of World War I.

Wolfson was not merely a slavish copyist preserving literary relics, or a conventional scholar, making a judgment about the character and origin of the manuscript. He searchingly examined the script of the writer, the manner in which difficult or obscure expressions were treated, and the personality revealed in a colophon. To cite one instance, among the Hebrew manuscripts in the Montefiore Collection at Jews' College, London, there was a manuscript of Crescas's *Light of the Lord* (later destroyed by direct hit of a German bomb in 1944) which was described by Professor H. Hirschfeld as marred by corruptions but probably "an autograph of the author." But Wolfson's study of the evidence led to a different conclusion. Comparing the texts of all the copies he had made, he concluded that Crescas's autograph did not exist. For one thing, Crescas had died soon after the completion of the *Light of the Lord,* which "precluded the possibility of a final revision and of the issuance of an authoritative text." For another, this manuscript, with annotations by one of Crescas's students, was an exact duplicate of the Parma manuscript. After examining the evidence exhaustively, Wolfson concluded, as stated in his *Crescas' Critique of Aristotle: Problems of Aristotle's* Physics *in Jewish and Arabic Philosophy* (1929), that the variants in the manuscripts seemed to represent "alternative tentative readings contained in the copies of the work made by students of Crescas to whom the *Or Adonai* was first delivered in the form of lectures and who participated in its composition" (p. 704).

Wolfson was not merely indulging himself in a farfetched theory. When confronted with what appeared to be conflicting evidence, he had already learned—as he had in preparing the outline of his paper for Santayana—to search for a reason for the conflict. He arrived at his appraisal of the Crescas manuscripts by a route that had its pitfalls, but he had marshaled enough evidence to avoid falling into them in the manner of Crescas's own students. While working on the manuscript at the Biblioteca Palatine at Parma, he could reconstruct, as he did in writing later, the difficulties and distress of a student of Crescas who wrote in a marginal note on a page of his copy of the *Light of the Lord,* "When I studied under my Master I could not fathom the full meaning of his view on this subject. . . . The Master, of blessed memory, was accustomed to express himself with the utmost brevity both in speaking and in writing." Wolfson identified himself with this student and imagined both teacher and student engaged in their classroom lectures and discussions, and the teacher using his quill to write down on parchment the substance of his lectures under the light of a candle. But all of this was incidental to his main aim of understanding the mind of Crescas and bringing into historical perspective the thought embodied in his major work.

Clearly, the two years devoted to so imposing an undertaking required concentration and patience to an extreme degree. Since photostats and collation devices had not yet been invented, he studied, copied, abridged, and cross-indexed by hand a mountain of unpublished material, thus providing himself with a miniature collection of important manuscripts and notes which would serve him and many of his students for more than half a century without the need of going abroad again.

Yet at the same time he kept his eyes open and managed to keep abreast of many other things that were of interest to him. He enjoyed art exhibits and theatrical productions, and he continued to read avidly, especially the Tauchnitz editions of English literature and a series of cheap, well-bound books published then in England. He devoured the works of Bernard Shaw and Arnold Bennett, and when he was in London he saw memorable performances of Shaw's *Pygmalion* and Bennett's *The Great Adventure.* Moreover, in each of the places he worked the life of students in the universities drew him as by a magnet—an interest which remained alive throughout his life. Nor was this all. Wolfson kept his eyes open wherever he went, and they took in the minutest details, from the habits of academic ladies and gentlemen to the beauty of church spires against the skies. His observations occasionally crept into some of his later essays in the *Menorah Journal,* where they were effectively deployed for illustrative or symbolic use. Splendid in historical and human insights, they are withal self-revelatory, as in the following excerpt from "Escaping Judaism":

I once had a vision in the German town of Nuremberg. A weary wayfarer, I came to that mediaeval town one early spring. Walking northward from the Central Bahnhof, along the Königstrasse and toward the Sebalder Seite, I found myself in a truly mediaeval environment. There was before my eyes an entrancing scene of mediaeval quaintness, not desiccated and deprived of all signs of life, petrified, wrapped up, and displayed for exhibition, but throbbing with activity and motion, where trade and barter went on amidst houses of lofty peaked gables, bay windows, and red-tiled roofs, and where men of a modern age and appearance rushed in their latest means of conveyances through the narrow and crooked old-trodden lanes. I was especially cheered by the sight of long lines of the week's wash, shirts, drawers, petticoats and waistcoats, bed sheets and pillow cases, all hanging in the air for drying, in the vicinity of the majestic ruins of the old Kaiserburg. A more fitting setting this, for the remains of the old, said I to myself, than the liveried servants, the glass cases, the carved caskets, which guard the ancient treasures in the Louvre and the British Museum. There is nothing more fitting in all human endeavor than the turning of the old into the service of the new. And as I was feasting my eyes on these new scenes of beauty, I discovered I was tired and worn out. I stopped on the Spital-Brucke, spanned over the Regnitz, northwest of the small island of Schütt, for rest and meditation. When I looked up, I saw before me two buildings, the Heiligegeist Kirche to the right and the synagogue to the left. The former was a noble stone pile, rising tapering from the ground, as if grown out of the soil, and blending with the entire scene; the latter stood out as an anachronism, weighing down upon the ground as something superimposed from without, alien to the entire environment, shrieking aloud with its brazen modernity, its squareness, its symmetry. Not even its Moorish style and its sombre look did disguise its recency. It was still reeking with paint and its beams were still aching with nail thrusts. Once there was a synagogue in the town of Nuremberg, which had its roots deep down in the ground and its spires rose high and merged with the clouds, but that synagogue was long, long ago uprooted and destroyed by the ruthless hand of the enemy and on its site now rises the towering structure of the Frauen-Kirche. This new synagogue is not the old renovated. It is not a growth; it is a new production. It is not built for eternity; it will never grow old; it is builded by the preconceived plan of the architect, for utility, for comfort, for convenience, and to meet the requirements of the latest fad. [pp. 82–83]

Wolfson arrived in Boston in June 1914. He stayed with his friend Rab during the summer, and they enjoyed catching up on their experiences during the past two years. When the war broke out they were profoundly concerned about the fate of their families and their people abroad, sensing the tragedies that would inevitably follow. One day they went to the big Blue Hill Avenue Synagogue in Roxbury and joined the congregation in reciting *kinoth*, odes of mourning and lamentation.

When he returned to Cambridge in September 1914, Wolfson

found a room in Divinity Hall. His mind absorbed with Crescas and the complicated problems inherent in every word and page of the manuscript, he felt as though he had never left his old sanctuary. Wolfson's findings and progress were well received by Professor Moore, who advised him to take the examinations for the doctorate, which he received at the 1915 commencement. "For his thesis," wrote Moore soon afterwards, "he presented part of his *magnum opus* on Hasdai Crescas. . . . On the substance of it I would not pretend to be a judge, but about the method I think I may say that it impressed me as one of those self-evident things which only original minds discover, and that it was carried out with extraordinary insight as well as perseverance. . . . I, for my part, have not seen a candidate who showed so much brains." Moore had already told the young scholar that he and Lyon wanted to make a place for him on the faculty of Harvard College, and soon after completing the Ph. D. Wolfson was appointed instructor in Hebrew literature and philosophy. Since this post was especially created for him, there were no funds for salary in the normal budget of the Semitics or philosophy departments. Professors Lyon, Moore, and Felix Frankfurter (who was then on the faculty of the Harvard Law School) succeeded in persuading Judge Julian W. Mack and several of his friends to underwrite a salary of $800 a year, which two years later was increased to $1,000.

The first course that Wolfson gave dealt with the problems of Jewish medieval philosophy, and the main emphasis was on Maimonides. There were three students in the class: Thomas Slater, William Gresser, and Marvin Lowenthal. Slater became a minister but found he could not bear the weight of theology, gave up the pulpit, and turned to business. In the thirties his son took one of Wolfson's courses. Gresser made his mark in law, Lowenthal in letters, and both of them became lifelong friends whom Wolfson saw on his visits to New York.

By the end of 1915 Wolfson had completed two studies dealing with Crescas, specifically the problem of divine attributes and the problem of infinity. Each study was divided into two parts, the first part an essay and the second part text, translation, and commentary. The essay entitled "Crescas on the Problem of Divine Attributes," a little book in itself, was published in the *Jewish Quarterly Review* in 1916. When the editor, Dr. Cyrus Adler, offered either to pay an honorarium of a dollar a page or to reprint the paper in book form, Wolfson chose the first alternative because he felt that the work was not definitive; and for the same reason he decided to extend the second part of the study as well as the essay on infinity and incorporate them into his projected work on Crescas.

Soon after his return to Divinity Hall he was invited to write for the projected *Menorah Journal.* It had happened that while he was working in Paris he had read an article on Jewish students in America in an issue of the distinguished Hebrew journal *Ha-Shilo'ah* ("The Messenger"). To correct some of the misstatements he had written a letter to Joseph Klausner, the editor, who had published the substance of the letter with flattering comment. It was natural, then, that within a few months after his return to Cambridge, he should write an article on "Jewish Students in European Universities," which was published in the first two issues of the *Menorah Journal* (January and April, 1915). Although the article purported to be "random impressions," the description of the manners and ideologies of the students is in fact an analysis of the spiritual posture of European Jewries on the eve of the impending war. It is spiced with deft irony. He observes, for example, the differences between liberal Judaism in Western countries:

In Germany, reformed Judaism has its nascence in free thought, and its aims appeal to the intellectual. With us liberalism is stimulated by our pragmatic evaluation of religion and is held out as a bait to the indifferent. In England it arises from the growing admiration on the part of a certain class of Jews for what they consider inwardness and the superior morality of Christianity and is concocted as a cure to those who are so affected.

His observations are given edge by examples from living customs:

In England it is quite fashionable to admit Judaism into the parlor. Parlor Judaism, to be sure, is not more vital a force nor more creative than kitchen Judaism, but it seems to be more vital than the Judaism restricted to the Temple. At least it is voluntary and personal, and, what is more important, it is engaging. So engrossed in the subject of his discussion was once my host at tea, that, while administering the sugar, he asked me quite absent-mindedly: "Would you have one or two lumps with your Judaism?" "Thank you, none at all," was my reply. "But I am wont to take my Judaism somewhat stronger, if you please."

In this way Wolfson alternately displays criticism and approval of the rising generation of university men in Germany, France, and Italy. It is several cuts above journalism. Indirectly there are clues to his own personality, and the writing, as in the parting shot about the Zionist debate that was raging at the time, bears the trademark of his wit:

Where people are obsessed by the fear of being misunderstood in doing what they otherwise think to be good and impeccable, no arguments, of course, can avail. They are in this respect characteristically Jewish. In the Brand-like racial frame of mind the Jews could never stop midway between the two antipodes of roving world-citizenry and hidebound monopatriotism. It is probable that their attitude will change as soon as it is generally realized that personal devotion and loyalty to two causes are not psychologically a self-deception, and that the serving of two masters is not a moral anomaly unless, as in the original adage, one of the masters be Satanic.

The editor of the *Menorah Journal* sent complimentary copies of the issues containing those articles to certain members of the Harvard faculty. Among them was Charles Townsend Copeland ("Copey"), whose writing course was in itself an institution. After reading the Wolfson article, Copey, a supreme egoist, is reported to have exclaimed, "This man can *really* write! How is it possible for a Harvard man not to have taken my course and be so fine a writer?"

In 1916 Wolfson made his bow in the *Harvard Theological Review* with a review of Joshua Abelson's *Jewish Mysticism.* In our days of the reign of what Marvin Lowenthal has called "Die Wissenschaft des Buberthums," Wolfson's penetrating observations on the phenomenon of mysticism in the Hebraic tradition have surprising freshness and relevancy. Wolfson preferred to see life through the serene light of reason. In this regard it may be pertinent to recall that just then the great Danish critic Georg Brandes, a Jew, was flaying

Sören Kierkegaard for making all that fuss against reason as the truth.

These literary excursions aside, only the preparing and teaching of new courses—new for him and his students and new in American universities—diverted him from the task of putting the results of his Crescas studies into a volume. In addition to linguistic courses on post-biblical Hebrew and Aramaic, the catalogue listed courses on "Jewish Literature and Life from the Second to the End of the Seventeenth Century" and "An Introduction to Mediaeval Jewish Philosophy." Wolfson also collaborated with Professor James Woods in a seminar on Aristotle, which would become a tradition in Emerson Hall during the twenties and thirties. His mastery of the *Physics,* on which he would lecture without notes for two-hour stretches, was something marvelous to witness.

But his mind for the most part inhabited his room at Divinity Hall, where he spent with Crescas the daytime hours away from the classroom and the quiet hours of the night. The collection, collation, and editing of the eleven manuscripts of *Light of the Lord* was of course an achievement. But scholarship is something more than the collecting and collating of manuscripts: it involves method, interpretation, and elucidation; it presupposes the discovery of problems and ways of solving them, when neither problem nor method lie on the surface. In the autumn of 1917, when he completed his manuscript and tied the pile of almost a thousand handwritten pages with thick string, he could be content with a feat of true scholarship.

Wolfson could hardly be content, however, with the fate of his work. It gathered dust for twelve years, despite vigorous efforts on the part of Moore and Lyons to find funds for its publication. But that is another story, to be told later. At this point it may be well to turn to the contents and character of the manuscript the author had tentatively titled, "Crescas' Critique of Aristotle's *Physics.*"

This work deals fully with the theme announced in its title, but in actuality it ranges further. An example of what is currently called "intellectual history," the work unfolds the entire panorama of medieval thought. Of Crescas's life little is said, for little is known.

There is extant a letter he wrote describing the pogrom of 1391 which wiped out his native community of Barcelona and in which his only son was a victim; the letter is signed, "I am the man who has seen affliction by the rod of His wrath—Hasdai ben Abraham ben Hasdai ben Judah Crescas." But he wrote his book more than a decade later, when he was concerned not with personal grief but with justification by faith. His opponents were not fanatics and killers but thinkers and philosophers. It is this war of ideas, with all of its battlefields, strategies, and weapons, that is described in Wolfson's work.

A man of profound religious conviction and a philosopher by temperament, Crescas chose his own time, place, and weapons for intellectual combat; and he was equal to his chosen opponents: Aristotle, Maimonides, Averroes, and their followers in the thirteenth and fourteenth centuries. Crescas did not know the writings of his opponents in the original Greek or Arabic, but his study of the Hebrew translations of their works was so painstaking that, as Wolfson tells us, the retranslations of Crescas's Hebrew quotations are almost identical with the original Greek and Arabic. Thus Crescas was equipped to undertake the iconoclastic enterprise of puncturing, if not undoing, the universe built out of the marriage of faith and science by Maimonides and thus of toppling his master, Aristotle. Crescas's main object, in the words of Wolfson, "was to show that the Aristotelian explanation of the universe as outlined by Maimonides in his propositions was false and that the proofs of the existence of God which they were supposed to establish were groundless."

Maimonides had grounded his religious philosophy in reason by a reconciliation of religious faith with scientific thought. He achieved this reconciliation in the *Guide of the Perplexed*, a work in which Aristotle's scientific conception of the universe merged with Moses' religious and moral conception of society and man. Maimonides treated every problem of philosophy with logic and independence of mind and, as Wolfson has remarked elsewhere, he "touched nothing that he did not adorn with some penetrating comment, with some original insight, with some new orientation." To Crescas, however, the universe of Maimonides, logical and scientific as it was, rested on the shaky foundation of reason and, as a consequence, injected into the religion of tradition elements of compromise. To free faith from this concession to reason, Crescas undertook in his *Light of the Lord* to employ syllogistic logic to disprove the conclusions of logic and science and thus construct a home for religion on its own foundations. He examined the proofs of twenty-five propositions in which Maimonides compressed the main principles of Aristotle's philosophy, analyzed Aristotle's concepts of space, vacuum, time, motion, infinity, matter, and form, and then demolished both Aristotle's principles and the arguments of Arab and Jewish proponents of them.

The entire intellectual exploit, in all of its subtle convolutions and ramifications, is reconstructed with clarity and precision in Wolfson's work. His introduction gives a full description of Crescas's aims and literary sources, the meaning of Maimonides's twenty-five propositions and Crescas's refutation of them, and an evaluation of *Light of the Lord* and its influence on subsequent European thought. Every statement bearing on Crescas's book is linked by cross-references to the Hebrew text and English translation of the book; and every point in Crescas's arguments is linked in turn by references to almost four hundred pages of notes. These "Notes" to the twenty-five propositions in Book I of Crescas's work are really the heart of the volume. No reader need any longer suffer the distress of Crescas's own students, for Wolfson fulfills his promise to give "the historical background of Crescas's ideas." The reader will find an exposition and discussion of everything that has been said by every Arab and Jewish philosopher on the themes of Wolfson's essay and Crescas's text. The result is a condensation of the pith and problems of medieval philosophy, with no sacrifice of clarity at any point.

To achieve this clarity and comprehensiveness was no simple task. Crescas nowhere gives a complete account of his sources. In order to understand Crescas, it was necessary for Wolfson to read not only all the books Crescas mentioned in the manuscripts but all the manuscripts Crescas might have read. This provided the knowledge of everything that was behind what Crescas wrote, and in this way Wolfson found the relationship of phrases and the ideas imbedded in them to phrases and ideas elsewhere in philosophic writings.

The mastery of texts aside, there were other rocks on which the work could have foundered. Crescas expressed himself with tantalizing brevity, his style is allusive and elliptical, his argumentation often only alludes to or completely omits the essential assumptions, and his method of reasoning has a logic of its own. It is not enough, Wolfson believed, to paraphrase obscurities in the text or to give an impressionistic modernization of the thought.

We must think out their philosophy for them [the Jewish medieval philosophers] in all its implications and rewrite it for them in their own terms. We must constantly ask ourselves, concerning every statement they make, what is the reason? What does it intend to let us hear? What is the authority for this statement? Does it reproduce its authority correctly or not? If not, why does it depart from its authority? What is the difference between certain statements, and can such differences be reduced to other differences, so as to discover in them a common underlying principle? We must assume that their reasoning was sound, their method of expression precise and well-chosen, and we must present them as they would have presented them had they not reasoned in symbols after the manner of their schools. [*Crescas' Critique of Aristotle*, p. 27]

This highly conscious and fiercely critical method of textual study, which assumed that a philosopher's thought "is not fictitious like the plot of a historical novel," is a key to Crescas's mental processes, and Wolfson devotes a long passage to its elucidation in the introduction. At first he thought of calling the method noeto-analysis but dropped it because the word, though precise, was not euphonious. He came to call it "the Talmudic hypothetico-deductive method of text interpretation" (*Crescas*, p. 25), suggesting that the attitude of the mind trained in Talmud is in some respects like the sort of historical and literary criticism that applies the method of psychoanalysis to the study of texts.

Confronted with a statement on any subject, the Talmudic student will proceed to raise a series of questions before he satisfies himself of having understood its full meaning. If the statement is not clear enough, he will ask, "What does the author intend to say here?" If it is too obvious, he will again ask, "It is too plain, why then expressly say it?" If it is a statement of fact or of a concrete instance, he will then ask, "What underlying principle does it involve?" If it is a broad generalization, he will want to know exactly how much it is to include; and if it is an exception to a general rule, he will want to know how much it is to exclude. He will furthermore want to know all the circumstances under which a certain statement is true, and what qualifications are permissible. Statements apparently contradictory to each other will be reconciled by the discovery of some subtle distinction, and statements apparently irrelevant to each other will be subtly analyzed into their ultimate elements and shown to contain some common underlying principle. The harmonization of apparent contradictions and the interlinking of apparent irrelevancies are two characteristic features of the Talmudic method of text study. And similarly every other phenomenon about the text becomes a matter of investigation. Why does the author use one word rather than another? What need was there for the mentioning of a specific instance as an illustration? Do certain authorities differ or not? If they do, why do they differ? All these are legitimate questions for the Talmudic student of texts. And any attempt to answer these questions calls for ingenuity and skill, the power of analysis and association, and the ability to set up hypotheses—and all these must be bolstered up by a wealth of accurate information and the use of good judgment. No limitation is set upon any subject; problems run into one another; they become intricate and interwoven, one throwing light upon the other. And there is a logic underlying this method of reasoning. It is the very same kind of logic which underlies any sort of scientific research, and by which one is enabled to form hypotheses, to test them and to formulate general laws. The Talmudic student approaches the study of texts in the same manner as the scientist approaches the study of nature. Just as the scientist proceeds on the assumption that there is a uniformity and continuity in nature so the Talmudic student proceeds on the assumption that there is a uniformity and continuity in human reasoning. Now, this method of text interpretation is sometimes derogatorily referred to as Talmudic quibbling or pilpul. In truth it is nothing but the application of the scientific method to the study of texts. [*Crescas,* pp. 25–26]

Wolfson's opus reveals the vigor and subtlety of the philosophers who fashioned the medieval vision of the world. In the gallery of incisive minds, he paints Crescas as an independent and original thinker who, by liberating himself from the thralldom of Aristotle, foreshadowed "some of those views which form what is called our new conception of an infinite universe containing an infinite number of worlds." Having carried the battle to his enemy's own ground and employed his own weapons to defeat him, he left the battlefield littered with the opponent's broken ideas and felt secure in the reason-free universe he designated. But the story, as Wolfson shows, has a sequel that is "full of mystery, danger, intrigue, suspense, and thrills." While Crescas's disciples were putting their master's lectures on parchment and composing commentaries on them, thinkers like Bruno and Spinoza took up the weapons with which Crescas had demolished Aristotle and used them for laying the foundations of modern science. The infinite universe of Crescas has now been supplanted by the finite universe of Einstein. Perhaps the last word on the matter belongs to the cosmographers who may return from their intergalactic journey into the seas of space to verify whatever the truth may be.

4
Adventure

The vitality of thought is in adventure.
Alfred North Whitehead

As he assiduously wrote the last pages of the Crescas manuscript at Divinity Hall, Wolfson had no inkling that the first—and what proved to be the last—interruption in his scholarly pursuits was imminent. The United States had declared war against Germany on April 6, 1917, and within a year millions of Americans were in uniform. During that time Wolfson labored on, as though on the double, and in November 1917, soon after the publication of the Balfour Declaration, he finished the Crescas manuscript. In a letter to a friend written on November 28, he says in a postscript, "Am celebrating now. Have finished the Notes on Crescas—600 pages strong." Anything brawlish was alien to his conception of "celebrating." He merely sought relief from the years of painstaking labor, and he found it in literary expression. Hidden in a pile of unanswered correspondence were a number of letters from the editor of the *Menorah Journal,* appealing for further contributions to its pages.

His preoccupation with Crescas had not sealed him off from the turbulent events of the world outside Cambridge. On the contrary, he appears to have kept abreast of the happenings, especially in the areas that had always been of interest to him. Now his hand was restless; he could no longer resist the impulse to put into writing some of the ideas that had been sizzling at the back of his head, and the mere thought of releasing them was exhilarating.

Apart from all the reasons that originally impelled Wolfson to select Crescas for a subject of study, it is probable that he was unconsciously attracted by Crescas's iconoclasm. Wolfson himself displayed that Puck-like quality of mind that reveres tradition but at the same time assails venerated idols. This quality, in the form of criticism and satire, marked some of his writing up to this time. It blossomed as he turned his pen from the court of learning to the court of public opinion.

The agitating climate of the war had stimulated clashes of opinion on many issues. The virility of debate was reflected in such new journals of opinion as the *New Republic* and *Smart Set,* and, in Jewish life, the *Menorah Journal.* In the last of these Wolfson chose to canvass the Jewish questions of that time. The result was the publication of two articles, in the form of brief essays on diverse topics, which have unity and express the author's individuality. They appeared in 1918 under the title "Pomegranates" and over the *nom de plume* "El. Lycidas."

The title and the disguise were characteristic. The word "pomegranates" was used in post-biblical Hebrew with several figurative meanings, and the editors of the *Menorah Journal* chose their motto from the *Jewish Encyclopedia:* "Pomegranates are eaten raw, their acid juice being most refreshing." As soon as Wolfson saw the galley proofs of the first article he posted a note suggesting that the motto as well as the announcement of the article be dropped. "Let it be a still-born baby," he wrote, "and let us watch how the readers will wake up and take notice, without being told to do so." But sensing that the editors would exercise their prerogative, he suggested that they at least give an accurate version of the original and proposed

as a translation, "Pomegranates, like wine, set the teeth on edge."
Then he took the editors to task for resorting to an encyclopedia,
suggesting that an encyclopedia "is not an Epictetus from which
mottoes are culled." Finding that the editors were adamant, he
remarked wryly, "How would you like this midrashic gem, 'Pomegranates, indeed, are a marvelous laxative.' Don't you think it would
increase circulation?"

As for the pseudonym, the editors raised no objection; indeed,
they appeared to welcome it. They promised to print every seed and
fiber of the "Pomegranates"—a promise which they honored—but
they included a note stating that the *Menorah Journal* was not in
any way committed to the "bold *ex cathedra* views" expressed by the
anonymous contributor. The editors appeared to be unaware that
"El. Lycidas" was an exact Greek translation, or contraction, of the
author's Hebrew name, Zvi Wolfson.

These essays are as arresting as they are readable. Wolfson casts
his net far and brings home a rich catch. He never gores down his
adversaries, but he leaves them shaken and, true to his version of the
motto, with their teeth set on edge. Fears and foibles are subjected
to biting satire. Since these essays are little known today and the
early issues of the *Menorah Journal* are very rare, it may be well to
give a few examples. Here is one of the shortest, which appeared in
June 1918, entitled "The Cephalic Index and Baseball."

The most important thing about man is the parting of his hair; the least
important—its color. For there is still truth in Carlyle's saying that a man's
religion is the chief fact with regard to him, and by religion here we mean
any act of consciousness, any desire, hope, or ideal, from his choice of wall
paper to his conception of heaven. In contrast to this maxim, we may
likewise generalize that a man's race is the least significant fact with regard
to him, and by race here we mean any congenital fact, any unaccounted
for action, from moles and birthmarks to the most persistent inherited
characteristics of mind and body. To describe a man with reference to his
religion is to describe him in terms of voluntary association; to describe him
with reference to race is simply to brand and catalogue him. Now, the
branding and collocation of human beings may be of some satisfaction to
a certain instinct of orderliness and classification within us, but it is hardly
a useful and purposeful task. The only useful classification of human beings

is that with reference to units in which they socially group themselves; and the forces which make for social organization, we say with good authority, are conscious ideals. While there may exist a certain freemasonry of the sore-headed, and a certain oddfellowship of the ill-bred, there seems to exist no social affinity, for all we know, between the short-headed or the ill-tempered. Perhaps one should be on his guard not to lay himself open to criticism by overdogmatizing on such matters, and so let us admit that it is quite possible for the fact of race to become an object of consciousness, even as it is possible for wood, a stone, a tooth, or a claw to become a fetish. Still it can never become an object of religion, and the difference between a fetish and a religious object is that the former is the idealization of a thing whereas the latter is the objective symbol of an ideal. By the same token, the fact of race, on becoming a fetish, may prove to be a social force of some kind, but that social force will be the tribal and never the national. For nationality is purely a subjective group, and in its highest form a religious institution. Land and government are merely objective symbols, and race is not even that. It is for this reason that nations may survive their loss of country and king provided they can preserve their ideal—hence, Themistocles' exclamation: "Athens is burned, Athens is in our ships." The unity which makes for nationality is not that of a quiescent, uniformative quality which men happen to share in common, but rather that of a dynamic, vital principle by which men consciously act together. Those who see the possibility of the future rise of an American nation in the fact that recent skull measurements have shown that the descendants of various races in this country tend to approach to a uniform cephalic index will have more reason to be hopeful when it will have been shown that the descendants of the diverse nationalities in this country all learn to chew gum, to drink ice water, to play ball, and to venerate the Constitution of the United States. [pp. 162–63]

Although Wolfson was shy in the presence of women, he was a shrewd observer of their foibles. In a section of "Pomegranates" entitled "Three Daughters of the Same Race," which appeared in February 1918, he describes three female types in order to drive home his conviction that Judaism should be taken "naturally, seriously, and intellectually, without a sense of condescension or elation, without a feeling of doing the unusual and adventurous thing, and above all, without making a fad out of it."

They are three daughters of the same race, students in the same institution. One is Lady Ambitious. In her submerged consciousness are surging the errant dreams of a bygone existence, of an adventuress intruding among princes and knights, long trailing gowns and pages, powdered wigs, courtiers, and gracious smiles. In her waking reality she is possessed by the modest ambition of escaping the disadvantage of an unfortunate accident of birth, to gain admittance into a social order to which she was not born. The other is Lady Maternal. She is a latter-day sister in a modern convent devoted to the religion of service. Because of that unfortunate accident of birth she lends a hand in the uplifting of those Jewish mothers who know not how to raise their offspring and of those Jewish children who wallow in the dirt of the gutter. The third is Lady Playful. She lives in her doll's house, a Nora reversed, playing with things rather than a plaything herself. She flirts with abstractions. She regales in the economic theories of *The New Republic* and in the literary views of *The Seven Arts*. She discusses poverty at pink teas, and talks sex in her family circle. Of that unfortunate accident of birth she has made a sportive vagary—a dimple out of a mole. She now entertains her genteel friends with delightful essays on that peculiar race of bohemians who are so advanced in thought and in manners. How she pities that so few of them are socially possible!

To the first—Judaism is a misfortune; to the second—a slum; to the third —a toy. [pp. 25–26]

Wolfson was literally acidulous, and the reactions in some quarters were expectedly astringent, especially those of the Yiddishists, who he "proved" to his sardonic satisfaction to be a people separate from the Jews. The Yiddish press roared and fumed, but the essays had to be taken seriously because their literary power was matched by their psychological and intellectual insights. All in all, the performance was a brilliant young man's *tour de force*.

"Pomegranates" appeared in 1918 while Wolfson was a civilian in the academic community. In August, two months after the publication of the second series of the essays, he was called to the local draft board in Cambridge and, judged ineligible for active service on account of eyesight, he was classified 1A, limited service. Early in September he was ordered to hold himself in readiness for service, and he was inducted into the army on September 30. He began his military life two weeks later as a buck private at Fort Slocum, a permanent military station on an island off New Rochelle, New York. Although his training lasted just five months and interrupted his academic and literary pursuits, he found something about the orderliness and earthiness of army life that fascinated him.

Fort Slocum had a normal cadre of regular army soldiers, whose mission it was to regulate the life of a regiment of assorted intellectuals who had been classified for limited service until their assignment to units elsewhere. The stringencies of basic training at this "recruit depot," from close-order drill to kitchen police, which are frequently a source of irritation to sensitive men, did not annoy Wolfson. He took it all with philosophic calm and turned some of his fatigue duties into pleasures. For instance, he made KP duty something of a sport by having himself assigned as often as possible to the meat slicer; he enjoyed watching the precision of the machine and especially helping himself to slices of salami. Among the other jobs was the stable detail, which required policing the stalls and grooming the horses. A visitor who found him in the stables noted that he looked uncouth but the horse he was rubbing down looked splendid.

Among the recruits there appeared the son of the eminent philologist Professor Leo Wiener, Wolfson's Harvard colleague. By this time Norbert Wiener was an "ex-prodigy"—the title he gave to an autobiography published in 1953—and, herded with the recruits, he felt, he says, as if he had been clapped into a penitentiary. In the dullness and isolation of the island, the fortuitous meeting of the mathematician and the philosopher afforded a pleasant diversion. They created their own private campus and held a running colloquy on topics of mutual interest. Wiener's description of these days at Fort Slocum suggests a pair of Mutt-and-Jeff characters out of the popular cartoons of that time. "The alleviation of my life on the island," he writes, "was the presence of another equally unmilitary recruit, Dr. Harry Wolfson of the Harvard Department of Semitic Languages. My uniform was strained by my corpulence, but Wolfson's reached nearly twice around him. Not even these uniforms could conceal the college professor in us as we walked around the seawall, discussing Aristotle and medieval Jewish and Arabic philosophy."

The incongruity of these professors in khaki did not escape the regular army cadremen. Every now and then one of them with a yen for windowsill philosophy would attempt to engage them in talk about the higher things. Once, when Wolfson had been assigned to a heavy construction detail, a sergeant with a paternal feeling for his curious wards called Wolfson from his onerous assignment, walked with him for a while, and then asked awkwardly, "Private, what do you think of immortality?" Wolfson would probably have preferred to grapple with the spade than with the query; to avoid the necessity of spiritual dialogue, he replied simply that all men need the consolation of the belief in immortality.

Aside from these diversions, life at Fort Slocum was monotonous. About the middle of October Wolfson received a letter from Rab, who, after basic training as a medical corpsman at a camp in Georgia, had been assigned to the chemical warfare department in Washington, D.C. Wolfson replied immediately, saying that he and Norbert Wiener were tired of peeling potatoes and cutting baloney and asked whether it would be possible to get a transfer to Washington. Rab was in the Walter Reed Hospital, recovering from an attack of Spanish influenza, but he obtained and forwarded the information Wolfson requested.

Wolfson was elated when on November 11, 1918, he saw the order transferring him to the Adjutant General Department in Washington, D.C. There was a shortage of billet for soldiers; Rab was bunking in the recreation hall of a Methodist Church, and when Wolfson arrived he found a cot for him there. He was assigned to the Adjutant General's Office and worked there at night checking the lists of the wounded and dead against files of about two million men in the armed forces and identifying casualties whose names or serial numbers were incorrectly listed. Since Rab worked during the day, they spent their evenings together eating in canteens for soldiers, visiting the Young Men's Hebrew Association, and attending movies.

From time to time friends visited Wolfson. One evening his former student William Gresser came to see him at his quarters. Gresser, who was an officer in the Naval Reserve at Pelham Training Camp and eager to get an assignment overseas, had taken matters into his own hands and had just come from seeing Franklin Delano

Roosevelt, the Assistant Secretary of the Navy. He found Wolfson still looking somewhat awkward in an ill-fitting uniform—his puttees seemed to cover his legs from ankles to knees—but Wolfson was in fine spirits and very enthusiastic about his work. He had just devised a novel method of classifying casualties which had impressed his superiors.

Walking down a street once, absorbed in his thoughts, Wolfson suddenly heard a sharp voice saying, "Private, don't you know what to do when you pass an officer?" Balaam was not more startled by the unexpected loquacity of his ass than was Wolfson by this command. It almost made him fall over himself, but he managed to pull himself together and raise his hand stiffly. The commanding voice spoke reassuringly, "Don't you recognize me, Dr. Wolfson?" For a moment the face of the man framed in the accoutrements of an army officer seemed strange, but a second look brought smiles to both faces. The joke was perpetrated by Major Ralph Barton Perry, Wolfson's Harvard colleague.

Rab has told a little more of the story in an unpublished memoir:

On returning to the church one day I found that Wolfson and his effects were gone. After a while I chanced to look out of the window and saw Wolfson standing across the street, motioning me to come over. When I joined him I learned that in the morning, while he was shaving at the back of the church, a Southern soldier had threatened to cut his throat if he didn't make room for him. He got frightened, and left immediately to look for another place to stay, which he managed to find at the home of a Jewish tailor.

The tailor turned out to be a great admirer of Lenin and Trotsky, but this was counteracted by the patriotism of his daughter, who did her best for American soldiers: in the evening when I returned to the tailor's and we walked up to the second floor of the house, we used to come upon her entertaining them.

I was discharged from the army in December 1918; Wolfson remained for another month or two.

Wolfson was, in fact, honorably discharged on January 13, 1919, to return to Harvard at the request of Professor James Woods, then the chairman of the Department of Philosophy. En route to Boston he stopped off in New York to see his family. While visiting at the New York Public Library, Dr. Joshua Bloch, head of the Jewish Room, introduced him to Louis Ginzberg, professor of Talmud at the Jewish Theological Seminary. Wolfson related some of his experiences in the army. Among other things, he explained how his night work with the lists of casualties had taught him much about the hazards of identifying persons and said that the method of identification that he used would be applicable to the identification of historical persons and their works. The men became fast friends.

On his arrival in Cambridge, Wolfson enjoyed a long visit with his cousin Harry Savitz, who brought him up to date on personal matters and took a photograph of him in uniform. It shows him to be well-dressed and in robust health. Wolfson always had a sense of pride in having been an American soldier, and he was a member of the American Legion for the few years that the Harvard chapter was in existence.

Wolfson returned like a homing pigeon to Divinity Hall, moving up to the third floor. Room 35 was one of the larger rooms, with a tall window and a pleasant rural-like view. A few hundred yards away there loomed above the trees and shrubs the top of the dignified Harvard Divinity School. Also visible from the window was the rear of the boxlike red brick Semitic Museum. And in between, almost directly opposite, was the house of George Foot More. Inside the room all was severely plain: a small bed, two chairs, a work table, a floor-to-ceiling bookcase on one wall, and a stand supporting a huge Century Dictionary (which he called his "pocket dictionary"). The room was what the original planners of Divinity Hall a century before had envisioned—home, workshop, and sanctuary. And no occupant, before or since, more abundantly fulfilled the purpose. Years later, when I visited Domus Spinozana in the Paviljensgracht at The Hague, my mind involuntarily conjured up Divinity 35.

Perched like an owl high on a bookshelf, the Crescas manuscript became an object of concern. Frequently Wolfson's eyes rested upon it, as if drawn by some irresistible magnet. Moore and Lyon had not succeeded in finding a patron. Some of his Menorah Society friends attempted to interest Julius Rosenwald, the Chicago philanthropist and Maecenas of Negro educational institutions, and for a while in 1920 there was a glimmer of hope; but the negotiations fizzled out. Wolfson's disappointment in having the result of his labor lie fallow for so long was indirectly revealed in a paper entitled "The Needs of Jewish Scholarship in America," written for a conference at the University of Chicago in 1920 and published in the *Menorah Journal* in 1921. There is no overt word in it to suggest his own need; he showed that certain natural resources were going to waste and that scholarship, unless productive, is useless. "Now, one of the most essential conditions of productive scholarship," he wrote, "is the possibility of publishing the results of investigation. There is nothing so deadening to the spirit as a manuscript lying dormant. It is the proverbial millstone around the neck. It crushes ambition; it checks progress." The words no doubt express his own disappointment, but it was disappointment that had no visible effect on his continuing study and writing. Yet it did stir in him concern about his academic status. Within him were the seeds of discontent, and they brought on a mood of depression. He again considered enrolling in a medical school, feeling that the medical profession would bring financial security for him and his family. But the mood passed.

His appointment was on a year-to-year basis, and his salary in 1920 was $1,000 per annum—just enough to keep out of debt. Yet his achievement seeped through by word of mouth to scholarly circles, and he was confronted with the choice of staying on at Harvard, hoping for a permanent appointment, or of accepting one or another tempting offer elsewhere. One of these offers was proferred by Dr. Julian Morgenstern, president of Hebrew Union College in Cincinnati, the oldest of the Jewish theological seminaries. Morgenstern had in mind a successor to David Neumark, an eminent scholar who had been teaching Jewish philosophy there since 1907 and was reaching the close of his career. Neumark had often consulted Wolfson by correspondence on intricate problems in their field of mutual interest—Neumark had embarked on a multivolume history of Jewish philosophy in Hebrew—and had the highest regard for the younger man's scholarship. But Morgenstern, despite offering a solid salary, failed to bring Wolfson around. One part of the conversation between the two men is nonetheless worth recording. Morgenstern had introduced the question of Wolfson's religious affiliation, since the college was an institution of Reform Judaism. Wolfson's reply was unequivocal: if he were to live in Cincinnati and to attend religious services, his first preference would be an Orthodox synagogue; if there were none, a Conservative synagogue; and only if the latter did not exist, a Reform temple.

In addition to such professional inducements, Wolfson was bombarded with requests for articles from diverse publications. He was invited, for example, to write a number of essays on Arab and Jewish philosophy for a new encyclopedia which hoped to compete with the *Encyclopaedia Britannica.* Incidentally, after his return from the army, Moore met him one day and said he had enjoyed reading some of the recent issues of the *Menorah Journal,* particularly—and he smiled knowingly—a series of articles by an anonymous writer. "Dr. Wolfson," he added, "you can't fool us. Be careful or you'll become a successful journalist." The advice was heeded; for after the publication of "Escaping Judaism" in the *Menorah Journal* in 1921 and a review of the new Moffatt version of the Bible in the *Boston Sunday Post* in 1924, Wolfson confined himself to writing for technical publications. This was regretted by his friends and admirers, and perhaps he himself had a tinge of regret, for these pieces today, with their depth of connotation and richness of exposition, still afford endless delight.

With the translations of the Bible flooding the market, Wolfson's comment on Dr. Moffatt's remarkable rendering provides a semaphore for translators who still grope and flounder in the Hebrew original. Wolfson admired the literary beauty of the King James version, and he questioned the wisdom of attempting to cope with the obscurities of the original by employing the kind of colloquial English that amounts to vulgarization. Instead of cumbering the pages of the review with argumentative divagations, he simply chose some typical verses, placed the Moffatt version side by side with the King James version, and added brief observations in the manner of a medieval Hebrew commentator. Here are a few examples:

GENESIS V:28–29

New Version

After living a hundred and eighty-two years, Lemech became the father of a son, whom he called Noah, saying "Now we shall know a relief from our labor and from our toil on the ground that the Eternal cursed."

Old Version

And La-mech lived a hundred and eighty and two years, and begat a son: And he called his name Noah, saying, This same shall comfort us concerning our work and toil of our hands, because of the ground which the Lord hath cursed.

Wolfson

When little David Copperfield was taken to Mr. Peggoty's barge and met young Ham, Dickens makes him ask the following question:

"Did you give your son the name of Ham because you lived in a sort of ark?"

The new etymology here of Noah's name has a similar Dickensian touch about it.

GENESIS 11:8

New Version

In the land of Eden, to the far east, God the Eternal then planted a park, where He put the man whom He had moulded.

Old Version

And the Lord God planted a garden eastward in Eden: and there he put the man whom he had formed.

Wolfson

The Hebrew word may mean either "park" or "garden." What English tourists in the time of Adam and Eve used to call that delightful spot in East Eden, of course, there is no way of telling.

GENESIS XXV:29–30

New Version

One day Jacob was cooking some food, when Esau came in famishing from country; Esau said to Jacob, "Let me have a bite of that red omelet there! I am famishing." (Hence he was called Edom or Red.)

Old Version

And Jacob sod pottage; and Esau came from the field, and he was faint; And Esau said to Jacob, Feed me, I pray thee, with the same red pottage; for I am faint; therefore was his name called E-dom.

Wolfson

Esau may have been rough and crude in many respects and rather careless about his birthright. But he had a good mother, refined and cultured, who had taught him from childhood to be polite in addressing other people, even his younger brother Jacob.

It is quite certain that, however famished he may have been, he never said to his brother, "Let me have." If he did not actually use the expression "I pray thee," he undoubtedly used the expression "If you please." The Hebrew text demands here some such expression of politeness.

Then, another point. Many a precious thing has not been bartered away in the past for a mess of pottage. Now has come the turn of the mess of pottage to be exchanged for a "bite of red omelet." The exchange, however, is unfair. What Esau was really begging for was a mouthful of lentil soup.

The substitution of the word "famishing" for "faint" is a happy one. The Hebrew commentator, Abraham Ibn Ezra, who died in the twelfth century, interprets the underlying Hebrew word in the same sense.

GENESIS XXXVI:20

New Version
Here are the sons of Seir the troglodyte, the natives of the country.

Old Version
These are the sons of Se-ir the Hor-ite, who inhabited the land: Lo-tan and Shobal, and Zib-e-on, and A-nah.

Wolfson
Inasmuch as Dr. Moffatt prefers to translate the doubtful Hebrew "Horite" by the tremendous word "troglodyte," instead of the simple expression "cave-dweller," he should have gone the full length and used "aborigines" for "natives."

The literal meaning of the word rendered here "natives" is "inhabitants" and for all we know, they may have been aborigines, natives or simply naturalized citizens.

JUDGES XV:16–17

New Version
With the jaw-bone of an ass, I have piled them in a mass! With the jawbone of an ass, I have assailed assailants!

When he said this he threw aside the jaw-bone, and so the spot was called Jawbonethrow.

Old Version
And Samson said, with the jawbone of an ass, heaps upon heaps, with the jaw of an ass have I slain a thousand men.

And it came to pass, when he had made an end of speaking, that he cast away the jawbone out of his hand, and called that place Ra-math-le-hi.

Wolfson
"Jawbonethrow" is an excellent English translation of the Hebrew "Ramath-lehi."

But, by the same token, Jerusalem should be called Peaceburgh.

Wolfson's conversation savored of the same sort of wit. He enjoyed the companionship of students, and among his pleasures were walks with them along the Charles River in pleasant weather. Among those to whom he had a strong attachment was Norman Survis,

whose Hebrew tutor he had been in Scranton and who after graduation from Harvard College attended the Harvard Medical School.
As they walked on the paths along the river, Wolfson munched
grapes and, talking freely, went off like an alarm clock. He also was
a remarkably good mimic, and he used to make Survis laugh by
imitating the *maggidim* whom he had heard in his childhood. Like
most men who exercise great self-control, he had an involuntary
habit that betrayed supressed excitement: he slipped his arm under
that of his companion and lowered his voice. Once while walking
with Survis—he always addressed him as "Norman, my boy"—
Wolfson observed one of the Gold Coast snobs passing by, a stuffed-
shirt and a pompous version of a family portrait who always spoke
of himself as _____ _____, III, accenting the *third*. Wolfson
remarked with sardonic amusement, "There goes _____ _____,
Ai, Ai, Ai." Behind the irony of his wit, or perhaps the strongest
element in it, is the cynicism of self-preservation, even though he
had concealed it deep within himself.

An insightful and touching portrait of Wolfson at this time was
drawn by another of his friends, Julius S. Hoffman, in a poem
entitled "The Toiler," published in the *Menorah Journal*, in June
1920:

> I am a hewer of wood and drawer of water,
> A toiler drudging at an unending task,
> The Temple of men's learning; whereof the base
> lies buried in the past, and whose tall spires,
> Ever unfinished, cut the clouds to shreds;
> So that a lifetime seems a little space,
> And all great effort futile. Wherefore labor,
> Grow pallid-faced and tired-eyed, traversing
> Dim hallways centuries old with Aristotle,
> Crescas, Maimonides, Ibn-Roshd, Halevi?
> Wherefore shut out the throbbing present world?
>
> Typewriter, fountain pen, electric lights,
> A study in the Widener Library,
> Lined with great volumes richly bound: these things
> You say surround me. But I am truly this:
> A skull-capped bearded rabbi, with quill and parchment,

Seeking the truth by flickering candlelight
In some medieval cloistered synagogue.
Deep in old volumes I have learned to smile,
Watching the ebb and flow of human tide.
Even if I ventured forth, still in my spirit
I should be laughing as men jostled me,
At these and at myself for striving so.
I have for such a time with old books dwelt
That all the juice of life has been pressed out
As from some rose, closed in forgotten pages.

I have no part in all the busy street;
Yet sometimes, when the voices of the world
Drift faintly through the window of my room,
Sometimes I would I were, as other men,
Full of the cares and crudities of life.

With all the ways of all men's lives in flux
I spend my days companionless, apart,
Pondering the meaning of an ancient phrase:
What meant the words that Aristotle spoke?
What grumbled Crescas at? What Hebrew thought
Lay hidden in Spinoza's gentile tongue?

And what the sum of this sequestered toil?
A musty tome perchance, on these great shelves
Utterly lost and overwhelmed; forgotten,
Save for the careless glance of passing students.
Here in my study sits the hard Taskmaster,
Stern cold impersonal duty, born of labor
Begun and uncompleted; urging; drawing
My eyes back from the window and the world.
For when I slacken at my unending task,
Mocking its sad futility, he sneers,
Saying, "O fool, in all this witless world
There is no better thing than what you do!"

[pp. 225–26]

Hoffman, a native of New Orleans, had made a brilliant record
at Tulane University in classics, mathematics, and literature; in 1919

he was an instructor in mathematics at Harvard and at Tufts University and was outstanding as a poet and chess player. He took an interest in Wolfson's work and Wolfson admired his talents. Hoffman was a frequent visitor at Divinity 35 where, among other things, he brought along the manuscripts of his new poems and read them to Wolfson. But Hoffman's promising career sadly was cut short.

One day Wolfson was talking with some friends in Perkins Hall when a student rushed in and shouted, "Hoffman's had a heart attack and is at the Stillman Infirmary." Wolfson's face blanched, he swayed and fainted. After commencement Hoffman was moved to the hospital, where Wolfson visited him regularly. It was there that Hoffman composed "The Toiler" and had it posted to the *Menorah Journal*. On the morning of June 29, 1920, Wolfson learned that his friend had died of influenza; later in the day he went to the mortuary to pay his last respects. Stunned by the sight of Hoffman's emaciated face, he walked back to Divinity Hall and paced in front of the building in the dark, haunted by the image of the dead man. The next morning he took a train to Waterville, Maine, and visited Professor Louis Ginzberg at his summer home. Wolfson could never again, even in the case of his own mother, look at the face of a corpse.

During the years 1920–21, Wolfson's decision to bind his future to Harvard began to bear fruit: he was appointed associate professor. In addition, Dr. Stephen S. Wise, who had just founded the Jewish Institute of Religion, persuaded him to become professor of Jewish history on a part-time basis. During the following three years he divided his time between Cambridge and New York.

Wolfson became more sociable than ever. He saw a good deal of Horace Kallen, who had joined the faculty of the New School for Social Research. The rabbinical students at the Institute joined the growing circle of Wolfsonians. Joshua Bloch became his crony, and the two men frequently could be seen at the Childs Restaurant on Sixth Avenue, just west of the New York Public Library, drinking coffee and talking animatedly. Bloch, who combined a gift for bibliographical excellence with an uncanny ear for academic and organizational gossip, was for Wolfson a perennial source of offbeat information. The friendship was ended by Bloch's death in 1957, which occurred while he was delivering a Rosh Hashanah sermon at the Creedmoor State Hospital.

While in New York, Wolfson spent many pleasant hours at the office of the *Menorah Journal,* which was then in an old-fashioned house at 167 West Thirteenth Street. Frequented by scholars, writers, and students, the place was a beehive of intellectual activity. Wolfson generally met with Henry Hurwitz, Marvin Lowenthal, and Adolph Oko, and sometimes they enjoyed good food and good talk at Petitpas, the French restaurant on West Twenty-ninth Street where W. B. Yeats, at the head of a long table, used to read his poetry to his acolytes.

Meanwhile, despite his diffidence in visiting the homes of people, Wolfson found himself at ease at the home of Professor Louis Ginzberg of the Jewish Theological Seminary. Ginzberg was a man of great charm, a powerhouse of learning as well as a fine raconteur, and Wolfson regarded him as the greatest talmudic scholar of our time. Their mutual friend, George Foot Moore, concurred in this estimate and was in close touch with Ginzberg regarding talmudic studies for many years. In the summer of 1920 Moore and Wolfson arranged for Ginzberg to deliver an address before the Harvard Theological School. It proved to be a superb exposition on "The Religion of the Pharisee"; soon afterward, while Moore was working on his study of Judaism, he wrote in one of his letters to Ginzberg, "You are the one who should be writing this book." But it was not only Ginzberg the scholar who interested Wolfson; he was charmed by Ginzberg's intelligent family, by the warmth of Mrs. Ginzberg, and by their attractive children, Sophie and Eli, who in turn adored him. Once, when Mrs. Ginzberg cajoled Wolfson into addressing a women's organization, he promised Sophie—she was fourteen then—a quarter if she would come to the meeting and ask the question, "What is the future of Judaism in America?" To his astonishment and delight, she did just that—though she insists that he never paid her the quarter. Sophie married Bernard Gould, a professor at the Massachusetts Institute of Technology, became the mother of three sons, and at each of Wolfson's visits to their home in Brookline, she continued to play the game of collecting the long-standing debt. Her older brother Eli, an economist at Columbia University, was especially interested in the subtlety of Wolfson's mind. At a Passover seder he once asked, "Why do the matzos have holes in them?" and Wolfson quickly replied, "Because we are *b'nai horin.*" It was one of Wolfson's fine puns, the Hebrew expression from the ceremonial Haggadah having the double meaning of "holes" and "liberated."

Several years later, in the summer of 1928, Ginzberg, feeling that Wolfson was working too hard, urged him to have a respite from Cambridge and to join his family at their new summer cottage at Oakland, Maine. But nothing could take him away from the preparation of *Crescas* for publication. One evening toward the end of July, Wolfson was returning to Divinity Hall from the library. The moon was at crescent. Divinity Avenue was uncannily still. As he walked up the stairs, the building seemed dark and lifeless. Suddenly, as he opened the door of his room, a shrill twittering pierced the darkness as clusters of bats hanging from the ceiling exploded all over the room, brushing against his body. Wolfson slammed the door shut and ran as though in terror. He hastened to North Station and took the next train to Maine. There were a series of cloudbursts that night; when he arrived at the Ginzberg cottage he found the family floundering around in water. While removing his shoes and stockings and rolling up his trousers to help remove the water, he recounted the story of the invasion of the bats. After dinner that evening he insisted that the army had made him an expert dishwasher, so he and Eli removed the dishes and tableware and took possession of the kitchen. There Wolfson became so engrossed in the mechanism of the water pump, and so delighted with operating it, that when the ladies returned they had to put on boots to get into the kitchen.

Wolfson's visits to New York during the twenties also led to the renewing of his acquaintance with Reuben Brainin. We know from Brainin's memoirs, included in his collected Hebrew works, that they met in April 1921, and from one passage we are fortunate to have the only record of a conversation at this time:

*Harry Wolfson's maternal grandparents,
Shmuel Aryeh and Michleh Savitsky,
photographed in Grodno, ca. 1900*

*Sarah Dvorah Wolfson,
mother of Harry Wolfson,
photographed in New York
in September 1947*

*Endpapers of Harry Wolfson's Hebrew grammar book,
displaying his sketches of local personages of Ostrin*

Photo by Karl A. Dimler/Courtesy of the University of Iowa

detail

*Harry Wolfson at Harvard
University Commencement
in June 1915, when he
received his Ph.D. degree*

*Harry Wolfson (left)
and his brother Nathaniel,
photographed on
26 December 1918
during the time of
their military service*

Harry Wolfson (right)
and his cousin Norman Survis, ca. 1920

Courtesy of Mr. and Mrs. Lewis H. Weinstein

The faculty and student body of the Jewish Institute of Religion
ca. 1921, shortly after Harry Wolfson (seated, third from left)
was named professor; Dr. Stephen Wise, president of JIR,
is seated on Wolfson's left

A gathering in Maine, at the summer cottage of Louis Ginsberg
(top right), ca. 1928: standing, from left,
Alexander Marx, Harry Wolfson, and Eli Ginsberg;
seated, Mrs. Mann, Mrs. Marx, and Mrs. Weiner

Courtesy of the University of Iowa

Today, before midday, Professor Harry Wolfson of Harvard University visited me. He sat in my room for more than two hours. We talked about Jewish students at Harvard and their strivings. Wolfson told me that among the students at Harvard there were about twenty who had been born in America and knew Hebrew, and a few of them had literary talent. How profound was my hope of seeing before me a native Hebrew writer or poet? The day that I would lay my eyes upon a writer who was worthy of being called a "Hebrew writer" would be a real festival for me—one of the greatest days in my life. . . . In the course of the conversation Wolfson said, "I believe that only individuals from among the eminent Jews are in a position to do something effective for the weal of our people. I do not believe in so-called Jewish democracy: as applied to our internal affairs, it is a false concept, for we have no parliament of our own and the 'democrats' simply do not have the power to implement their decisions. Democracy in the Diaspora is merely a clanging noise."

I was strongly opposed to this view. I tried to point out that he was in complete error. I was astonished that Wolfson, a man of incisive intelligence, scientific outlook, and immense philosophic learning—and a product of the yeshiva too—that this son of a poor Jew and of the people in whose bosom he had been bred and nurtured, that he of all people should be dragged along by the mistaken notions of the haughty regarding the Jewish problem, that he should see the great ones rather than the little people; finally, and above all, that Wolfson the just—I had almost written "the blameless and upright"—that he should hand-and-glove with the rich and fashionable who were perched on the high places of American society and that he should not feel for the soul of the living people or for the profound revolution taking place in our lives; and that from one who was influencing the climate of Harvard University! Not for nothing did that exchange stick in my memory for twelve years. [Reuben Ben-Mordecai Brainin, *Complete Works* (Hebrew), 3 vols. (New York, 1922–40), vol. 3, pp. 409–11]

Brainin does not record enough of the argument for one to pass judgment on its merit, but the disagreement in no way cooled their friendship. Toward the end of his life, when Brainin espoused the cause of the Soviet experiment of a Jewish homeland in Birobidzhan and the people he loved ostracized him as a traitor to Zionism, Wolfson was one of the few who did not desert him.

Another friend whom Wolfson saw often during the twenties was his former student, Ralph Marcus, an instructor at both Columbia and the Jewish Institute of Religion. Wolfson had a strong affection for the brilliant young scholar, whose phenomenal mastery of languages and irrepressible sense of humor he admired. There is much to be told about their unusually warm relations, but part of it must be postponed until a later chapter. Marcus was in financial difficulty at this time, and having been offered a loan by Dr. Wise but fearful of falling into debt, he sought Wolfson's advice. "But, why worry," wrote Wolfson. "Take the Institute loan. By the end of next year Dr. Wise will probably be so delighted with you that he will double your salary." He was also solicitous about Marcus's new wife. "Don't let Alice gain too much weight. But she may get suntanned."

Marcus was an admirer of Wolfson's writing and continually prodded him about doing articles for this and that magazine. When he became an editor of the *Jewish Institute of Religion Quarterly*, he kept bombarding Wolfson for a contribution. Then one day, during the winter vacation, he received this letter:

Your Xmas greeting with the other kind notes with which you favored me makes me wish I could reciprocate it by sending you an appropriate Hanukkah token. But alas, I have neither the dishes nor the utensils nor the wherewithals to prepare it. And then I don't know whether they have as yet discovered here a recipe for kosher lard. Trefah butter I don't care for.

But I am really going to do something, if not for you personally, at least for the child of your young age, the Institute—and headlines and heresy trials and charges of blasphemy! I have a bombshell in the shape of half a typewritten sheet of paper, double-spaced. I should hurl it in some top corner of the *Quarterly* and let it hit whomever it may. When is your next issue coming out?

Upon second thought (you see the wheels of my typewriting machine move very slowly and give me a chance for a second thought)—yes, upon second thought, I have decided to wait with it until I come to New York. I may perhaps be able to swathe it in some innocent looking wrappings and make the concussion less shaking.

How deeply Wolfson was drawn to Marcus is revealed by a remark in another letter written in April 1927. "Got started on Spinoza's Eternity—as an escape from the temporal. Miss you terribly."

As an escape from Cambridge, especially when he hit a snag in his work or felt "low," Wolfson would take a train and arrive unexpectedly in New York. He would telephone Ralph, and his high-pitched "Ralph, my boy" was a signal for his young disciple to drop everything and meet him at a cafeteria or kosher delicatessen. There they would discuss some knotty problem, continuing at the Marcus apartment, where Wolfson would pace back and forth ventilating his ideas; he would then rush off to catch the midnight or 2:00 A.M. train back to Boston. Marcus, who was not robust and ultimately died of a heart ailment in his fifties, would drop into bed exhausted. When Wolfson appeared suddenly in this manner and Marcus or Ginzberg or Bloch were not available, he would remain at the station and take the next train back.

Such trips to New York, ending in an abrupt return to Cambridge, became fairly frequent over the years; thus among his friends there grew a legend that makes of him something of the proverbial absentminded professor. It was said that he would decide on the spur of the moment to escape to New York, and often, remembering something left undone or having solved a problem that was on his mind, he would take the next train back from New York or even stop at New Haven or Hartford and return to Boston on the first train that appeared. But the facts are enough to dissolve this particular legend, or at least to cast a shadow of doubt upon it. It is true that at that time, and later as well, his trips to New York were mostly short, not so much because he acted on impulse but mainly because he knew exactly the purpose of the journey and wasted no time in accomplishing it. Most often he had some special business to attend to or particular friends to see. During the summer of 1934, for example, he accepted an invitation from his friends Mr. and Mrs. James Feibleman of New Orleans to visit them for a weekend at their summer home in Norwalk, Connecticut. Upon arrival he went directly into the station, got a return train schedule, took his toothbrush and shaving things from his suitcase, and checked the suitcase at the baggage counter. He talked most of the day about the Spinoza manuscript and continued into the night trying to convince Feibleman, who was turning from poetry to philosophy, that poetry was a more suitable medium to express creative thought than philosophy. Feibleman was sparked by his wit but unconvinced by his argument. On Sunday, after breakfast, Wolfson took a train to Boston.

In December 1926 Judah Magnes, who had sought Wolfson's advice on many matters for a decade and had recently been appointed president of the newly-established Hebrew University in Jerusalem, invited him to set up the Department of Philosophy on Mount Scopus. Imbued with the ideal of Zion, Wolfson was tempted. He turned over the idea in his mind for a month and finally, on Janurary 28, 1927, wrote the following letter:

Dear Dr. Magnes:

I have kept your letter under this long consideration because I wanted to give myself a chance of thinking over thoroughly your question with regard to my accepting a permanent appointment in the Hebrew University. If I were to follow my personal inclination, I am sure I would not hesitate for a moment in deciding to accept your offer. My immediate duty, however, lies here. While I cherish the traditional hope that some day, and "even speedily and at a near time," I may find it possible to return to Palestine and to cast in my lot with you, I feel that I must stay on here to try to justify some of the hopes that have been placed in the new Chair which was established only a year ago.

But it will certainly be possible for me to come to you for one or perhaps two semesters. By the end of this term I shall have earned a sabbatical year. Although it is too late now to arrange for a leave for next fall, I hope, as soon as conditions allow me to get away, to go to Palestine and to place myself at your service for whatever duties you may call upon me to perform.

It is difficult for me to answer directly your question with regard to recommending suitable candidates for the proposed Department of Philosophy. In my judgment all those who are at present engaged in the field of Jewish philosophy are good men and are decidedly of academic calibre. But the question of choosing from among them the personnel of the Department is to be determined largely by what you conceive to be the aims and purposes in view. As the Department of Philosophy is still in the process of formation, I may perhaps allow myself to make a few suggestions even at the risk of adding nothing but another counsel of perfection to the many of the same stamp of which you are undoubtedly the daily recipient.

An ideal Department of Philosophy in the Institute of Jewish Studies, like all its other departments, should be organized primarily as an academy of research. It should, from its very inception, become identified with some definite scheme of a grandiose and ambitious literary undertaking planned on as large a scale as the subject demands, even though a century may be required for its complete realization. There will, of course, have to be some teaching in the Department, but this should be confined to the training of properly qualified men in a certain definite direction for active participation in that literary enterprise. In such an ideal Department there should be room for every student of Jewish philosophy who is willing to work there himself, to direct the work of others, or to work under the direction of others. It does not seem to me that it would be the wisest of plans simply to allow the Department to grow up of itself by having men, however excellent, lecture semester after semester on topics in which they happen to be interested to a casual though appreciative audience. The Institute of Jewish Studies should be organized after the manner of the Rockefeller Institute for Medical Research, with such supplementary teaching as the circumstances may require. If conditions in Palestine require that the youth of the country be provided with undergraduate instruction by means of lectures and courses in a varied curriculum, the need, I believe, can best be satisfied by the establishment of a College as a separate department of the University, with a teaching faculty either of an entirely independent composition or recruited from the scholars of the various research Institutes.

If I may further venture upon submitting a few practical suggestions, I should say that the first thing to be done in organizing the Department is to make a survey of the present state of philosophic Jewish learning, to discover what there is to be done, and to work out plans for doing it. A series of publications should be undertaken and announced as the special task of the Department. Jewish scholars of achievement or of promise should be invited as coworkers in this undertaking. All available human material in Palestine—old-fashioned *lomedim*, yeshiva-trained youth, and university graduates—should be encouraged to join the Department, to receive practical instruction in certain branches of the work, and to become, as it were, a new kind of intellectual Halutzim—for the work will undoubtedly require the help of all willing hands. There is nothing of which Jewish learning is in greater need at present than a research institution of this kind. There is no dearth anywhere of educational Jewish institutions with financial and intellectual potentialities to grow and develop into institutions of collegiate rank. What is most necessary now, not only for the Palestinian population but for the world of Jewish scholarship as a whole, is an institution of research to enable us to clear up once and for all, systematically and in a thoroughgoing fashion, the accumulation of centuries of Jewish writings in philosophy as well as in other branches of knowledge, to reexamine texts, to edit them, to study them, to explain them, and to extract from them, by methods of modern investigation, everything that they are capable of yielding. There is nothing which can so well establish the reputation of the Hebrew University in the academic world as a steady flow of solid volumes. And if there will be any creative genius among those who will attach themselves to the University, it is nowhere more likely to appear than in the midst of such scholastic activity.

> With kindest regards, I am
> Sincerely yours,

Magnes, an admirable organizer and a man of charm and vision, was greatly disappointed; but he was enriched by an idea. Afterward Wolfson and Ginzberg recommended Gershom Scholem, a specialist in Kabbalah and Hasidism, and he was joined by Jacob Guttmann, one of the leading German scholars in the field of medieval Jewish philosophy. But Magnes did not succeed in fulfilling Wolfson's concept, nor have his successors followed the idea of creating a milieu that would produce a modern counterpart to master-builders of thought like Philo and Maimonides. Wolfson's proposal was based on the belief that original philosophers are not produced by university departments but emerge out of a congenial intellectual climate. On another occasion some years later he remarked about a philosophy department then being organized at a new university— that it had the appearance of a Zulu king decked out in a top hat, Prince Albert coat, and no pants.

During the twenties a number of Wolfson's former students and erstwhile Scrantonians, who addressed him as "Doc," renewed their association with him. The beginnings of academic recognition and financial security and the admiring cordiality of the "Doc circle" (which over the years ripened into warm affection) seemed to have chinked the armor of Wolfson's reserve. He saw a great deal of William and Gisela Gresser (who became U.S. women's chess champion), Norman Survis, Isaac Witkin, Harry and Cecile Starr, and Pearson Neaman; and on the distaff side Edith Berlack, Annabelle Neaman, and Sarah Kitay. It was a bright, art-minded young group, and Wolfson joined their parties and trips to art galleries in Greenwich Village, where he delighted them with critical interpretations of the exhibits. One day in July 1922 they took him on his first visit to Coney Island, where among other entertainments he rode the roller coaster. Wolfson appeared to enjoy fully these lively young men and women, and to them he was utterly delightful. That year he frequently saw Sarah Kitay, an attractive and gifted girl who was doing graduate work in philosophy at Columbia. She came from a well-known Orthodox family in Paterson, New Jersey, whom Wolfson jokingly called "kosher—eating snobs." In their lively exchanges in regard to his studies in philosophy she found him the greenest of pastures; and in the "Doc" circle all of this was regarded hopefully as a sign of romance. However, after she was awarded her master's degree from Columbia in June 1928, she went abroad and in Switzerland met Leonard J. Stein, a London barrister and the secretary of the World Zionist Organization, whom she married.

Wolfson was then in his late thirties; his "salad" days had come to an end.

After the appearance of *Crescas* in 1929 his life appears to have passed into a more eremitical phase. He had thought of marriage, and his friends had urged it on him. In a letter written from Cincinnati on April 18, 1928, Oko remarked: "How are you? Are you still a bachelor? Why don't you get married? Pretty soon you will be a 'contemporary' of mine—and then it will be too late; that is, no girl will have you. At any rate, think of it." And Marcus, who saw Wolfson at closer range, quipped, "You keep Crescas; I'll take Alice." But his energies were absorbed and expended in his work. The longing for family life became more and more deeply buried, and by force of circumstance and character he made the hard adjustment to being a bachelor. His study became his home, his books and students his children.

Among his colleagues the withdrawal from the rough and tumble of life was often attributed to his shyness, but it was equally the expression of his lofty conception of the scholar in society. He never considered knowledge and intellect in themselves sufficient, but always strove for a religious dedication to the pursuits of learning. "Our ancient wise men," he wrote then, "enumerated forty-odd virtues, and many more are still required by one who nowadays intends to enter upon a scholarly career." Again, in a letter to Dr. Isidore Singer regarding the *Jewish Encyclopedia* on the twenty-fifth anniversary of its publication, he reiterated his view: "Scholarship by its nature is a priestly craft. It is only right for its guardians to be zealous for its purity and fearful of its being contaminated by the gaze and touch of the uninitiated. Left to themselves, they would rather practice it behind a cloud of burning incense on a smoke-enveloped altar in their cloistered studies."

He may have forgotten these remarks; but his life was then, and became ever more so, a living illustration of them. From now on knowledge and thought followed him all the days of his life and he dwelt in the house of learning continually.

5

A New Quest

When I saw that all these ordinary objects of desire
would be obstacles in the way of a search
for something different and new . . .
I came to the conclusion that by abandoning
the ordinary objects of pursuit and betaking myself
to a new quest, I should be leaving a good,
uncertain because of its own nature . . .
for a good not uncertain in its nature . . .

Spinoza

After Wolfson had completed his work on Crescas in 1917, he might simply have awaited publication of the book and thereafter rested on his laurels. Or perhaps, satisfied of the eventual acclaim of his peers, he might have spent the rest of his life publishing medieval philosophical texts and commentaries. He did neither of these things. *Crescas* was only a prelude to greater undertakings.

After Crescas it would have been natural for him to turn to another of the medieval philosophers and apply his method of investigation to, say, Maimonides. He had devoted most of his first course in 1915 to Maimonides, who, together with Aristotle, constituted the background on which Wolfson projected his picture of Crescas. Wolfson had the greatest admiration for Maimonides's original mind and the consummate skill of his philosophic writings. So the author of the *Guide of the Perplexed* would appear to have been a likely choice. Instead Wolfson skipped over to the seventeenth century and chose Spinoza as his subject. The earliest clue to this venture is an essay, "Spinoza's Definition of Substance and Mode," which was published in the first issue of the *Chronicon Spinozanum* at The Hague in 1921. Are we to attribute this unexpected leap in time to chance or to design? If we trace the origin of Wolfson's study of Spinoza, we shall find a combination of both.

There is no need for detective work in order to discover Wolfson's first contact with Spinoza. As a student of Santayana he could hardly have attended his course without being exposed to that philosopher's love of Spinoza. Moreover, his decision to write on Crescas in 1912 could but point toward Spinoza. Not only had he steeped himself in the work of scholars like Manuel Joel and Jacob Guttmann, who took the view that Crescas was a more original thinker than Maimonides, but he was equally familiar with David Neumark's monograph on *Crescas and Spinoza*, published in both Hebrew and English in 1909. Spinoza figures in his own study of Crescas.

Wolfson was released from the army early in 1919, and, with no teaching to do that semester, he began to think about his next project. Until then preoccupied with medieval philosophy, his thoughts turned to the originators of the modern period. At first he considered Descartes, but he felt that Descartes was too much part of the medieval tradition to present any specially new problems. It was precisely in this respect that Spinoza attracted him—Spinoza who ended the long reign of Philo. No doubt his choice was influenced also by the fact that Spinoza's early life as a yeshiva student in Amsterdam was reminiscent of his own early life. Like him, Spinoza studied the Jewish philosophers. Further yet, this side of Spinoza had been neglected by students of his philosophy. Once he had come to a firm decision, Wolfson moved his material to a room at the top of the Semitic Museum where he could work without interruption. He also announced a course on Spinoza in the 1920 catalogue.

At about this time Carl Gebhardt was organizing the publication of the *Chronicon Spinozanum* in The Hague. One of Wolfson's friends, Adolph S. Oko, a bibliophile and literateur who was serving as the librarian of the Hebrew Union College, was appointed to act as the American agent for the publication. He visited Cambridge and urged Wolfson to contribute to this important Spinoza enterprise. The invitation was a catalyst, and soon thereafter Wolfson wrote the essay, "Spinoza's Definition of Substance and Mode," and sent the manuscript to Oko. When the essay appeared in the sumptuous pages of the *Chronicon Spinozanum* it was received in the scholarly community with unusual interest. The essay was followed by four more studies of key problems in Spinoza, published in the same organ between 1922 and 1926, which were regarded as models of scholarly precision. The announcement in the *Chronicon* that these were installments of a work to be entitled *Spinoza, the Last of the Mediaevals: A Study of the Ethica Ordine Geometrico Demonstrata in the light of a hypothetically constructed Ethica More Rabbinicoque Demonstrata* put scholars on notice. The essays were reviewed and the book eagerly awaited.

Among those who were impressed with the first of these essays and took the trouble to communicate with the author was his former teacher, George Santayana. His letter, written from Nice on October 25, 1922, bears the imprint of a mind of extraordinary strength and subtlety:

I have spent a very pleasant hour reading your first chapter on Spinoza. . . . You know, perhaps, that Spinoza is a great force in my private economy, and I daresay I sin in adapting and transforming him to my own uses. It is a legitimate absorption of what one finds nutritive, but it makes it all the more necessary for historical criticism to restore the genuine character of great men's thoughts, as their own age conceived them. I admire your wise scholarship, and the way you employ it: in the first place, in order to make an imaginative and even playful reconstruction—what Spinoza's book *might have been;* and then to return to the formal and quaint dialectic, to the scholastic flavour, of Spinoza, in contrast to the sentimental turn given to him by Goethe & Co. I hope you will persevere and make a great success of the work.

Santayana's praise was of course gratifying, but in Wolfson's own mind the lauded essay was tentative and would probably have to be scrapped before he completed his two-volume work, *The Philosophy of Spinoza: Unfolding the Latent Processes of His Reasoning.* In *Crescas* Wolfson had fashioned or refashioned a method of study which he referred to by the traditional term *pilpul.* It consists in the interrogation of a text so thoroughgoing as to leave no aspect of it or of the mind behind it unexplored. It amounts to the recreation of both. In applying this method to the mind of Spinoza in the period before he was excommunicated by the Amsterdam Jewish community and before his escape from Judaism, Wolfson brought to light Spinoza's medieval affiliations, an aspect of his philosophy which had hitherto been neglected. But the method needed to be extended and refined if he was to cope with the enigmas of Spinoza's reasoning.

First of all, as in the case of Crescas, Wolfson considered it essential to read all the books that Spinoza mentions in his writings as well as the books he might have read. As he had already written in his *Crescas,* such investigation in the sources, actual as well as possible, is "not a matter of mere idle play or even of intellectual curiosity," but it is "necessary for the understanding of the text" being studied. Spinoza cannot be understood otherwise. Wolfson writes:

In our study of the *Ethics,* we must try to follow the same method that Spinoza followed in writing it. Spinoza did not start out with classified lists of bibliographies, outlines, abstracts, quotations, and all the elaborate equipment with which methodical scholarship of today prepares itself for the writing of an informative work of reference. He started out with a certain fund of knowledge acquired through miscellaneous reading, which in his mind formed itself into a composite picture of the salient features of traditional philosophy. In this composite mental picture, we may assume, the problems of philosophy presented themselves in a certain order, each problem modelled after a certain pattern and expressed in a certain ter- minology. Tagged on to this picture, underneath its surface, and deep down into the recesses of Spinoza's consciousness, we may further assume, there was an aggregation of notes swarming with references to sources of texts, to parentages of ideas, to conflicts of opinions, and to diversities of interpre- tations, all of them ready to come up to the surface, whenever the occasion arose, and take their place in the picture. In our endeavor to retrace the steps of Spinoza's reasoning, we must, therefore, first of all, equip ourselves with a similar fund of knowledge, or philosophical mass of apperception, as it may be called. [*The Philosophy of Spinoza,* vol. 1, pp. 4–5]

Because it illustrates so perfectly the character of his method, we might dwell a little on Wolfson's treatment of infinity in *Spinoza*. Spinoza's discussion is puzzling, in that it is one of the enigmas of philosophy. Anxious to dispose of the view of those philosophers who deny the infinity of corporeal substance, he restates and criticizes their arguments, but mentions no names. Who were these philosophers? Presumably they were followers of Aristotle, so that it is ultimately the views and arguments of the latter that Spinoza is combating. Yet the curious thing is that for every view ascribed by Spinoza to his unnamed opponents there is in Aristotle a statement to the contrary. Having identified these opponents, Wolfson finds that they not only explicitly deny that kind of divisibility of extension that Spinoza accuses them of affirming, but they are equally emphatic in rejecting the term "infinite" in the sense which Spinoza attaches to the term in maintaining the existence of an infinite extension which is indivisible. The easy way out of the difficulty would have been simply to assume that "Spinoza purposely misrepresented his opponents in order to be able to refute them, or that out of sheer ignorance he attributed to them views of which they did not approve." But it was not the way taken by Wolfson, who "preferred to believe that Spinoza was both intellectually honest and accurately informed." Accordingly he asked himself whether it might not be possible to interpret Spinoza's statements in such a way as to absolve him of the charge of ignorance or dishonesty. "We made several vain attempts," he says, "until we finally hit upon a possible distinction in the use of the term 'indivisible' and correspondingly in that of the term 'divisible.' By assuming that Spinoza had used these terms according to this new distinction which we invented *ad hoc*, we were able to explain his statements about his opponents in a fully satisfactory manner." At this stage the invented distinctions were purely hypothetical with no evidence in their favor "except the internal criterion of [their] workability." The next step was to find some external corroboration "in the form of a statement by some author, mediaeval or ancient, where that distinction in the use of the terms 'indivisible' and 'divisible' was made." Away in New York at the time, and occupied with teaching and other assignments, he failed to find the corroborating statement. But later in Cambridge, with all the literary sources at his disposal and after some search, he "found that this distinction in the use of the term 'indivisible' is made by Aristotle and Thomas Aquinas" (vol. 1, p. 29).

Spinoza's discussion of infinity is only one among the many problems which his philosophy poses. They are problems not immediately evident, since they lie under the surface, and it is not only their solution but their very discovery that marks the preeminence of Wolfson's study of Spinoza. No philosopher could have presented a greater challenge to his method. It was not merely a matter of learning, of what in professional jargon is called "sources," but of an imaginative reconstitution of Spinoza's mind. For, as Wolfson writes in *Spinoza* (vol. 1, p. 22), the *Ethics* "uses language not as a means of expression but as a system of mnemonic symbols. Words do not stand for simple ideas but for complicated trains of thought. Arguments are not fully unfolded but are merely hinted at by suggestion. Statements are not significant for what they actually affirm but for the denials which they imply." In a word, Wolfson was undertaking to do for Spinoza what Spinoza had failed to do for himself— namely, communicate the fullness of his thought. He had undertaken to do much the same thing for Crescas, and now, as his work on Spinoza progressed, the linkage between the mental processes of the two thinkers became more and more apparent. Perhaps Wolfson aimed at just such a linkage. In any case, Spinoza could not be understood without Crescas.

The manner of Wolfson's day-to-day procedure was this: he would sit down in the morning and write out an interpretive essay on the basis of the working hypothesis and insert dummy passages. Later on, as he located the proof-texts, he would insert them. Given the method he was employing throughout his investigation, the necessity of setting up hypotheses was paramount. For the method was not merely a matter of classifying data but of discovering problems and, in addressing himself to their solution, Wolfson commonly started with a conjecture. Thus, speaking of the missing links in Spinoza's argument, he observes that sometimes "they could be forged out of material which we happened already to have at our disposal, but most often they had to be invented imaginatively out of material which we only assumed to exist and the corroborative evidence was to be discovered afterwards" (vol. 1, p. 27). In fact, he could have written his *Spinoza* by presenting each problem in the form of a mystery story.

During these years Spinoza was at the center of Wolfson's thoughts. They were years relentlessly devoted to the task of reconstructing the *Ethics*. His promotion to a full professorship in 1925 in no way altered his way of life, except for the change of residence the next year from Divinity Hall to an apartment in a newly constructed building at 85 Prescott Street. With him went the yellowing Crescas bundle which now found itself ensconced in a modern refrigerator as a safeguard against fire. It seemed that, with funds still not in sight for its publication, Spinoza might be his first printed book.

Suddenly the prospects brightened. Through the efforts of friends and colleagues, Lucius N. Littauer, a millionaire glove manufacturer from Gloversville, New York, and a Harvard graduate of the class of 1878, took under consideration the establishment of a chair for Wolfson. Littauer was a kindly, sensitive, unpretentious person who was devoted to his alma mater. An outstanding member of the crew and football teams in his undergraduate years, he later served as the first coach of the Harvard football team. Neither politics (he had served a term in Congress and was a friend of Theodore Roosevelt) nor business stopped him from attending the regattas and the football games. His only contact with Jewish learning was through the discourses of Rabbi Hyman Enelow of Temple Emanuel-El in New York, a scholarly rabbi whom he revered. Among Littauer's younger friends was Harry Starr, also a native of Gloversville, New York, whom he had helped through the Harvard Law School. Starr had taken Wolfson's course in post-biblical Jewish history and had often spoken of him with admiration to Littauer.

The groundwork had been laid by Henry Hurwitz and Harry Starr, an intimate friend of both Wolfson and Littauer. Starr was then practicing law in New York and sparked Littauer's interest in the idea, meeting with him frequently and keeping Wolfson advised of the progress. On June 11 Starr wrote: "Congratulations! The professorship is practically sure. I have just had a talk with L. N. L.

over the telephone. . . . I am going to see him tomorrow afternoon and all the details will be settled. . . ." Littauer arrived in Cambridge the following Wednesday and in the morning visited with Wolfson at Divinity Hall. His impression of Wolfson apparently corroborated all that he had heard, and soon afterward, with warm encouragement from his friends, especially Judge Julian W. Mack and Rabbi Enelow, Littauer presented the university with an endowment to establish a chair for the Nathan Littauer Professor of Hebrew Literature and Philosophy—the first of its kind at any university in the Americas or Europe—and Wolfson was appointed its first incumbent.

Though Littauer was initially impressed with Wolfson's concern for and impact on students, he also came to discern the importance of publishing the Crescas work, and in the fall of 1927 he agreed to underwrite the costs. At the time *Crescas' Critique of Aristotle* was completed in 1917, the Harvard University Press had estimated the cost of publication at about $2,700; by 1929 the cost had soared to $8,000. However, Littauer did not consider that too high an investment for a work of which Professor Moore had written, "I do not know of any work of comparable magnitude and difficulty that has been undertaken of late years by one of our scholars and carried through on so sound a method, and with such untiring persistence. . . . The value of such a piece of work as Wolfson's lies, not solely in the light it throws on Crescas and on the thought of the period in which he lived, but in the exemplification of the way in which such an investigation should be conducted."

For two years Wolfson was sidetracked from Spinoza, editing the Crescas manuscript, rewriting the introduction, and taking it through the press. The bound book was a weighty tome of 759 pages, and in later years he jokingly referred to it as a "monstrosity." The original title had been *Crescas' Critique of Aristotle's Physics,* but just before publication he confided to a friend that he had decided to "jazz it up" and forthwith dropped the last word and the possessive. Among the handful of scholars in the world qualified to judge it, the qualities described by Moore were confirmed. For example, when *Crescas* was read by Professor Heinrich Meyer at the University of Berlin, the preeminent scholar of Aristotle and author of *Die Logik des Aristotles* appeared with the book in his seminar room and exclaimed, "At last, a genuinely great work of scholarship has been produced in America!"

Unlike the novelist, the true scholar does not achieve popular fame overnight, if ever; nor are riches his reward. Yet there are modest satisfactions, and in Wolfson's case at this time it was the acquisition of a permanent study. The Spinoza table at the top of the Semitic Museum had the advantage of isolation, but it was far removed from the resources in the stacks of Widener Library in Harvard Yard. During 1927–29 Wolfson worked alone at night on Crescas at the Museum. Then his friend Professor Robert P. Blake, the eminent Byzantine scholar, became the librarian of Widener and told him that Room 15 on Floor B at Widener would soon be available. It was at that time occupied by Henry James, the son of William James, who was finishing a biography of Charles W. Eliot. Wolfson moved in on December 14, 1931.

Having expended his energies on getting the Crescas work to press, he had experienced something of a letdown during the previous year. Now, the transfer of his material from the Semitic Museum accomplished, he felt in the mood for a vacation and went to New York for the winter holidays. After spending several days visiting with family and friends, he was suddenly possessed by his project on Spinoza. A few days before New Year's he returned to Cambridge, and from the moment that he entered his study at Widener until the end of the following summer, nothing but his teaching and food and sleep interrupted his work.

But it was by no means smooth sailing. Of course the basis for five chapters existed in the installments that had appeared in the *Chronicon Spinozanum,* and these in the meanwhile had been interlined with revisions. Actually, he could now see the first volume in his mind. He had already worked out—frequently using his course on Spinoza as a laboratory—a logical order for the propositions of the *Ethics* as a framework for analysis and interpretation of the book for his first volume. As he proceeded, he had to toil at precise and graceful expression, for he was determinded to make this a work of literature as well as scholarship.

His hands moved surely and speedily. He had followed through with his plan. Now it was necessary to spin the threads of his mesh tighter. The book in his mind formed on paper. The first volume was completed.

But he was then stumped by the second volume. For some time he could not account for a haunting notion that he was repeating himself; and the inability to solve this riddle was extremely disturbing. He had difficulty in swallowing, a condition that was diagnosed as globus hystericus, or feeling as if a ball were lodged in the esophagus, obstructing the passage of food. Then one day, while he was taking a shower, the analogy of macrocosm and microscosm occurred to him, and the application of it to his work dissolved his difficulty. As a result, the solution to the problem of establishing the historical background of Spinoza's thought seemed to come more readily. And even the search for the exact meanings of the most baffling of Spinoza's terms was less nettling. "The history of philosophic terminology," he remarked later, "is full of all kinds of tricks, and no sooner do we find a term meticulously and scrupulously defined than we discover somewhere either explicitly or by some subtle implication that it also has some other meaning." Each day some such uncommon distinction rose like a jinni to plague him, but before the library closed at night he would usually have substantiated his findings. At any rate, by the end of the semester in June he had only the last few chapters in the second volume to complete.

About this time a scout from the publishing house of Macmillan sought him out at Widener and offered him a contract for the work. But he hesitated, for his preference was to have *Spinoza* appear, as *Crescas* had done, under the imprint of the Harvard University Press. One day soon afterward Professor James Ropes, the New Testament scholar and then chairman of the Board of Syndics of the Harvard University Press, met him at the Faculty Club and said that the Press would like to publish the Spinoza. Wolfson replied that he would feel honored but that he did not want Mr. Littauer or any of his friends solicited for the funds. Ropes then suggested that he might get the money from the Commonwealth Fund if Wolfson would make the application for a grant. But Wolfson remembered the humiliation suffered by Professor Leo Wiener when his applications for funds for the publication of his books were turned down. He had made a firm decision that he would never apply for a grant unless he knew in advance that the money would be given. Ropes assured him that the money was certain, that he would only have to put his signature on the application sheet, and that Ropes would take care of the rest. Ropes was as good as his word; shortly thereafter, Wolfson was notified of the grant.

One day in August 1932 Wolfson was writing the last few pages of his final chapter, "What Is New in Spinoza?" Since he was approaching the end, he did not stop to have lunch but continued working until about four o'clock in the afternoon. Just as he wrote the last line, Nathan Isaacs, a professor of law at the Harvard Business School and an Orthodox Jew, came to his office. Wolfson told him joyfully that he had just completed the manuscript, adding that he had not eaten all day. Isaacs replied, "I haven't either. Today is Tisha B'Av." Wolfson thought afterward that perhaps it was not only eagerness to finish the manuscript but also the unconscious memory of the traditional fast on the Ninth Day of Av, the commemoration of the destruction of the Temple in Jerusalem, that kept him from eating that day.

That year the completion of a work begun twelve years earlier was saddened by two deaths. The passing of George Foot Moore marked the loss of a great scholar who had had a profound influence on Wolfson's life. And in New York his maternal grandmother died. She had outlived her husband by fifteen years, and her life spanned a full century, her mind still alert in a shriveled body until the end.

After the work on Spinoza was completed, Wolfson kept making revisions for another two years. The manuscript that reached the Harvard Press had the look of a patchwork quilt and became the despair of the editorial staff. Besides, Wolfson was anxious not to repeat the mistake of presenting the world with another "monstrosity." He made a study of fonts, makeup, stock, bindings, and color schemes. He discussed all the details of appearance with his friends, asking them what color they preferred for the cover of the book. Should it be blue, or red like the Haldane edition of Descartes? Should it be one volume or two? Should the type be large or small, and the leading conventional or generous? He would have some of his students read aloud—"with expression, please"—long passages in order to test the prose, and the cadence of it was manifestly delectable to him.

The Philosophy of Spinoza appeared in two volumes in the summer of 1934, and this work was widely acclaimed as a classic of philosophical scholarship.

At this point it would have been natural for anyone but Wolfson to sit back for a while and enjoy the pleasant things that were being written and said of his *Spinoza*. But the demon within would not allow him to relax. He did not "celebrate," as he had done after the completion of *Crescas*, with a bout of satirical writing. On the contrary, the period 1934–35 was marked by unusual productivity and widening of his fields of research. Among his courses announced in the university register that year was one dealing with the fundamental concepts of metaphysics and theology, with special reference to Thomas Aquinas, Maimonides, and Avicenna, and another seminar in the history of philosophy with special reference to the development of Aristotelian philosophy. At the same time he lectured more frequently than was his custom at the philosophy clubs at Harvard and at the neighboring universities and made contributions to the worldwide commemoration of the 800th anniversary of the birth of Maimonides, an event that Harvard noted by a colloquium in which outstanding scholars on the faculty participated.

In the midst of his labors there was one escape into sociability, and it should not surprise us to find that the occasion concerns his friend Ralph Marcus. Now a professor at the Jewish Institute of Religion in New York, Marcus still was plagued by financial difficulties, which just then became more severe because the Depression had precipitated a cut in professors' salaries. In the hope of replenishing his resources, he wrote a novel; but although the publishers' readers were uniformly full of praise, they resisted accepting it for publication. (Years later the book was published privately.) These setbacks, however, dulled neither his humor nor his adventurousness.

One of the things Marcus admired about Wolfson was his success as a matchmaker, and Marcus strove to vie with him, making Wolfson himself his principal target. During February 1935 Wolfson suggested to Rabbi Louis Epstein, a friend from yeshiva days, that he invite Marcus to Brookline to speak at his synagogue at a meeting to be devoted to Maimonides. Wolfson, on a visit to New York a few weeks earlier, had missed seeing Marcus, and soon after his return to Cambridge a letter arrived, containing a characteristic paragraph. "Alice tells me that you made quite an impression on her friend Cornelia (who isn't at all bad-looking and is a nice girl. Verbum sap.) She thinks you quite 'cute' (marvelous description) and she and Alice were disappointed that you didn't call on them Sunday afternoon."

Wolfson's failure to turn up for a second look at Cornelia deprives the story of a romantic motive. Actually, there were professional matters that Wolfson wanted to explore and an honorarium for the lecture would make the trip feasible. In any case, several letters from Marcus, posted withing the subsequent two weeks, lift the curtain on the friendly relations of the men.

February 16, 1935

Dear Doc,

There must be such a thing as telepathy. Yesterday I mailed a letter to you—about nothing in particular, and this morning I got a letter from Rabbi Epstein saying that you had put him up to inviting me to speak to his congregation on Maimonides on March 8. I've accepted the invitation, although, as I wrote him, I feel like a faker, speaking on Maimonides with you around Boston for them to call on. The question is, shall I give my own lecture or ask you to write the lecture for me?

I'd like to take Alice along, leaving Danny with her folks. Epstein offers $25 for expenses. With reduced weekend fare we can just about make it on that; I asked Epstein to wangle another $10 or so from his treasurer.

If Alice comes along, may we and can we stop with you? Have you got an extra couch? We might even all sleep three in a bed, providing you promise not to disturb my sleep by making love to Alice in the middle of the night. Anyway you'd only need one bed and one couch, no matter how narrow. We're both quiet sleepers.

Listen, why don't you write a big commentary on Maimonides like the classic modern commentaries on Plato and Aristotle or like your work on

Spinoza? It would be a swell thing to have and only you could do it just right.

I'm full of ideas. But if and when we get to Boston, "no shop talk" says Alice. She's out for a vacation spree. What say? Be seeing you. Love from all. As ever,

Ralph

We do not possess the letter Marcus mentions in the next note, yet it can be read between the lines.

Dear Doc,

Our letters must have crossed. But after writing to you to make inquiries about accommodations at Hotel Wolfson, we are puzzled by your cryptic warning about bringing "knitting along." Does that mean that Alice has to stay at home? She's a high-spirited woman, and besides, is always anxious to see Boston. So I guess I'll have to invite her.

Please write frankly about the bed situation. Or maybe you don't allow Jews in your hotel? Then I guess we'll have to stay at the Statler, but you'll be sorry not to have your bachelor privacy pleasantly invaded by feminine perfume. Or shall I bring along a girl for you?

As ever,
Ralph

February 28, 1935

Dear Doc,

Hurrah for our host! But its too bad you went to the trouble of reserving an extra room. You know we really could sleep two on a couch if we had to. Anyhow we'll be seeing you on Friday the 8th. We'll take a train at about 11:00 A.M., which will get us in about 5:00 P.M.

Rabbi Epstein is a fine sport. He not only got me an extra $10, but he even sent a check in advance.

I still don't know what to say about Maimonides or whether to be serious, amusing, profound, eloquent, or just boring. But maybe I'll get a few ideas from the *New Yorker*.

The Epsteins invited us for dinner Friday evening, before the service, I presume. Shall you be there too? Come over and then we can go back to Cambridge together and have a bite in the Georgian [cafeteria] like old times.

Alice wants to go sightseeing Saturday around Boston. Shall we ditch her and go scouting for waitresses or be polite and escort her around?

Many thanks. As ever,

Ralph

This sort of diversion was rare for Wolfson, and thoroughly enjoyable. Another activity not strictly in line with his occupations at that time was dealing with certain critics of his *Crescas* and *Spinoza*. Nothing could rouse him more than the words of the uninformed and misinformed, especially when they gave the impression of speaking with authority or when authorities departed from the canons of true scholarship. Detailed reviews of *Crescas* had been slow in appearing, George Sarton's in 1930, Isaac Heinemann's in 1932, and Julius Guttmann's in 1933. Wolfson made marginal notations on their disagreements but delayed writing them up until *Spinoza* was finished. Then, in 1934, he dealt systematically with the points they raised in a paper entitled "Studies in Crescas," and he did so in a way that would make them of general interest to students of Hebrew philosophic texts. Among other things Wolfson dealt with Heinemann's and Sarton's criticism of his method. Heinemann asserted that Wolfson's claim to be employing the talmudic method was unconvincing because he had failed to develop the distinction between this method and that of Aristotle and his commentators. Wolfson's reply was telling:

Evidently, the reviewer wanted to object to something I have said, but could not make up his mind whether to object to my identification of the Talmudic with the scientific method or to accept my identification and then, on that score, to object to the description of my method as Talmudic, and so he combined the two objections and finds fault with my use of the expression "Talmudic method" on the ground that I failed to explain how it differs from the scientific method. Now, I do not feel that I have to apologize for my describing the subtleties of reasoning displayed by Crescas in handling philosophic texts as a manifestation in the field of philosophy of the traditional native Jewish method of studying texts which is generally associated with Talmudic literature. Nor do I feel the need of apologizing for the statement that in attempting to retrace the processes of Crescas' reasoning I have consciously followed this old method of Jewish learning, though externally I have tried to conform to all the accepted canons of modern scholarship. But realizing the prevalent misconceptions about this native method of Jewish learning I felt it my duty to show by an analysis of it that it is essentially a scientific method of text-study. That I have succeeded in my attempt to rehabilitate this misunderstood Talmudic method is quite evident from the reviewer's complaint that he finds no difference between it and the method followed in the best type of scholarly research. But while Heinemann seems to have become so much convinced of the scientific nature of the Talmudic method that he objects to my singling it out as something peculiar, my friend and colleague, Dr. George Sarton, in his review of *Crescas' Critique of Aristotle* in *Isis* [14:240–4 (1930)] . . . contends that in my statement that "Pilpul is nothing but the application of the scientific method to the study of texts" I confuse "the truth in the worst manner." "For," he continues, "the essence of the scientific method is precisely not to stop at words but to investigate as directly as possible the realities which these words are meant to represent. . . . From that point of view, pilpul is as antagonistic to scientific thinking as anything can be." In this criticism Dr. Sarton has committed a fallacy which in the language of the logic of pilpul may be described as the fallacy of "wheat" and "barley." What I have tried to establish in my description of pilpul may be reduced to a formula which runs as follows:

> Pilpul to the *study of text* is as
> Scientific method to the *study of nature.*

What Dr. Sarton argues against is a formula which runs as follows:

> Pilpul to the *study of nature* is as
> Scientific method to the *study of nature.*

[*Proceedings of the American Academy for Jewish Research*, 5 (1934), pp. 171–72]

Within eight months after the publication of "Studies in Crescas," numerous reviews of his *Spinoza*, many of them highly critical, appeared in the learned and general press. Wolfson took exception to a number of reviewers whom he considered bread-and-butter philosophers, men whose knowledge was as faulty as their repugnance to originality was great. But whatever the character and length of his rejoinders to the critics, all of them contained objective discussions of crucial points in the interpretation of Spinoza which were of general interest to students of philosophy.

Paul Weiss, in a review of the book in the *New Republic,* October 1934, paid tribute to Wolfson's scholarship and originality, saying that the author "argues his thesis with persuasion, bolsters it with quotations from Greek and Latin, Arabic, Hebrew, and Dutch, and writes in a style that is a model of clarity. His is a work of first magnitude." But this "work of first magnitude" evidences, he complains, little or no interest in mathematics and science and presents a Spinoza "who is only a logical outgrowth of mediaeval philosophy," and this is "a seventeeth-century thinker pressed into fourteenth-century clothes." Weiss also claimed that Wolfson's distinction between Baruch and Benedict makes Spinoza a man who is intellectually divided against himself.

This brought Wolfson into the field. He did not skirmish; in a letter to the *New Republic,* published in January 1935, he trained his guns at the target of criticism with deadly accuracy:

Professor Paul Weiss advanced four arguments to show that in my book *The Philosophy of Spinoza* I have unjustifiably neglected to deal with science and mathematics, which, in common with others, he believes to be the basis of Spinoza's philosophy. Although Mr. Weiss's arguments are all his own, his point of view is that which now generally prevails among students of philosophy and even among professional scholars. I should like to examine his arguments one by one.

In the first place, he says I have ignored Spinoza's "consuming interest in current scientific work" and also "the influence which Cartesian physics . . . undoubtedly had on Spinoza." I admit that in his correspondence with his friends Spinoza displays an intelligent man's natural interest in current events of science and that in his textbook on Descartes he outlines also some part of Cartesian physics, but it happens that in his own philosophical works and especially in his *Ethics,* of which my book is a study, Spinoza deals neither with science in general nor with Cartesian physics in particular. All the science of the *Ethics* consists of a few sundry references to simple scientific facts and one physiological excursus. These I have not ignored. With the exception of these references and the excursus, the entire *Ethics* deals exclusively with problems of traditional philosophy and theology, from the definition of substance to the immortality of the soul.

By no alchemy of sophistication can these be transmuted into Cartesian physics. My book, furthermore, happens to contain 242 references to the writings of Descartes, and in these the reader will find all the legitimate connections between Spinoza's philosophy and "Cartesian physics."

In the second place, arguing against my contention that the geometrical form of the *Ethics* was not a necessary consequence of its philosophy, Mr. Weiss says that Spinoza was a "rationalist" and "a mathematically arranged philosophy is a natural consequence of rationalistic assumptions." I take it that by "a natural consequence" the reviewer means "a necessary consequence," for this is the point at issue. Now the term rationalist covers a multitude of irrationalities. But it has never been used in the sense of one whose philosophy must be mathematically arranged. What the reviewer really does here is this: he first applies the term rationalist to Spinoza in a unique sense, evidently for no other reason than the uniqueness of Spinoza's use of the mathematical arrangement, and then proceeds to argue from that unique sense of the term rationalist that Spinoza's philosophy had to be mathematically arranged. Logicians have a word for this kind of reasoning. Furthermore, when the reviewer says that the present writer "forgets . . . the tremendous importance of the discovery of analytic geometry" in its bearing upon Spinoza's use of the geometrical form he fails to take notice of my detailed discussion of this particular point in the chapter on "The Geometrical Method" in my book.

Two more points are discussed by Wolfson in the same manner. He concludes with a passage that shows the extent to which this reviewer and others missed the import of his central thesis:

Nor is my Spinoza divided against himself, as the reviewer says. This is not what I meant by the distinction between Benedictus and Baruch. Benedictus is only the mouthpiece of Baruch and he stands fully explained in my detailed and substantiated explanation of what the explicit Spinoza "meant by what he said, how he came to say what he said, and why he said it in the manner in which he happened to say it." The sequel of two volumes, which the reviewer suggests, would have to deal, I am afraid, with what Spinoza did not mean by what he said. If the Spinoza who emerges from my book is, as Mr. Weiss says, not "a respected seventeenth-century lens grinder and student of optics" but rather a disrespected "mediaeval scholar" and student of books, and if he does not conform to our conceptions of what a seventeenth-century philosopher should be, it is perhaps time to revise our views on both. The imaginary boundary line between mediaeval and modern in philosophy, anyhow, will some day have to be shifted and perhaps altogether abolished.

Most of the reviews of *The Philosophy of Spinoza,* however, were of the sort that brought the pleasing reward of recognition to Wolfson. Many of them, like Irwin Edman's appreciation in the *New York Times Book Review,* and the piece by his Harvard colleague D.W. Prall in the *Saturday Review of Literature,* are worth quoting; but it may be well to confine ourselves to another singular reaction that is part of the thread of our story and at the same time is an illuminating human document. Santayana did not see the books until 1936, and on June 16 he wrote Wolfson from Rome:

It is a real gift, this, of so much hidden light on Spinoza, and I am truly grateful. . . . I can't thank you for it adequately or make any final comments upon it, because I am leaving Rome, and it is impossible for me to take the two volumes with me. I shall return to them when I get back here in October. But I have already read enough to see how much learning and what perfect simplicity you bring to your book, and how clearly you show the continuity of philosophy through the middle ages and into the mind and language of Spinoza himself. I have often thought that he was the only *philosopher* of modern times. I now see one reason, that he was not really modern, except as we all must be in our day, but traditional and in the great highway of human speculation: which cannot be said, I think, of any other modern philosopher. Your learning, especially your Hebrew learning, enables you to show this clearly. I believe there is another reason also why Spinoza seems to me so preeminent: that in spite of being traditional, or because he was not distracted by side issues, he was an entire and majestic mind, a singularly consecrated soul. All these trite dogmas and problems lived in him and were the natural channels for his intuitions and emotions. That is what I feel makes a real philosopher and not, what we are all condemned to be, *professors* of the philosophy of other people, or of our own opinions.

When I return to your volumes I shall be particularly keen to discover just how you interpret the mediation of intellect in determining the attributes of God. I have supposed hitherto that there was a radical ambiguity here, and that Spinoza had two notions of substance, one of *mere* substance, and the other of substance involving its own deployment and making necessary, and intrinsic to its essence, every detail of the universe. These two notions seem to me on different ontological levels; *mere Being* is an essence only; the universe is the sum and system of existences. But didn't Spinoza attempt to identify the two, and isn't that sheer confusion?

In my remoteness, I wasn't aware that you had become a professor at Harvard. I am very glad for them and for you.

Santayana, in his query, had put his finger on the problem of substance in Spinoza, a problem of singular difficulty and one which the work of most interpreters had only enveloped in a fog. But, as Santayana doubtless discovered when he returned to the work, Wolfson for the first time threw light on one of the darkest areas of Spinoza's philosophy. He did this by showing that Spinoza's "substance with which he identifies the traditional God is nothing but a logical shell holding the particular things of the universe together, conceived as acting by the necessity of its own nature, an eternal machine incapable of changing the course of its own action, still less the action of others." Of Spinoza's reputed God-intoxication, Wolfson concludes that it "was really nothing but a hangover of an earlier religious jag" (vol. 2, pp. 345–46, 348).

This brings to recollection the way in which Wolfson treated a related problem in his course on Spinoza some years before the completion of his book, and the incident may serve to dramatize his method of teaching. The course was given at the Semitic Museum at an early hour; the time and place were suited to the task of disinterring Spinoza from the geometry of the *Ethics*. The translation of a system of mnemonic symbols into the universe of discourse is as intriguing as the solution of a difficult double acrostic; observing the process was akin to seeing Houdini perform his mysterious feats. Wolfson took the turgid, obscure text of the *Ethics* and shook it until it became as clear as the morning's sun. Moreover, his writer's instinct came to the fore and he employed a variety of literary devices to bring home his point. On the morning when he was about to discuss the problem of substance as formulated in Proposition 8, Part. 1, of the *Ethics*—"Every substance is necessarily infinite"— he opened the discussion with a reference to *Elmer Gantry*, which had just been published. "On page 299," he said with a sly smile,

"Elmer is reading a book on philosophy and, bogging down on a passage concerning the problem of Being, he throws the book to the floor and shouts, 'Oh, shut up.' I'd like to pick up the book and examine the problem that was too much for Elmer." As this was one of his smaller classes, he was not under the tyranny of the endless monologue. He drew his students out, welcoming their questions and discussion, so that they left the classroom feeling that they had not only heard a brilliant lecture but had been quite brilliant themselves.

The Philosophy of Spinoza is a remarkable feat of scholarship and a model of expository prose. Apart from its vast and varied learning, it is exquisite in its literary quality. The style throughout is as clear as a bell and of utmost precision. When the author employs a literary device, such as the fictional conversation in the first chapter or the imaginary sermon delivered by Spinoza in Doctor Cordes's church in the last chapter, the prose sparkles and the narrative is highly evocative. The whole work is studded with epigrammatic sentences, sometimes bristling with irony. For example, there is the definition of popularization: ". . . what is called popularization means nothing but the explanation of a text in terms of the ignorance supposed to be possessed by the readers for whom it is intended." And some of the high peaks of expression are achieved in the passages where the mind of Benedictus, the explicit Spinoza, is related to the mind of Baruch, the implicit Spinoza. Again there is the passage in which Wolfson relates his discussion with a group of friends concerning "the importance of philology and of bookish learning in general for the study of the history of philosophy":

I happened to remark that philosophers, after all, see the universe which they try to explain as already interpreted to them in books, with the only possible exception, perhaps, of the first recorded philosopher, and all he could see was water. "How about Spinoza?" challenged one of the listeners. "Was he also a bookish philosopher?" Without stopping to think, I took up the challenge. "As for Spinoza," I said, "if we could cut up all the philosophic literature available to him into slips of paper, toss them up into the air, and let them fall back to the ground, then out of these scattered slips of paper we could reconstruct his *Ethics.*" [vol. 1, p. 3]

He goes on to say:

Not long after that I found myself reconstructing the *Ethics* out of scattered slips of paper figuratively cut out of the philosophic literature available to Spinoza. The problem before us, as I discovered, was like that of a jig-saw puzzle. Suppose we have a box of pieces out of which we are to construct a certain picture. But the pieces contained in the box are more than can be used, and from among them we have to select those which are needed for our purpose. Furthermore, the pieces do not fit together, and they have to be reshaped. Finally, many necessary pieces are missing, and we have to supply them ourselves. But to offset all these difficulties, we have an outline of the picture which we are to construct.

The picture which we have to construct in our own jig-saw puzzle is the *Ethics* as it was originally formed in the mind of Spinoza, of which the present *Ethics* in its geometrical form is only a bare outline. Since, however, we do not know nor can we ascertain exactly what books Spinoza had actually read, what quotations he had come across in the course of his readings, or what casual information he had gathered from conversations with friends, we must take as our box of pieces the entire philosophic literature available at the time of Spinoza and out of this make our necessary selections. Furthermore, since philosophic texts and ideas are the most plastic of material, capable of assuming a variety of meanings with different philosophers, we must reshape our pieces in the form which we have reason to believe they assumed in the mind of Spinoza. Finally, since the *Ethics* before us is not the result of a syncretism of traditional philosophy but rather the result of criticism, and since this criticism, though implied, is not explicitly expressed, we shall have to supply it ourselves. [vol. 1, pp. 3–4]

And here is part of his imaginative portrait of Spinoza, the social man:

Spinoza is represented by those who knew him as having lived a life of retirement, though one not devoid of friendship. We should like to agree with his biographers, that he was guided into this mode of life by his philosophy, but unfortunately recluses are not made by philosophies, not even by philosophies which, unlike the philosophy of Spinoza, preach retirement from life as an ideal virtue; they are made, rather, by the inhospitableness of the social environment and by the ineptitude of their own individual selves. But for the circumstances, environmental and personal, which had cut his normal contacts with society, Spinoza, who defined man, after Aristotle, as a social animal, would undoubtedly have guided himself by the same dictate of reason that he had prescribed for others—by his maxim that man is freer when he participates in the life of society than when he lives in solitude. In conformity with this maxim of his, then, he would undoubtedly have joined in the active life of the communities in which he lived after his departure from his native Amsterdam—Rijnsburg, Voorburg, and The Hague; he would have become a substantial, respectable, and public-spirited burgher and a pillar of society. Perhaps, also, despite differences in theology, he would have joined the Lutheran church of his friend Doctor Cordes in The Hague. And I can picture him, once of a Sunday, at the invitation of the good old Doctor, taking the services in the church. He preaches a sermon which is an invective against what he styles "the prejudices of the theologians of our time." In it he inveighs against prevailing credulous beliefs in the spirituality of God, His personal relation to men, His direct guidance of human affairs, the divine origin of the Scriptures, human freedom of the will, the separability of soul from body, and the survival of the soul after death as an individual entity. The sermon over, he pauses and says, "Now let us pray." And in his prayer he thanks God, "the creator of the universe," for His bountiful goodness; he begs for the forgiveness of "our sins," asks for divine enlightenment in the true understanding of "Thy revealed Word," and petitions for divine grace in "guiding us" in the paths of righteousness, to the end that "we may inherit" life everlasting and enjoy eternal bliss in the presence of "Thy glory." As he is about to close his prayer, he catches a glimpse of the congregation and suddenly realizes that he is in a Christian church. Immediately he adds: "In the name of Christ, the mouth of God, whose spirit is the idea of God, which alone leads us unto liberty, salvation, blessedness, and regeneration. Amen." [vol. 2, pp. 350–52]

But no quotation or summary can convey the quality and power of the work as a whole. As a document of philosophical acumen and psychological analysis, it is unparalleled in the entire literature on Spinoza. If Wolfson had written nothing else, the *Philosophy of Spinoza* would have ensured his fame.

6
Enigmas, Human and Other

Problems may be solved in the study,
which have baffled all those who have sought
a solution by the aid of their senses.

Sir Arthur Conan Doyle

The popular image of Wolfson as a cloistered scholar obsessed with the past is a valid part of his legend. Yet the view that he was a solitary figure is not the whole truth, for his curiosity reached beyond his bookish concerns: he took an interest in his friends and students and found the same delight in taking their dilemmas by the horns as he derived from the solution of intellectual problems. To know and judge people gave him perhaps a subtle sense of being part of the practical world; and even though he rarely sought or permitted intimacy, he was a sympathetic, agreeable companion as he dealt shrewdly and dispassionately with his friends' problems. Perhaps the best way of discovering this facet of his personality is by what the novelists call the "peephole" method.

To the present-day student who conceives a college education as either the prolongation of infancy or as an opportunity for acting out his perplexities, Wolfson's pedagogical views must appear in the main as old-fashioned. "The purpose of the American college," he wrote in *Pomegranates*, "is to train for life's tasks rather than to meddle in them. It is a manoeuvre ground, not a battlefield." On one occasion he departed from this rule. While he was an undergraduate the appeal of the suffragette movement was becoming widespread and had won many adherents among public figures and college students. During his sophomore year a parade was organized by the suffragettes in Boston, to be led by Louis D. Brandeis and other prominent men and women. He found himself joining a group of Harvard students and marching jauntily through downtown Boston to the mixed jeers and applause of the observers. He never quite could explain the impulse that conquered him and made him sin against his own commandment.

In the early twenties he had an experience which illustrates his compassion for the underdog. On the principle that in history, as in life, one ought to let bygones be bygones, the incident should be forgotten; for Harvard since has eradicated any semblance of anti-Semitism that was charged at the time. The episode is resurrected here only to show Wolfson's capacity to join the lists when his sense of justice was violated.

Early in 1922 there had been some discussion at faculty meetings regarding the increasing number of Jewish students at the college. Acting on the valid assumption that airing the problem among students and faculty would clear the air and reduce, if not remove, the growing ill will, several of the gentile and Jewish students felt that a frank exchange between representatives of Jewish student societies and of the general student body might be helpful. Harry Starr, the president of the Menorah Society, took a leading part, keeping Wolfson informed and discussing with him the formation of a committee and questions of policy. Wolfson's view was, as later formulated by Starr and his associates in a letter to Dean Chester Noyes Greenough, that "any limitation of the number of Jewish students whether direct or indirect, whether based on any theory of racial differences, or on arguments of expediency . . . [is] unjustifiable on any ground." The view was vigorously advocated by Professor David Gordon Lyon at faculty meetings. Unfortunately, in May the news had leaked out and was in the newspapers. The faculty discussed it. The press was full of it. There was tension on the campus and in the dormitories. On June 6, 1922, the *Harvard Crimson* printed an editorial notice and letters to the editors from several students who had been involved in the meetings. It appears that the view advocated by Wolfson, Lyon, and the Jewish representatives helped the Jewish students, in the heat of controversy and recrimination for several months, to maintain their sanity and dignity, both privately and at the meetings. There is a sample of this approach in the last of the communications, signed by Starr: "We cannot have tolerance until we recognize the real issues involved, until we perceive why social and ethnic prejudices persist, why Jew and non-Jew cannot get together and have 'plain talk and high thinking' without being hampered by stultifying self-consciousness. And we are Harvard men, too; can we not reason together on that basis, and in respect for the tradition we all love, instead of skulking in our tents, like academic Achilles? For tolerance is not to be administered like castor oil, with eyes closed and jaws clenched."

Aside from such direct encounters with his civic conscience and his special trips to the city hall to make sure that he was registered to vote, Wolfson's temperament disengaged him from turbulent social and political issues. During the depths of the Depression some of his philosophy students became interested in Marxism and joined the radical movements which invaded the campus. Although in his boyhood days he had been a member of a Zionist circle which was considered subversive by the traditionalists, he felt that Jewish students in America should not commit themselves to the risks of revolutionary movements. When the first student peace strike was called in 1934 and the air was filled with tension, he noted that one of his students was scheduled to address a mass meeting on the steps of Widener Library. He earnestly urged the student not to speak. But, for all his regard for Wolfson, the student felt that right was on his side and that he must do his duty. For the radical-minded students the campus had become a battlefield.

The problems of individuals created no such predicament for Wolfson, stirred up no such inhibition. When he faced the personal quandaries of students, colleagues, and friends, he was full of appreciation for the subtle perplexities of the human situation and enjoyed trying to unravel their intricacies. And this faculty was detected in him very early by his friends.

Among the Scrantonians who turned up at Harvard between 1909 and 1919 were several boyhood friends—David Levy, Harris Berlack, and Norman Survis. One day the latter, an intelligent and handsome student at the Harvard Medical School, told Wolfson that he was fed up with his medical studies and had decided to quit. Wolfson considered him admirably suited for a career in medicine and was determined that he should remain and complete his course. "If it takes all day and night," Wolfson said to him, "I'm going to talk with you until I change your mind." Talking late into the night and drawing out of Survis an account of his current doings, he finally located what he thought was the source of his friend's restlessness. Survis was by nature very sociable and indeed a member of the Zeta Beta Tau fraternity, but he was living alone in a room in a private house. Wolfson advised him to get quarters at the fraternity house, even if he had to double up with another student, and made him promise to stay on for the remainder of the semester before making a final decision. Survis agreed to the pact, found himself enjoying his new existence and his studies, and later became, as his friend had anticipated, a successful doctor.

There are many such stories. Browsing among the bookstalls along the Seine in the early fifties, I chanced upon an avant-garde literary journal published in Paris, with an announcement of a curious assortment of articles and stories on its pale brown cover. The first name of one of the writers was "Austryn," and that was the only time I had seen it except in Wolfson's name. Inquiries upon my return to New York led back to Wolfson in the twenties, and to a law student who had taken a course with the professor. The student was an intelligent, handsome fellow whom the girls always pursued. One day he turned up at Wolfson's apartment at Prescott Street and sought his advice regarding an *affaire de coeur*. The tables had been turned and now, as a pursuer, he felt embarrassed and perplexed. He was interested in an attractive girl but she was half-committed to another admirer. He couldn't decide whether to push his case or retreat. Wolfson suggested that he ought to continue his pursuit with more vigor and artfulness. He then mapped out a plan of attack.

Within the year the couple were married, and they named their first son "Austryn" after his godfather. The young father—who, with his wife, was Jewish—approached him with another problem: his father-in-law vehemently opposed the infant's circumcision, regarding the ritual as barbaric. Wolfson asked who the obstetrician was and, learning that he was a fashionable gentile doctor, suggested unhesitatingly that they seek his advice. The doctor's revelation that his own son was circumcised appeased the father-in-law, and, to add an O. Henry touch, he advised that "an old bearded rabbi" was more skilled than the physicians; thus the ceremony even had the aura of tradition. The boy ultimately turned up at Harvard and subsequently went to Paris to pursue a literary career. (He and his father, an American diplomat, were included in the little black address book that Wolfson called his "private social register.")

Another tale derives from an equally odd source. During a visit to Israel, soon after its founding, I noticed in the window of a bookstore in Tel Aviv a Hebrew translation of some of T. S. Eliot's prose. Writers in Israel are not difficult to locate, and I soon met the translator at a café frequented by intellectuals. His story, too, threaded its way back to Wolfson's residence at Prescott Street in the late twenties. An excellent student, he had graduated from Harvard with a magna cum laude degree in English and had won the Bollingen Prize for literature. He was also a talented Hebrew writer. Unable to decide on a career, he consulted Wolfson. He had a clear recollection of the discussion that took place.

"Suppose," asked Wolfson, "there were no economic or other problems and you could choose your ideal future, what would it be?"

He replied, "I would like to be a Hebrew writer."

Wolfson explored the alternatives, probably conscious of the analogy to his own youthful aspirations:

Let us assume that you pursue graduate studies, obtain a doctorate, and achieve success. You will get an appointment, teach courses, and correct papers for five years and ultimately become a professor. In the meantime, even though you have intentions of writing Hebrew prose and poetry, the pressure of work will make this increasingly impossible. In the end your ideal will disappear.

On the other hand, let us suppose that you are a failure and do not get an appointment. You will probably combine Hebrew teaching with odd jobs and you will thus find little time for creative writing. Again your ideal will disappear.

Now let us suppose you go to Palestine. Your life there will be harder than in the United States. But you will be in an atmosphere where you can develop your talents. You can become a writer for one or more papers and at the same time publish essays and verse. There is a good possibility of realizing your ideal.

The young writer found his mentor's logic compelling and settled in Palestine. At the time of our meeting—the days of austerity following the War of Liberation—his life was very much as Wolfson had predicted it would be. The source of his greatest satisfaction was an ambitious plan to render into Hebrew the best work of modern writers. He had completed the T.S. Eliot and was confident of going on with Rilke, Hesse, Kafka, Joyce, Mann, Montherlant, and Hemingway.

Wolfson always had an instinct for detecting a student in distress, finding out the nature of the difficulty, and taking the trouble to suggest a remedy. My personal experience of this came when I was his neighbor in Divinity Hall. One of my sisters, a beautiful and vivacious young woman of twenty-three, died, and I was inconsolable. I stayed in my room and wept like a child. Wolfson must have noted my absence from classes or perhaps caught the sound of crying as he went past my room. In any case, on the second day after my return from the funeral he knocked on my door and gently inquired what had happened. Despite my reverence for him, I could not discuss it. After a while he induced me to take a walk with him and ultimately elicited the story. I gave full vent to my sorrow and bitterness. Soon afterwards I found myself back at classes and study. The sympathy he had extended to me with sensitive discretion had helped me to perform what Freud calls "the work of mourning."

Many, many others have similar tales to tell, and Wolfson's "clientele" was not confined to the campus; there were among his visitors innumerable clergymen, professionals, and even businessmen who sought his counsel on questions that required not only shrewd judgment but also the ability to see all the wool of a problem, plait it up quickly, and know exactly what string to pull. Once a former student, who was interested in buying a house in Brookline and had been advised against it by several real-estate agents, called to ask Wolfson to help him make up his mind. Wolfson accompanied him to the property, queried him about the details of local values and the terms of purchase, looked around the neighborhood, and said simply, "Grab it." He did and lived in the house happily for twenty years, when it had quintupled in value. On another occasion a New York tycoon who had a complex problem involving corporation law and family ethics, preferred to discuss it with Wolfson rather than his attorney. His handling of the problem was so canny that when Austin W. Scott, the eminent professor at the Harvard Law School, heard an account of it, he commented that Wolfson would make a first-rate corporation lawyer. In all this there was of course no thought of reward; but in the latter instance the grateful financier came to the rescue of the Mediaeval Academy of America and enabled it to publish one of the most expensive volumes of the Averroes *Corpus*.

These same qualities mark Wolfson's role in the establishment of the great collection of Hebrew books at Harvard.

Being a Puritan institution of the seventeenth century, and thus in essence biblical, Harvard quite naturally fostered the study of Hebrew from its very beginning. John Harvard's library of 329 titles introduced Hebrew books to North America; it included numerous Hebrew grammars, commentaries on the Old Testament, and Bishop Lightfoot's *Miscellanies*, which comprised selections from rabbinic literature in the original Hebrew and in translation. The collection was enlarged by gifts from the Hollises of London in the seventeenth century and from the oldest Harvard families such as those of Charles Eliot Norton, Charles Francis Adams, and Georgiana Lowell Putnam. Only two volumes from John Harvard's collection and none of Bishop Lightfoot's library survived the fire of 1764. In the nineteenth century, with the establishment of the Divinity and Semitic libraries and continuing accessions by the College Library, it was possible for scholars like Toy, Lyon, and Moore, despite

the dispersion of books and their varying classification in the catalogues, to find most of the resources necessary for their studies.
Nevertheless, Moore had to buy for himself numerous rare editions
of Hebrew and talmudic works which were essential to research for
his work on Judaism in the talmudic age. And Wolfson frequently
was compelled to resort to books which were available only in the
collections of the New York Public Library, the Jewish Theological
Seminary in New York, and the Hebrew Union College in Cincinnati.

Wolfson developed the idea of enlarging the Hebrew collection
soon after he began to teach. He first tackled students whose homes
housed Hebrew libraries. In 1920–21 one of his students promised
to present his alma mater with about 2,000 volumes which had been
in his family for several generations. In 1926 this student, Leon N.
Alberts, '09, allowed Wolfson to select about 350 rare volumes out
of the library left by his father, who was a Hebrew scholar and writer.
In the spring of 1929, at Wolfson's suggestion and with the help of
David Levy and his wife, Adele Rosenwald Levy, Julius Rosenwald
bought and presented to Harvard in honor of Judge Julian W. Mack,
LL.B. '87, a collection of 3,000 volumes in Hebrew. This collection,
consisting both of rabbinic and modern Hebrew literature, was especially rich in Oriental prints.

In the fall of 1929—the black days of the Wall Street crash which
ushered in the Great Depression—Wolfson's friend Joshua Bloch
apprised him of the availability of the collection of Ephraim Deinard, who had recently died in New Orleans. Deinard was the kind
of bibliophile who deserves a book to himself. He had scoured every
corner of the world where Hebrew books and manuscripts were said
to exist and possessed an uncanny way of acquiring almost everything important he saw. For some fifty years he had supplied the
British Museum, the Bodleian, the Jewish Theological Seminary,
and the Library of Congress with Hebraica and Judaica. Here is the
story as Wolfson tells it in "Hebrew Books in Harvard," which
appeared in the *Harvard Alumni Bulletin* in April 1932:

Deinard's name is identified with the discovery of the only extant copy, in
its Hebrew version, of Averroes' Long Commentary on "De Anima,"

which is now in the National Library in Berlin. He was then in his late eighties, a Johnsonian figure in massivity and character, half-blind, but knowing his books by touch, keen of mind and memory, and a picturesque raconteur. He lived then in New Orleans, where his books were kept in a shack. The collection consisted of about 12,000 printed volumes and twenty-nine manuscripts gathered by its owner during a lifetime of travel in all the parts of the world. It was representative of every phase of Hebrew literature and of every period and center of Hebrew printing. It contained sixteen incunabula, eleven in Hebrew and five in Latin, including the first dated Hebrew book printed, and it abounded in sixteenth-century prints and in first editions and in many other bibliographical rarities. Collected by a man who understood Hebrew books, it showed in every part of its makeup intelligence and skill in planning. The opportunity was rare, and we could not let it go.

Mr. Lucius N. Littauer, '78, who four years previously had established a professorship in Jewish literature and philosophy in the University in memory of his father, seemed to us the one most likely to be interested in the purchase of the books for us. A conference with him during his visit to Cambridge for the Yale-Harvard football game in November 1929 resulted in a promise to purchase them for us if they proved to be all they were represented to be. A trip to New Orleans just before the Christmas vacation, together with Professor Alexander Marx of the Jewish Theological Seminary, one of the greatest living authorities on Hebrew books, brought the deal to a conclusion. [pp. 886–87]

During these weeks Wolfson spent most of his time in Deinard's shed, examining the books and reveling in the incunabula; he felt that he had found "an orphanage of children." In the evenings, however, he wrenched himself from the trove and visited with friends. Among them was Ephraim Lisitzky, a Hebrew poet and teacher, who had studied at the Rabbi Isaac Elhanan Yeshiva a few years before him. He took Lisitzky with him to the home of Dorothy and James Feibleman at 717 St. Peter Street in the French quarter of the city. Feibleman was undergoing an intellectual crisis just then; he had left the University of Virginia at the end of his freshman year and had written articles and poems for various newspapers and magazines. He was readying a book of poems, *Death of the God in Mexico* (1931), for publication. At the same time he had reached the view that philosophy was a more creative medium than poetry, and he was at work on a philosophical book with Julius W. Friend. Feibleman aired his thesis; Wolfson opposed it vigorously, stating that modern philosophy was either traditional philosophy in a new garb or a flight to science. The discussion provided an intellectual banquet for the guests; but Feibleman continued on his course and, despite his lack of any degree, became the head of the Department of Philosophy at Tulane University. Some of the guests at the Feibleman home, among them Joseph Cohen and his wife Rosalie, became ardent admirers of Wolfson; during the forties and fifties he welcomed several of the sons of this New Orleans group at Harvard.

What gave Wolfson special joy was the discovery of his relatives from Ostrin and their families. He visited their homes, both in New Orleans and Bogalusa, regaled them with stories of Ostrin, and took delight in learning about their interests. He was a little too late to find his Aunt Zivia—she had died a few years earlier in her late nineties. Wherever he went, however, he heard her spoken of with warmth and reverence. She had, in her prime, helped establish the first Orthodox synagogue and ritual bath in the city. When she became old and near-blind, she was seen walking through the street, frail, trim, amiable, kindly, and attending to her lifelong concerns —acting as custodian of the ritual bath, collecting money for the dowries for poor girls, and preparing the dead for burial. She had been, like Wolfson's grandmother and mother, a woman of distinction whose joys and sorrows sprung from the vices and virtues of human life.

Soon after his return to Cambridge in January 1930, seventy-three boxes of the Deinard books arrived at the College library. Wolfson employed Samuel Kurland, who had received his doctorate under him in 1929 and had just returned from research abroad on a Littauer fellowship, to tackle the task of readying and classifying the collection. It took three full days to unpack the books and several weeks to assemble the Hebrew books spread throughout the libraries of the university. Wolfson devised a method of classifying the books, and Kurland, with the help of twenty-odd students from the Hebrew

Teachers College in Roxbury, began the onerous job of cataloguing them. The first stage of arranging the Deinard collection on shelves and having a written card for every one of the volumes was completed by the time college opened in the fall of 1930. But the entire process of cataloguing, and indeed of even identifying certain volumes, took many years. Other collections were acquired in the course of time by purchase or gift.

I learned from personal experience that for the sake of this library Wolfson could drop his usual reserve. In the late twenties I developed a strong interest in Hasidic lore and managed to build up a collection of the rare editions of the books written by the first four generations of Hasidic writers. As I reported interesting acquisitions to Wolfson during periodic visits, he in turn would suggest clues to where other little-known books might be found. Toward the end of the thirties he lamented the paucity of Hasidic works in the Harvard library, so that in a moment of weakness I promised that as soon as I finished my work for a book I had in mind, I would give my collection to Harvard. From that time his suggestions became more pointed; he discussed in great detail exactly how I should arrange the books, have them bound, and the like, just as though they were already on the shelves of Widener. Aware of the humor of his position, he commented that he was acting like the aristocratic beggar in Israel Zangwill's *The King of Schnorrers*, following his patron around to keep spots and stains off the clothes he was wearing because the beggar would eventually inherit them. When I was drafted into the army in 1942 my book was still unfinished, but I anticipated a long absence and succumbed to the professor's enthusiastic brainwashing. That one of his students subsequently wrote a doctoral dissertation based upon these books made the gift doubly rewarding to the giver.

To Wolfson a library was not only a museum for assembling and preserving books but above all a laboratory where books are tools for research. Apart from the value of Hebrew books for the understanding of the national culture they represented, he saw them as part of the mainstream of human culture. Thus he wrote in "Hebrew Books in Harvard":

Here is a literature that spans the entire history of mankind. Its oldest book is contemporaneous with, if not older than, the epics of Homer, and its latest publication bears the date of the current year. The record of the life and thought of one single people over a period of more than 3,000 years, it also mirrors the life and thought of all the peoples with whom it came into contact during the period of its national unity and among whom it lived during the history of its dispersion—Egyptians, Assyrians, Babylonians, Achaemenian Persians, Hellenists, Romans, Byzantines, Sassanian Persians, Moslems, both those of the east and those of the west, and every Christian nation of Europe. It is called an oriental literature, but it is also an occidental literature, for ever since the tenth century, when the first Hebrew book appeared in Italy, it has had its home in those countries where the literature called European has been produced. For over four centuries, investigators, both Jewish and non-Jewish, have been searching its pages for material for the enrichment of our knowledge of general history, literature, and philosophy. . . . What an abundance of new material may one yet find, for instance, in the rabbinic Responsa for rounding out our knowledge of the economic and social history of European and other countries, or in Hebrew philosophic texts for the reconstruction of the history of mediaeval philosophy. The task of scholarship, which is an eternal prying into man's past, will not be ended until every page in these 15,000 volumes will have been studied for all that may be extracted from them and the result embodied in footnotes, essays, and monographs. [p. 887]

In this essay the collection is portrayed as both part of the Harvard tradition of Hebrew learning and of the wide realms of history and literature. The essay is a gem, sparkling in its spirit, perfect in its execution, and shining in its felicity and grace. Very widely read, it elicited a deluge of appreciative letters from readers in America and Europe. No one expressed the marrow of the epistolatory encomiums more warmly than Felix Frankfurter, then Wolfson's neighbor at the Harvard Law School:

May 31, 1932

Dear Wolfson:

Not often do I find bibliographical essays throbbing with life, but your "Hebrew Books in Harvard" did. I am grateful to you for letting me have a reprint. Unfortunately I see the [*Harvard Alumni*] *Bulletin* only intermittently. I liked it all. The story of the acquisition of this collection or collections was indispensable to an understanding of the lyric interpretation of the meaning of these books with which your paper closes. I don't know when I have seen such a persuasive and humane account of the purposes which books serve—the lives they have lived and the lives they have enabled their readers to live. I am deeply your debtor for giving me rare enjoyment and making known as widely as you have what books were really meant to be—the "tools of scholars," not the playthings of bibliophiles.

If you have some extra copies to spare of your reprint, please be good enough to send them to the persons named on the enclosed sheet.

> Cordially yours,
> Felix Frankfurter

Among the persons Frankfurter listed were Benjamin N. Cardozo, Harold J. Laski, Bernard Flexner, and Morris R. Cohen.

In 1936 a translation of the essay by Noah Stern, a former student of Wolfson's who had taken up residence in Palestine, appeared in *Gilyonot*, a Hebrew literary journal.

There is a vast gap between having the tools of research at one's disposal and being able to use them with intelligence and imagination. Many valuable talents are lost and some remain unfulfilled because of the want of expert guidance or the inability of scholars to direct students on the basis of their abilities and interest. The kind of zealous interest Wolfson took in guiding young men and women capable of independent study is rare in the academic world. Professor Morton Smith of Columbia University spoke of this quality at the presentation of a citation to Wolfson by the Tarbut Foundation in New York in 1962:

Some twenty-five years ago I went, as a graduate student, to my first class with him. At that time I had no premonition that study under him was to be a unique experience. Now, recalling that experience, I want to try to tell you precisely what made it unique. It has been my privilege to observe closely a number of the greatest scholars of our time, in several fields of the study of antiquity. Of all great scholars one expects keen intelligence and exceptional memory—these are the sine qua non of greatness in scholarship. Therefore, although Professor Wolfson has one of the sharpest analytical minds I have ever encountered and although his memory is literally prodigious, yet it is not these qualities which made his teaching unique. Nor is it even the content of his teaching, though his famous "hypothetico-deductive" method is, I think, one of the most powerful and exact tools of historical criticism. The great peculiarity of his teaching is not a matter of content, but of concern. No other man I have known has been so much concerned by purely intellectual problems, so determined to discover the solutions, so excited by the hunt and so delighted by the capture. When Professor Wolfson has solved a problem his joy is something I cannot describe. It calls to my mind those passages in which Plato speaks of the delight of knowing, the experience of the philosopher who at last escapes from the cave and catches his first glimpse of the intellectual sun. This joy in the pure exercise of the intelligence is something I have seen in Professor Wolfson as in no other man, and since he has made his life work the application of Talmudic method to the exposition of Greek philosophy, I think it particularly appropriate that he himself should be a living exposition of Plato, and that the heart of this exposition should derive from the Talmudic tradition, from *simhat talmud Torah* [the joy of Torah study].

There is also the story of Ralph Marcus, who in the fall of 1926 came to Wolfson's study in Widener 45 and introduced himself. Born in San Francisco, where one of his high-school teachers was the sister of Dean Willard Sperry of the Harvard Divinity School, he had been a brilliant student in English and classics at Columbia University. His ambition was to become a Jewish scholar, and in order to study with Moore and Wolfson, he applied for and received a fellowship at the Harvard Divinity School. When he told Wolfson that he wanted to specialize in rabbinic scholarship, Wolfson pointed out that his greatest asset was his knowledge of Greek; that since he had not started to study the Talmud in his childhood he could not make himself a rabbinic scholar; that a scholar who combined a knowledge of Hellenistic Greek and the contemporary Jewish sources was needed, and it was in that field that he could make a genuine contribution. He advised Marcus to take Moore's seminar on Philo, and he himself undertook to teach him rabbinic Hebrew, of which Marcus, being an extraordinary linguist, soon acquired a good working knowledge. Besides being an excellent student, Marcus had an engaging personality and an exquisite and sometimes uncontrollable sense of humor. He became one of Wolfson's lifelong friends.

Marcus returned to New York, where he got appointments at Columbia—teaching Arabic—and at the Jewish Institute of Religion. But instead of allowing him to pursue Hellenistic studies, Dr. Wise had him teach Bible and historical subjects. He was less frustrated in his personal life, however, for he married a charming, intelligent woman. When Marcus presented her to Wolfson, of whom she already stood in awe, he turned to Marcus and asked, "Does she type?" and upon hearing the answer "No," Wolfson said with disarming innocence, "Then why did you marry her?" Nevertheless, he had in mind a welcome wedding gift. He had just received a letter from Professor Richard McKeon, of the Oriental Institute at the University of Chicago, asking whether Marcus could fill an opening for a professor of Arabic. He replied that if Marcus took the job he would probably be the best Arabic scholar in the country within a few years; but he felt that Marcus should continue in Hellenistic studies. Soon thereafter McKeon told Wolfson that he had an idea of getting a man to combine Hellenistic and Semitic studies. Keeping Marcus informed of the negotiations, Wolfson wrote McKeon, indicating that Marcus was the right man for the post and included a formal recommendation. When Marcus received an invitation to go to Chicago for an interview, Wolfson made a special trip to New York to discuss the strategy of presenting himself. Among other things, he suggested that when he met the committee, which included President Hutchins, he should control his joke-telling and be serious and dignified. When Marcus returned he reported that he had tried very hard to be sedate but in the end, with some encouragement from the committee, he had made a few jokes. He got the appointment anyway, to Wolfson's relief, and in the subsequent twenty-eight years his contribution in his field brought world renown to the Oriental Institute.

Besides personal and academic diplomacy, putting a student on the right road sometimes involved the improvisation of new methods of teaching. And in this regard the story of Morton Smith is revealing. After majoring in English at Harvard College, Smith became a student of the New Testament at the Divinity School. In his second year Smith went to Wolfson and expressed a desire to study Hebrew. Knowing him to be a brilliant student, Wolfson suggested that he study rabbinic Hebrew for the background of the New Testament and that he would teach him by his own method. The first reader was the *Sefer Ha-Aggadah,* an admirable collection of nonlegal passages from talmudic literature prepared by the Hebrew poet Hayyim Nahman Bialik and Y. H. Ravnitsky. Wolfson read each sentence and translated it and parsed each word, Smith then studied it by himself, and following the rabbinic doctrine that knowledge of a text is assured by repeating it 101 times, he virtually memorized each passage. Wolfson also gave Smith one *pisgam,* maxim, to memorize each week. By the end of the year Smith could read Hebrew.

Toward the end of the second year Wolfson spoke to Professor Henry Cadbury about recommending Smith as a Sheldon Fellow. One day he met Dean Ferguson at the Faculty Club and discussed Smith with him, pushing Smith's case for the fellowship. At Ferguson's request, Wolfson wrote him a long letter, saying in substance: since the death of Lightfoot, Strack, and Billerbeck, there have been only a few scholars in Christendom with a rabbinic background for New Testament studies, and Smith thus should be encouraged.

Smith received the fellowship, and Wolfson then suggested that he study at the Hebrew University in Jerusalem. After Smith's first year there World War II broke out, and he was stranded in Palestine. Wolfson helped him to get an extension of the Sheldon Fellowship as well as a grant from the Lucius Littauer Foundation. Smith received his doctorate from the Hebrew University—a rare distinction—and wrote his thesis in Hebrew on the New Testament. After teaching at several universities, Smith was given a full professorship in the Department of History at Columbia.

Father Frank Gavin, another friend of Wolfson's, had grown up in Cincinnati, where he had acquired some knowledge of biblical Hebrew, and then had gone to Cambridge, England, to stay with the Paulist Fathers and continue his studies. Later he became a professor of Church history at the General Theological Seminary in New York. Once, when Father Gavin was invited to preach in

Appleton Chapel, he asked Wolfson to take lunch with him. At that time there was among the students enrolled in Semitics 9, a course on post-biblical Jewish history, one named McCoy, but as the class was large and composed mainly of Jewish students, his name was unknown to Wolfson. Father Gavin appeared at the Faculty Club with McCoy and introduced him as his nephew whom he had advised to take the course. McCoy was a mathematician and later went to Cambridge to study higher mathematics. Upon his return three years later he visited Wolfson and told him that at Cambridge he had changed his field from mathematics to Hebrew and the classics. He had an idea of opening up a school in the Midwest, like Groton in the East, with emphasis on the classics. Subsequently he went to St. Louis, opened a cooperative institution called the Thomas Jefferson School, and sent many able students to Harvard. McCoy had made a habit of reading the Hebrew Bible daily and covered it all once or more each year. Thus, whenever he turned up in Cambridge, Wolfson would greet him with the query, "How many times?"

Innumerable tales could be told to show the extent of Wolfson's influence as a teacher, but only one more will be cited here. When Wolfson was a freshman one of his classics teachers was Francis H. Fobes. He was a member of an old Yankee family from Maine, which had moved to Lexington, where their chocolate factory produced a popular brand of candy called "Necco." When Fobes was teaching at Union College in Schenectady, New York, he made a translation of the Latin text of Aristotle's *Meteorology.* When he found in it the expression *firmus semper aeternitas,* which he didn't understand, he sought Wolfson's help. Wolfson quickly suggested that the Latin was probably a translation from the Hebrew, and the word *semper* was probably a mistranslation of the Hebrew word for "or" and thus should read *sive,* that is, "firm or everlasting"; in other words, the Latin translator was not using both words but one or the other. (This was later substantiated.)

In the early twenties Fobes became a professor of classics at Amherst, and he and Wolfson saw each other frequently. The Fobes family in Lexington was impressed with Wolfson's historical and anthropological observations on the artifacts of Indian and colonial times which filled their house. A decade later Wolfson discussed with Fobes a method of teaching Greek to adult students which was analagous to his method of teaching rabbinic Hebrew; that is to say, to begin with advanced texts in the field in which the student was interested. Fobes experimented with the method for some years and ultimately wrote an introduction to the reading of philosophical Greek with illustrative examples from Aristotle, Plato, and Menander, called *Philosophical Greek,* which was published by the University of Chicago just before Fobes died in 1957. The book is dedicated to Wolfson, and in the preface the author expresses his indebtedness to him "for the main idea of the book, and for help in selecting the Aristotelian passages."

Even as Wolfson was a devoted friend to many, he also developed his own effective method of warding off people who were bent upon invading his privacy. As generous as he was in helping his own students, he was wary about students who lacked a sense of academic decorum. On one occasion a graduate student who had written a paper on Spinoza for a specialist in seventeenth-century thought asked him whether he would read it and say what he thought of it. "No," replied Wolfson unhesitatingly. "You are not my patient." A shadow of a smile twisted the corner of his mouth.

But there is one instance in which he succumbed to the cunning of a woman artist. In the summer of 1934, when Wolfson was literally working day and night to complete the second volume of *Spinoza,* he was visited by his cousin Harry Savitz, who was accompanied by several men and by Theresa Bernstein, an artist whom Wolfson had seen a year or two earlier at a studio in Gloucester which she shared with her husband, William Meyerowitz. Before this visit she had been told by Dr. Savitz, "If you can induce him to pose, the commission is yours." For a while the men chatted about personal matters and Miss Bernstein looked on quietly. Suddenly Wolfson turned to her and inquired, "And what are you doing in Cambridge?"

"Oh, I'm going to paint a portrait of a Harvard professor."

"That's interesting. Is he outstanding?"

Harry Wolfson in his thirties and forties
Courtesy of Mr. and Mrs. Lewis H. Weinstein

*Portrait of Harry Wolfson, painted by Theresa Bernstein
in the summer of 1934; commissioned by his cousin Harry A. Savitz
and later given by Savitz to Harvard, the portrait
now hangs in the Judaica Division of Widener Library*

"In my opinion and many others' he is quite exceptional," she replied.

"When are you going to paint it?" he asked (as she put it, "just to be polite").

"Probably next Monday morning at 10:00 A.M."

"Well," he exclaimed, "I wish I were the subject."

"You are!" she retorted promptly. And so he was trapped.

On Monday morning she started the portrait, eliciting his interest by taking up the roll of canvas and the stretchers and asking him to assist her in stretching the cloth. He read galley proofs of *Spinoza* as she painted. Sometimes his head was buried in the galleys so that all she saw was the top of it. She was anxious to get the expression on his face so when the telephone rang she took advantage of his absence to put a wooden tray under his seat cushion. This succeeded in straightening him up long enough for her to get his posture without his suspecting what she was up to. When it came to getting his eyes, she had to violate her promise that she would not disturb him and suggest that they take a break so that he could smoke and she rest. Although she did not smoke, she made an attempt to puff on a little cigar—his favorite then was a cheap cigarillo called "Between the Acts"—which he offered her. Within no time the room was so gray with fumes that she had to open the windows. But this little ruse helped her to get his character on canvas.

The tie he was to wear also became a problem. The artist suggested a tie in the tan group, which would fit into her color scheme. The artist buried in him came to the fore and he launched upon a discourse on color and composition. Finally he went out and shopped for ties and brought back a half dozen ties at the next sitting from which she could choose. She found one of them perfect.

There were six sittings in all. After each one she put the canvas in Wolfson's closet with the warning, "No one is to touch it or look at it until I'm finished." Nevertheless she found thumbprints on the background each time she returned.

The artist brought the painting off well: one sees the meditative, pensive scholar in an image that is suggestive of underlying dignity and of intellectual power; the head dominates the portrait, as it should, and the characteristics of Wolfson's spare physique are established with economy. Yet, while it portrays the writer of *Spinoza* deeply absorbed, with vision turned inward, the whole man is less visible.

To see the whole man, one needs to unfold the years of study and writing that *Spinoza* only faintly foreshadowed.

7
The Long Search

Explorers of the past are never quite free.
The past is their tyrant. It forbids them to know
anything which it has not itself,
consciously or otherwise, yielded to them.

Marc Bloch

An avid reader of mystery stories, Harry Wolfson's feats of scholarship can certainly be considered feats of detection. They are scholarship in which learning and play of mind march together. A passion for unraveling, together with a preternaturally sharp eye for clues and connections, led Wolfson to see the development of Western thought from ancient times in a radically new light. He worked in the manner of one who likes to walk upstream and track a river to its source; uncharted regions held no terror for him. By the early thirties he had formed his tools of investigation into precision instruments, developed a private radar system of "hunches," and mastered his medium of expression. As he dealt with one problem after another in the history of philosophy, he took nothing for granted, least of all the obvious. Not only did he look at a problem backwards and forwards, but sideways as well. Only in this way could the questions to which the problem originally gave rise be properly formulated, and only in this way could the answers be understood. There is nothing in all this of what Horace Walpole called "serendipity"— the faculty of discovering agreeable things by accident—as the story of Wolfson's long search during the subsequent decade will show.

Soon after the autumn of 1934, Wolfson realized that the documentation upon which his reconstruction of Spinoza as the last of the medievals was based might more properly have been published prior to the appearance of the finished work, *The Philosophy of Spinoza.* What to do then? Take the texts and passages not used in *Spinoza* and set forth in detail the relationship between Spinoza and the philosophic systems of his predecessors? But that would mean only the enlargement of his footnotes into monographs, or perhaps a third volume, and it would in no way modify his analysis and interpretation of Spinoza. As a matter of fact, within a short time he did collect more than three hundred additional corroborating passages, mainly from Latin scholastic literature; and although some of these required the revision of certain statements in the *Spinoza* and the expansion of a view expressed here and there in it, on the whole the new documentation only confirmed his interpretation of the *Ethics.* To follow such a course would be like going from a peak to the valley, which he was all the more disinclined to do since another peak was already beckoning.

By means of the method applied to Crescas and further applied to Spinoza, Wolfson was able to express the linkage that existed between certain key philosophic problems as they appear in both these thinkers. The course of thought over the three centuries that separated them embraced in its convolutions a multitude of ideas which shone only dimly, if at all, in the dark tunnel of time. To throw light on that darkness was the sort of challenge that excited Wolfson's passion for inquiry. As a consequence, he conceived the idea of working on a number of problems as they reached back from Spinoza and Crescas to their origins in Greek philosophy. To master the thought of twenty centuries and to elucidate it in terms of certain seminal ideas was a project to test even Wolfson's powerfully gifted mind and unusual apparatus of scholarship.

The salient features of his research can be traced in some fifteen monographs and papers published between 1934 and 1942. These provided the basis of a series of volumes whose making is a separate story. Our concern here is with the intellectual development, at least in some of its essential phases, that led up to them. But a word first about the physical setting.

Widener 45, in the depths of the library's stacks and difficult to approach, was the right setting for the adventurous enterprise into which Wolfson was about to plunge. The study was relatively small and the ceiling unusually high, with shafts of sunlight slanting down from high windows. A work table in the center was flanked by wall-to-wall bookshelves on top of which manuscripts and old periodicals were piled up to the ceiling. At the side and head of the table stood two wooden chairs, likewise overflowing with books and learned journals. To the side, facing the entrance, was an old leather easy chair where the visitor could sit and converse, provided he could get by the ponderous volumes heaped on the floor and remove similar impediments from the chair and if his head was higher than the work material piled on the table. One was hardly aware of the ancient wooden filing cabinet just to the left as one entered the room, bulging with Wolfson's own manuscripts and now the repository of a folding bag containing his manuscripts and notes from abroad.

Wolfson would never allow the cleaning woman to touch his books or papers; he instructed her to dust only the open spaces, provided she could find any. But he could put his hand on anything he wanted: he knew exactly where to locate the minutest scrap of information or the most elusive reference when conversing with a student or scholar; and if he sought an old journal on one of the upper shelves, even the topmost, he moved quickly and surely through and over the impedimenta and up the ladder to find it. This picture was never quite reproduced by the reporters who turned up with increasing frequency after the publication of *Spinoza;* but one photographer from *Holiday* magazine managed to catch the scholar in his lair—only partly tidied up—in a color photograph illustrating an article on the Ivy League colleges by Henry Morton Robinson. To Wolfson's astonishment, out of the dozens of pictures Robinson had had taken on the other seven campuses, he selected this untypical study to illustrate what he called "a typical professor in the great Ivy League tradition."

Widener 45 had the look of a secondhand bookstore hit by a tornado and, in a way, it was symbolic of the philosophic forest Wolfson was setting out to conquer. He had hewed his way toward the heart of the forest and hoisted two markers: *Crescas* and *Spinoza.* He knew the general extent of the forest, but to see the trees would require a method of approach different from the one he had used to reach his point of orientation. *Spinoza* is a vertical book; he now needed a horizontal approach to move safely through the depths of the forest. He could take nothing for granted, he would leave nothing unturned. He would move from tree to tree until he had devised and recorded a reliable map.

A neatly planned stretch of his life lay before him invitingly. He was sure of his tools—they had proved their worthiness. Among the principles guiding his use of these tools was one that he had formulated fifteen years earlier and that had become like a pin that holds together the crossbeams of the huge structure he was erecting: "Mediaeval philosophy is one philosophy, written in three languages, Arabic, Hebrew, and Latin." Wolfson wrote this sentence in his article on "The Needs of Jewish Scholarship America," which appeared in the *Menorah Journal* in February 1921. As usually expounded, Latin scholastic philosophy is a subject bounded by walls, but Wolfson did away with such walls. In the light of his principle, no idea is a stranger to another, whether it appears in Arabic, Hebrew, or Latin dress. Whether one starts from the middle or the beginning or the end, whether backwards, forwards or sideways, the disparate tales become a single story. Of the three languages in which the story was told, Hebrew, says Wolfson, "holds the central and most important position." Again, until one sees this statement demonstrated in *Crescas* and *Spinoza,* one's Latin-centered education causes a wrinkling of the brow. These two works teem with examples, but they are works addressed to readers who have a technical interest in philosophy. We are in luck, however, for Wolfson stated his case urbanely in the *Menorah Journal* article. "In Hebrew mediaeval philosophy," he said, we have the full efflorescence of Arabic thought and the bud of much of scholasticism. It is in the interest of general culture and general scholarship that these hidden Hebrew treasures should be brought to light . . . so that the world may readily recognize their value for a reconstruction of the history of philosophy. For the time will come when the history of philosophy, mediaeval as well as early modern, will have to be radically rewritten, and rewritten it will be as soon as the contents of these writings become more widely known, just as Biblical history had to be rewritten when the ruins of Assyria and Babylonia began to yield up their secrets, and just as New Testament history had to be rewritten when Christian theologians began to discover that the Pharisees spoke for themselves from the pages of the Talmud. [pp. 32–33]

Wolfson began his new venture by cutting a swath through the jungle of terminology. He pinpointed one problem which he had dealt with in *Spinoza,* the problem of "soul." The definition of the soul and its faculties had challenged the acumen of all the medieval philosophers and the Greek thinkers before them. The nature of the human soul, as understood by all of them, is linked to sensory perception, which is designated external (the five senses) and internal (memory and imagination). Now the phrase "external senses" is clear enough, but the phrase "internal senses" is not. Nor have the historians of medieval philosophy thrown much light on the matter. Accordingly, Wolfson addressed himself to the problem of these terms and their classification, and within a year, in 1935, he published three papers, one of which, "The Internal Senses in Latin, Arabic, and Hebrew Philosophic Texts," took up more than half of the April issue of the *Harvard Theological Review.* (Incidentally, the reprint of this monograph brought him a total royalty of twelve and a half cents.) Here we find all meat and no sauce: the monograph, compact and comprehensive, is virtually an index of all the relevant terms in medieval and Greek philosophy; at the close, there is appended a table showing at a glance the variety of ways in which Greek terms are translated into Arabic, all of which illuminated the subject as never before. Moreover, for the adventurous reader there is more. Does the history of the traditional use of the term "internal senses" end with the Middle Ages? Not at all. The term shows up, says Wolfson, "in modern philosophy with its restoration by Locke

and Kant, perhaps unbeknown to themselves, to the original meaning with which it started its career in Augustine."

What is true of "internal senses" is true of philosophic terms
generally. They never die or at least have nine lives. It is ignorance
of this fact that stands in the way of a proper reading of the history
of philosophy.

Unlike the Spinoza volumes, the monograph did not attract much
attention, but its importance was recognized in certain learned circles and warmly appreciated by his colleagues on Divinity Avenue.
Two days after the April issue of the *Harvard Theological Review*
appeared, Wolfson received a letter from Robert H. Pfeiffer, then
chairman of the Department of Semitic Languages, expressing his
admiration for the comprehensive scope and thoroughness of the
monograph. "As all that you write," Pfeiffer added, "this study
seems to say all that needs to be said on the subject, so that no one
else need ever bother about the problems involved. You seem to have
developed a new method, a sort of detective work, following clues
to the solution of the mystery, in the field of mediaeval philosophy;
you trace words and ideas through half a dozen languages, like
hunters following a fox, and never return empty-handed."

Recreating the scene in Widener 45 during those years of sleuthing, one sees Wolfson engaged day in and day out with the vicissitudes of every important word and phrase used by the philosophers.
He assembles the evidence; and, as though Widener 45 were a court
of law, the philosophers through their own writings appear as witnesses, answer the questions of both defense and prosecution, reply
to their cross-examination. Then Wolfson acts as judge: reviewing
all the evidence given by the principals and the interpreters who
have been called in as witnesses, he separates the essential from the
inessential and renders a verdict. Throughout the long process, from
the assembling of evidence through the examination of principals
and witnesses, until the final dénouement, there are pitfalls aplenty,
dangers of misinterpretation, mysteries of long standing, tales of
distortion, acts of perjury.

Yet the judge, in his relentless pursuit of truth, proves his case
beyond a reasonable doubt. And his decision, written with clarity
and precision, becomes a word, a phrase, perhaps a footnote or a

sentence, in a paper or monograph. For example: "Isaac Israeli, who does make mention of common sense, excludes it from both the internal and external senses . . . and makes of it a neutral sense occupying an intermediate position between the two. The first to specifically include common sense in his classification of the internal senses is Avicenna" ("The Internal Senses," p. 95). Behind this statement is the odyssey that Wolfson has made between the Jewish court physician of the khalifs of Kairouan of the tenth century and the eleventh-century Arab commentator on Aristotle. On the way he has stopped off here and there to interrogate all the contemporaries who could be found so that his conclusion can be stated as definitively as is humanly possible. If the evidence is too thin, or if he is not convinced beyond a reasonable doubt, he either suggests a possible solution or says simply, "I do not know."

As case follows case in court, so problem follows problem, each one suggesting another. And as the genealogy of each term is fixed, it becomes clear that the family of every term is related to other families. No term stands in isolation. Sometimes terms are the victims of family quarrels, and as the generations of words succeed each other, stepchildren appear as do children born out of wedlock. If prudery or snobbishness (or the ignorance of scholars) enters the family portrait, the scientist simply smiles, makes mental notes but, being free of social prejudice, restores the terms to their rightful place and, if deserving, gives them an appropriate epitaph. Wolfson found that every term and every problem he ever studied led back to Greek philosophy. In this way he traversed the centuries, zigzagging his journey from Spinoza back to his philosophic forbears among the ancient Greeks.

"In this way"—if anything, these simple words conceal the concentration, perseverence, and ingenuity with which he has pursued his quarry. Out of the diffuse world of manuscripts and books with which he started and in which he slowly forged his way, there emerged a structure different from those sanctified in the textbooks. The way of the conventional historian is to deal with each thinker archeologically, constructing out of extant material his system of thought. The Wolfson method is different. It deals with the thinkers historically, *reconstructing* from the extant material their answers to problems. And this gave him a key to the overworked words "new" and "original." "Novelty in philosophy," he writes in *Spinoza*, "is often a matter of daring rather than of invention. In thought, as in nature, there is no creation from absolute nothing, nor are there any leaps. Often what appears to be new and original is nothing but the establishment of a long-envisioned truth by the intrepidity of someone who dared to face the consequences of his reasoning" (vol. 2, p. 331).

One might read these words as a splendid epigrammatic display and nod with approval. But there are scholars upon whom their explosive implications were not lost. Resistance to change or innovation is an old story. Since interpreters for centuries kept repeating that Spinoza was a pantheist and Descartes a mechanist, these judgments have come to be taken as axiomatic and any challenge to them, however soundly argued, was bound to have its critics. So, in 1937, Wolfson interrupted his studies to take on these critics. And, although he had suppressed any semblance of polemics in his technical writing, in this instance he wrote with incisive criticism and devastating irony. By way of example, here is a short passage from "Spinoza's Mechanism, Attributes, and Panpsychism," which appeared in *The Philosophical Review* in 1937:

If the term mechanism is applied to Descartes and to others like him despite their belief in a God endowed with will and acting by design, it is only by the courtesy of modern historians of philosophy. But, for that matter, the same courtesy might with equal propriety be extended to all the mediaeval philosophers who believed in necessary laws of nature preordained by an unknown will of God. Though these mediaeval philosophers continued to speak of final causes, the term really was nothing with them but a verbal designation for what they believed to be the revelation in the world of some divine purpose unknown to men—exactly the position taken by Descartes with all his verbal denial of final causes. To say, therefore . . . that Spinoza replaced the mere denial of final causality by the "positive doctrine" of mechanism is to reduce Spinoza to the intellectual level of the village free thinker who tantalized his bucolic listeners by declaring that he did not have to explain the origin and order of the universe by the existence of a God, as he could explain everything by the existence of atheism. [p. 309]

Such digressions from his main studies were infrequent, and while they display his gift for polemics, they do not tell us much of his progress. But there was an event in 1937 which does throw light on the development of his ideas. In that year occurred the semicentennial celebration of the Jewish Theological Seminary of America, and Wolfson accepted an invitation to read a paper on Maimonides at an institute in June, which was the climax of the commemorative events. From the time when Wolfson wrote his prize-winning essay "Maimonides and Halevi" as an undergraduate, Maimonides figured constantly in the mainstream of his work. During the celebration of Maimonides's 800th anniversary in 1935, Wolfson spoke at a symposium under the auspices of the Harvard Philosophical Club at Phillips Brooks House; and in April of the same year he published "Maimonides on the Internal Senses" in a special issue of the *Jewish Quarterly Review*. Based upon the historical and philological conclusions reached in the monograph we have discussed, this paper provides further documentation and analysis of the role of the internal senses in Maimonidean thought. The paper delivered at the institute in New York in June was technical but, reading between the lines, we can see that it represents a first step in rescuing Maimonides from the downgraded position accorded him by some modern scholars.

In an interview in 1937 with William L. Lawrence, a Harvard classmate who was then the science reporter of the *New York Times* and was anxious to decode the technicalities of the Maimonides paper, Wolfson provided a clue to some generalizations that he felt ready to make public. The colloquy can be fully reconstructed:

Wolfson: To begin with, what is generally regarded as Christian scholastic philosophy, in the light of comparative studies of Muslim and Jewish medieval philosophy, is basically not all Christian. The three faiths wrote their philosophies in three different languages, but all three of them had common intellectual roots and were actually united in one philosophy.

Lawrence: Can you say a word about their common source?

Wolfson: The common source is in the search for a reconciliation between the revealed truth of the Scriptures and the truth as arrived at by philosophy—in other words, in the age-old attempt to reconcile science and religion, faith and reason. From this same source they reached a common synthesis.

Lawrence: What is that synthesis?

Wolfson: The medieval synthesis between philosophy and religion is generally regarded as a Christian synthesis, and medieval philosophy is consequently often defined as the "Christianization of Aristotle." This is indeed a true description of medieval philosophy if one confines oneself to the writings of Christian authors; but it would be similarly true to regard it as a Muslim or Jewish synthesis if one confined oneself, respectively, to the writings of Muslim or Jewish philosophers. The truth is that neither medieval philosophy, nor modern philosophy, can be broken up into such religious or linguistic groups. Medieval philosophy is one philosophy which happened to be written in three languages—Arabic, Hebrew, and Latin. They all dealt with the same problems, derived from the same sources, and all three arrived at the same conclusions.

Lawrence: Would you kindly give an illustration?

Wolfson: When we reexamine the history of every medieval problem in which an attempt was made to reconcile the concept that God had personal, humanlike attributes, such as love, goodness, and mercy, with the concept of the Divine Being as immutable, indefinable, unrelated, and incomparable to anything else in the universe created by Him, the study brings out an interesting and significant fact: it was one Jew, Philo, who started it; it was another Jew, Maimonides, who raised it to its highest logical point; it was a third Jew, Spinoza, who dissolved it.

Lawrence: Does this fact have any bearing on modern thought?

Wolfson: Nowadays, ever since Kant proved that the existence of God cannot be demonstrated by "pure reason" but that it must be assumed as a postulate of "practical reason," we are in the habit of justifying religion not as revealed truth, but as a convenience. We are already acquainted with theologies which find a justification for the religious way of life without the assumption of a God or of revelation. But, for that matter, there are those who similarly justify science as a convenience without subscribing to its creeds. For example, there are communities where they build hospitals with all the modern scientific equipment but at the same time prohibit the teaching of evolution.

Lawrence: What do you mean by your use of the word "convenience?"

Wolfson: The average man of today, regardless of his beliefs or disbeliefs in science and religion, likes to enjoy the fruits of both of them. For in his unthinking moments science means nothing but to push a button to get electric illumination; and religion similarly means nothing but to offer a prayer to get divine illumination. In medieval times, on the other hand, religion and science meant truths and not conveniences; and thus one could not logically follow both unless one could reconcile them in thought. The method of reconciliation consisted in interpreting the language of the Scriptures in terms of philosophy. Nowadays this method is described as rationalization.

Lawrence: But didn't the medievals use the same method?

Wolfson: When we realize that to the medieval philosophers the Scripture was of revealed and divine origin, such rationalization had a logical basis in fact. It was not until Spinoza denied the divine origin of Scripture that this rationalization had to be simultaneously discarded by philosophy.

Lawrence: How about Maimonides, the subject of your paper?

Wolfson: In their attempt to reconcile philosophy and theology, all of the medieval philosophers except Maimonides did violence to the concept of God, and it could be truly said of them that they made philosophy the handmaiden of religion. Maimonides, on the other hand, did not want to sacrifice the logic of the philosophic God. Consequently, his concept of God's personality actually amounted to a denial of this personality by reducing God's personal attributes to something wholly unknowable to the human mind.

One would imagine that this dialogue took place in Widener 45 or in the seminar room, but the two men sat in easy chairs in an office of the *New York Times* building. A strange background for the airing of ideas forged in the scriptorium of a scholar. Be that as it may, the views expressed in the interview suggest certain developments at Widener 45 to which even the papers Wolfson published hardly provide a clue. He had reached a point in his studies where he had all the material from Plato to Spinoza assembled in portfolios and he felt ready to put it into written form. He began writing essays on problems in Greek philosophy and worked forward to Spinoza. By 1941 he had written a series of manuscripts covering twenty centuries, and he began to think of putting the manuscript material into books. In his own mind the years of sowing were over; he could now look forward to the harvest.

8
The Alexandrian Mystery

Cast no stone into a well from which you have drunk.

Babylonian Talmud, Baba Kama 92b

With the entire domain of traditional philosophy stretching before him on his shelves at Widener 45 and the intellectual assurance that came with the mastery of it, Wolfson relished the thought of the abundant harvest ahead. He could see, almost taste, the early fruits and the late fruits. Surely within another four or five years the manuscripts would be revised, put to press, and then take their places as companion volumes to *Spinoza*. Indeed, early in 1941 the entire manuscript of a work on problems in Greek philosophy was ready for the printer. But once again the inquisitive demon within asserted itself. In certain chapters of that work he had driven head on into one of the mysteries in the history of philosophy and, like the physicists of the mid-twentieth century, he had arrived at a fundamental law without defining its nucleus. If he could probe further and ferret out the elements of the nucleus, so to speak, he might be able to unravel the mystery.

He therefore put aside the manuscript on Greek philosophy, except for the six chapters dealing with Philo of Alexandria, one of which was already in galley proofs; it would appear as "Philo on Free Will" in the April 1942 issue of the *Harvard Theological Review*. These chapters on Philo had been treated as part of Greek philosophy because he had decided in principle to divide all his material according to languages and to write an exposition of the problems as they were conceived and solved in each literature. But Philo, as he came to see, sounded the knell of Greek philosophy, and he saw further that it was Philo who laid the foundations of religion and philosophy in Judaism, Christianity, and Islam. Accordingly, Philo would head the great series of books on the structure and growth of philosophic systems. The introductory volume of Greek philosophy would have to wait. In the light of Wolfson's reappraisal it was clear that no thinker had been so egregiously misunderstood as Philo. Indeed, the evidence suggested that the treatment of him amounted to mayhem. Why had Philo been maimed by historians of Greek philosophy and unobtrusively embalmed in footnotes? What was the secret of this Alexandrian mystery?

The main facts of the case can be briefly stated.

Of the life story of Philo we know little. The scion of an aristocratic Jewish family, he lived in the Hellenistic metropolis of Alexandria in the first half of the common era (*c.* 20 B.C.E.–50 C.E.), and thus was an older contemporary of Jesus of Nazareth and a younger contemporary of Hillel, who became a great teacher in Palestine. Philo was a leader of the Alexandrian Jewish community, and after the anti-Jewish riots that occurred in the autumn of 38 C.E. on the appearance of the newly crowned king Agrippa in Alexandria, he headed a Jewish deputation to Rome. But such public activities did not impede his intellectual pursuits. He was a master of both Jewish and Greek cultures, and when he was not drawn into political turmoil, devoted himself to philosophy. Such are the bare bones of his life.

Our case, however, involves not the man but the ideas he expressed in his writings. Some of these writings were lost, but the bulk of them have survived. They are easily accessible, both in the original Greek and in an English translation, in the set of ten volumes of the

Loeb Classics. Thus we have, so to speak, the *corpus delicti*. It had been exhumed by plodding scholarship since the sixteenth century. But the autopsy of these scholarly physicians is open to question; there are ambiguities of fact and interpretation.

Before these scholars are placed in the witness box and cross-examined by Wolfson, let us look at that part of the evidence which is incontrovertible. First, Philo produced a body of writing which in the main is cast in the form of an interpretive commentary on the Greek translation of the Hebrew Bible—though, it should be added, it is highly possible that he had some knowledge of the Hebrew original. Second, Philo knew Greek literature and philosophy and employed them in his allegorical interpretation of the Pentateuch. Third, Philo's writings influenced the early Church Fathers, though he had no direct influence on the subsequent development of Judaism. Neither prosecutor nor witness has any quarrel with these facts. And, to complete the picture, one should keep in mind that with the destruction of ancient Alexandria and of Hellenistic Judaism in the following two centuries, Philo's works seem to have disappeared, and he became so blurred a figure that he was often taken to be a Christian Church Father.

With these indisputable facts before us, then, let us see what constructions emerge from the time of Philo's rediscovery in the Renaissance to the rehabilitation of his writings in the past century. I shall sketch, without regard to sequence, the conventional portrait of Philo, which is characteristic of the entire literature.

Philo emerges in this portrait as a species of theosophist who conducted a fashionable school of adulterated education, where he delivered lectures on the topical issues of the day to upper-class ladies and gentlemen. His books were potboilers consisting of discourses on the bestsellers of that time, richly illustrated with references to the popular spectacles in the theaters, circuses, and art galleries of Alexandria, which was the Paris of the first century. He was essentially a preacher, interpreting the Bible in long-winded homilies which were garnished and embroidered—sometimes eloquently but more often tiresomely—with quotations from Plato, the Stoics, and numerous Greek writers. In this view Philo is completely devoid of originality, although in rare instances he is conceded a thought or two; indeed, at best he is portrayed as a compiler whose works are little more than a gallimaufry of literary allusions and muddleheaded philosophy, and an eclectic who syncretized in the manner of the current mystery religions the pagan philosophies with the religious ideas of the Bible. Such is the stock estimate of the Philonic commentators and scholars. And the upshot was silence about him in books on Greek philosophy, or, at most, burial in footnotes.

By 1942 at the latest—Wolfson's statement about Philo in the interview with a reporter in 1937 suggests a much earlier date—he had arrived at an estimate which was poles apart from both the modern and the ancient views. It was a revolutionary position, but before we say more about it, let us follow the method by which he arrived at it and how it ultimately became the version of Philo incorporated in the two volumes he published five years later, in 1947. When his chapter "Philo on Free Will" appeared, he stated in a footnote that this "is one of six chapters on Philo in a larger work dealing with the history of an integrated group of philosophic problems from Plato to Spinoza." Typical of the others, this chapter was calculated to undermine the conventional portrait of Philo, for it is a demonstration that Philo is the originator of the doctrine of free will. This doctrine is not to be found in Greek philosophy. In Philo's conception man is possessed of a will which by divine grace is completely autonomous. The freedom of the human is comparable to God's power to suspend the laws of nature. Both partake of the miraculous.

One can look in vain for anything like this in Plato or any other Greek philosopher. In Plato, for example, "there is," Wolfson writes, "no such third factor as a free will conceived as something autonomous and as something which is free and independent of both the rational and irrational faculties of the soul and which by some arbitrary action tips the scale on the side of the one or the other. Whenever the rational and irrational souls meet in conflict, the victory of the one or the other will be decided on the basis of their respective strengths and weaknesses. For man there is no choice in the matter." In the case of Philo, however, the view is that

voluntary acts are of man's own free choice and not decided me-
chanically by the respective strengths of the competing souls within;
to wit, man has a will "which by some unaccountable manner may
decide in favor of the one or the other, even when by all the laws
of causality the outcome should have been otherwise" (*Philo*, vol.
1, pp. 430–31).

Nor is this all. Philo extends the idea of human responsibility to
the choice of evil as well as good. Man can choose and attain good
or virtue by his free will, and, if he strives for it, with the help of
God; but the choice of evil is also in the power of man. In Philo's
conception of human freedom "we have an adumbration of all the
elements of the problem as it presented itself to the minds of religious philosophers, whether Christian, Moslem, or Jewish, throughout the ages" (vol. 1, p. 458). After showing how Philo's idea of
human freedom entered into the stream of medieval thought, Wolfson concludes that the medieval philosophers' conception of free will
and grace "amounts to nothing more than the simple assertion of
Philo and the rabbis that both God has foreknowledge and man is
free" (vol. 1, p. 461). And Wolfson gives this play of ideas an ending
that is an anticipation of his whole dramatic theme:

It is this traditional conception of God's, as well as man's, freedom of the
will, which originated in the philosophy of Philo and was maintained
throughout mediaeval philosophy, though occasionally somewhat modified,
that was made the subject of attack by those who before Spinoza began to
nibble at traditional philosophy and by Spinoza himself in his grand assault
on it. The result, in the case of Spinoza, was a return to the classical
conception of the immutability of the laws of nature, especially as it was
conceived by Aristotle, ere it was modified by Philo's introduction of the
principle of the changeability of these laws through the miraculous inter-
vention of God. The God of Spinoza, like the God of Aristotle, acts by what
traditional philosophy would call the necessity of His own nature but which
Spinoza himself defines as true freedom. Man also, according to him, has
not that power to overcome his passions which traditional philosophy would
call the power of one's free will; but still he himself, like Plato, Aristotle
and the Stoics, speaks of man's ability to overcome his passions by knowledge and thereby become free. It is not until the entire conception of
immutable laws of nature was called into doubt that absolute undetermined

freedom of the human will, like that asserted by Philo, makes its reappearance in philosophy. But the ground for the questioning of the immutability of the laws of nature is not the rediscovery of a God who, like the God of Philo and his followers, is endowed with a miracle-working power. The historical background of this new view is to be found in the ancient Epicurean denial of causality. [vol. 1, pp. 461–62]

The Philo described in this passage cannot be identified with any of the caricatures drawn of him by the modern portraitists. Philo knows the conceptions of the Greek thinkers, but he is not their follower or compiler; he is their critic. True, Philo derived certain conceptions from Greek thinkers, but he rejected or reinterpreted them in the light of what he considered true religious doctrine. As Wolfson reveals Philo's grappling with the problem of human freedom he establishes that Philo is neither a Platonist nor a Pythagorean nor a Stoic, even though he employs their vocabulary. At the same time Wolfson demonstrates that in Philo's use of this Greek vocabulary he is exact and discriminating, and, far more than an imitator, he is a critic of the pagan philosophers. In clarifying the meaning of terms used by Philo, Wolfson by a fresh deployment of the original Greek sources dispels the fancy that the use of expressions or terms from Greek philosophers makes him a follower of their schools of thought. Thus Philo is not a wooly-headed eclectic, except in the sense that, as Wolfson says, "like any great and original philosopher in the history of philosophy, Philo's own philosophy was a reaction against that of his predecessors and contemporaries." The portrait that suffers most from Wolfson's Philo is the one which makes of him the purveyor of a paganlike mystery religion and of a mystical gospel that paved the way for Christianity. If ever such a mystic existed in Alexandria, he is as insubstantial as Banquo's ghost. In any case, Wolfson seems to demonstrate unfalteringly that Philo is a philosopher to be reckoned with.

The six chapters on Philo extracted from Wolfson's manuscript on Greek philosophy amounted to some 300 pages. When he examined them he found that they amounted to an exposition of the major problems of Greek philosophy as criticized and reinterpreted by Philo. The problems ranged from the creation of the world to the unknowability of God, and with the addition of the introductory chapter the material could form a book. But it was of first importance to make Philo's presuppositions explicit, especially as these bore upon the character of his allegorical method in the interpretation of Scripture and as they issued in what amounted to a preamble of faith. Moreover, given their importance, Philo's ethical and political conceptions had to be included. Above all, the provenance of Philo's thought, especially in relation to Palestinian Judaism, required reconsideration.

The question of Philo's relation to the normative Judaism of Palestine is crucial. All the writers on Philo had taken the position that there was a deep breach between Palestinian and Hellenistic Judaism. But long ago Wolfson had reached an opposite conclusion, which he had been expounding as early as the 1920s in his course on post-biblical Jewish history. His first impulse was to provide the historical justification of his view; he followed that impulse and wrote a chapter of more than a hundred pages which was a complete description of the history of the Jews of Alexandria. But as soon as he had completed it he realized that this historical presentation was out of focus: his work on Philo must be analytical rather than historical. Besides, what he had to prove was how the Alexandrian Jews and Philo justified Greek philosophy and at the same time remained traditional.

In the initial draft of the chapter he had given the historical data to show how the Jewish community of Alexandria was socially and economically a self-contained and self-sufficient society and how they were never cut off from the mother society in Palestine. Consequently, he subjected the first "stream-of-consciousness" draft to radical revision: the rewriting actually took six months. Most of the early draft was deleted and summarized in a single paragraph of 325 words, the second paragraph of the first chapter. The paragraph is preceded by an opening one of similar length which formulates his view of the Jews and Judaism in that Hellenistic age. He shows how none of the peoples who "after the conquests of Alexander began to participate in Greek philosophy contributed anything radically new to it. All they did was to master its teachings and furnish teachers." After a review of the main centers and their teachers, Wolfson compresses into a few striking sentences an epitome of the history of the Jews of Alexandria:

If certain vestiges of foreign beliefs and certain undertones of foreign thought are sometimes said to be discerned in their teachings, they themselves had no consciousness of them; and in fact it takes all the skill and imagination and insight of searching scholarship to get even a scent of their presence. The single exception was the Jewish population of Alexandria. This Alexandrian Jewish population produced out of its midst a school of philosophers who consciously and deliberately and systematically set about remaking Greek philosophy according to the pattern of a belief and tradition of an entirely different origin. [vol. 1, pp. 3–4]

Here is the basis for Wolfson's revolutionary view of Philo, the view which was adumbrated in the first six chapters and which would take another five years to elaborate. The paragraph that follows upon this is an even greater feat of compression. It reads:

The rise of that school and the continuity of its existence for about three centuries, from the translation of the Pentateuch into Greek (*c.* 260 B.C.) to the end of the activity of Philo (*c.* A.D. 40), was made possible by the nature of the dominant element, if not the basic stock, of the Jewish population in Alexandria and by the nature of the social economy of the Alexandrian Jewish community. That dominant element came from Palestine at a time when Judaism in its native home had already been molded by the teaching and preaching and disciplinary training of the Scribes into that particular form which ultimately gave rise to Pharisaism. From its native home this dominant element of the Jewish population in Alexandria had brought with it not only a Scripture and a tradition, but also a knowledge of that Scripture and tradition, an ordered mode of life and thought based upon them, and a firm resolve to preserve that mode of life and thought under whatever conditions it might find itself. Conditions in Alexandria were such as to favor the maintenance and preservation of this mode of life and thought. Politically the Jews of Alexandria had the right to organize a community of their own within which they were free to live according to their own religion. Socially, they lived in compact masses within certain areas of the city, which provided them with the necessary facilities for the practice of their religion. Economically, though the community as a whole depended upon the outside non-Jewish environment for the main source of its wealth, the majority of Jews within the community gained their living there, without being forced to seek occupation among non-Jews outside. Culturally, though one generation after their settlement in Alexandria the Jews had adopted Greek speech, they remained a separate group, with a system of education and intellectual life entirely their own. Constant communication with the home country in Palestine had kept Alexandrian Judaism, despite the inevitable rise of certain local changes, from becoming completely separated from its original source. [vol. 1, pp. 4–5]

Of course, this summary does not express the total content of the writer's mind; but it does convey everything that is relevant to his analysis. The common experience of the learned reader of Wolfson is that he can read more between the lines than in them. The chapter in which all this is set forth is called "Hellenistic Judaism and Philo," and it took six months to write. During the four years that followed, Wolfson continued building upon a systematic structure of Philo's thought. Nowhere is his method of establishing complete identity with a philosopher and thinking through his every thought applied with more exciting results. He finds Philo's mind engaged with all the speculative problems of his time: "the existence of ideas, the origin of the world, its structure and the laws which govern it, the nature of the soul and the realm of living things, problems of human knowledge, man's knowledge of God's existence and God's nature, and the problem of human conduct, both individual and social." To be sure, Philo stands in the mainstream of a tradition that began with Plato, but he is the founder of a new trend within that tradition; for he not only examined the entire range of philosophic problems but also hammered out a reconciliation between philosophy and Scripture. As Philo effected this reconciliation, he had perforce to examine every philosophic view and determine whether or not each view was reconcilable with Scripture. And in the course of this painstaking search, Philo is shown by Wolfson to scripturalize Greek philosophy and to philosophize Scripture, and thus to usher in a new period in the history of philosophy.

Wolfson's presentation of this dramatic event in the history of human thought is introduced in two chapters which precede the original six and are called "Handmaid of Scripture" and "Scriptural Presuppositions." Every page broaches a fresh insight and his resources of learning are managed with dexterity; indeed, technical though these chapters be, they can be read like a novel. One can glimpse the distinctive flavor of his writing in the following passage, which seeks to explain why other scholars did not detect the true character and importance of Philo.

If all this is not apparent in his writings, it is perhaps because he is one of those philosophers who does his thinking in private and presents to the public only the maturity of his thought. If, with the exception of an occasional groan at some pet aversion, he does not dwell much upon the erroneous views of philosophers to which he objected, it is perhaps because his purpose was not to teach true philosophy to students of Scripture but to show the truth of Scripture to students of philosophy. If almost without any exception he adopts philosophic views without telling us that he adopts them only according to a new version of his own, it is perhaps because at his time philosophic views and concepts had not yet become rigidly fixed by the constant hammering of commentators and one could still freely reshape them for some particular use without having to offer an apology or explanation. Perhaps, also, at his time he could envisage a class of readers who were so well acquainted with the original meaning of the views and concepts with which he dealt that he felt no need of constantly reminding them of the revisions he had introduced. Do we not all sometimes quite deliberately pervert a familiar quotation, without stopping to insult the intelligence of the reader by pointing out the liberty we have taken with it? [vol. 1, p. 105]

Such is Wolfson's method of studying Philo, as profoundly psychological as it is dynamically historical, and the results sketched thus far warrant further examination.

From the writing of the first chapter in 1942 to the completion of the third chapter in 1944, the original core of 333 pages more than tripled in number. After about six years of work he had before him a manuscript of over 700 pages. These pages contain a systematic description of Philo's thought which demonstrates a coherent system of philosophy. The core of that philosophy is Scripture; and by showing that Philo made philosophy the handmaid of Scripture —the word "handmaid" is Philo's—Wolfson established him as the first thinker to subordinate reason to faith and thus the ancestor of all the later thinkers who directly or indirectly adopted this view, together with the basic concept that revelation provides the preamble to reason.

With the addition of a final chapter, "What Is New in Philo?" Wolfson might have sent the manuscript to the printer. He had given a full account of Philo's religious philosophy. But there is another fold of Philo's thought to which Wolfson alludes succinctly in his discussion of the development of philosophy as the handmaid of Scripture: the role of ethics as the highest branch of philosophy and the implication of this view for the science of government. Philo's name is conspicuous for its absence in works on ethics and political theory. Yet it had become clear—and Wolfson's statement in his brief account is already explicit regarding this—that Philo's ethical and political views are a departure from Greek thought and no less original than the rest of his philosophy. So Wolfson set about elucidating Philo's ethical and political theories.

Within a year he had filled another ream of paper. These two chapters, which grew into more than three hundred printed pages, comprise in themselves a full-length book. As elsewhere, Wolfson breaks new ground in these chapters. His exposition is oriented to the fact that Philo was both a political theorist and a practical statesman. In his criticism of Greek political theories, Philo gives new meanings to concepts of constitutional law as well as of governmental administration and institutions of the state. He illuminated every aspect of political existence, from citizenship and nationality to democracy and world government. Such is the tenor of Wolfson's exposition here. The following is a characteristic passage:

When Caligula forgot that he was a Roman emperor and acted like a Hellenic hero, demanding to be worshipped by his subjects, and when also popular feeling and thinking in Alexandria threatened the existence of the autonomous Jewish polity, Philo did his best to defend it. First, he appeals to the Jewish constitutional rights, which have been confirmed by the Roman emperors. Second, he condemns popular agitation against the Jews as falsely masquerading under the guise of patriotism, or, as he expresses himself, under the guise of wishing "to do honor to the emperor." Third, he dwells upon the antiquity of the Jews in Alexandria and elsewhere, arguing that in some places they were among the original founders. Fourth, he parades Jewish patriotism, maintaining that the Jews are bound by their religion to pay honor to the ruler of the country which treats them hospitably, evidently having in mind his own interpretation of the verse "thou shalt not abhor an Egyptian because thou wast a sojourner in his land" as constituting a commandment that "settlers" in a foreign land should "pay some honor to those who have accepted them."

This was his formal defense. But he knew that by such arguments one can win a debate, but one cannot change a social situation. He knew that the root of the problem was too deep to be overcome by such palliative arguments. The root of the problem, as he himself states it, was to be found in the peculiar laws practiced by the Jews. Many before Philo, and Philo himself, had tried to convince the world of the intrinsic merits of these laws. But he knew that the world was offended by these laws not because they were harmful, but because they were different; more so if it were constantly told that these laws were superior; and still more so if it actually felt that these laws were superior. These laws, says Philo, "are necessarily grave and severe, because they inculcate the highest standard of virtue; but gravity is austere, and austerity is held in aversion by the great mass of men because they favor pleasure." Indeed, one might argue, as Josephus later did argue, that similar religious differences exist also among non-Jews themselves. But Philo felt that the differences between the Jews and non-Jews are unlike the differences that may exist between various religious groups of non-Jews. The former are more fundamental. They place the Jews as a group apart from the totality of non-Jews, with all the varieties of religions and sects among the non-Jews themselves. Whenever any hostility breaks out between two groups of non-Jews, he says, the hostile groups do not stand alone, for "by reason of their frequent intercourse with other nations, they are in no want of helpers who join sides with them." Not so, however, is the case of the Jews. "The Jewish nation has none to take its part" and "one may say that the whole Jewish nation is in the position of an orphan compared with all other nations in other lands."

What, then, is the solution of the problem? Long before Philo, when for the first time Jews became conscious of the gulf created between themselves and non-Jews by reason of their Law, we are told, "there came forth out of Israel lawless men, and persuaded many, saying: 'Let us go out and make a covenant with the nations that are round about us, for since we separated ourselves from them many evils have come upon us,' " and this covenant which they advocated to be made with the nations, we are told, resulted in that "they repudiated the holy covenant; yea, they joined themselves to the gentiles." Individual Jews at the time of Philo in Alexandria undoubtedly offered the same solution for the Jewish problem of their own time. His own nephew, Tiberius Julius Alexander, thus solved the Jewish problem for himself in that way. He forsook Judaism and henceforth found no difficulty in rising to high office, and in his subsequent behavior toward his own people, both in Alexandria and Palestine, showed that he succeeded in completely emancipating himself, from what was then called Jewish "inhospitality," the common opprobrium of that time for the natural desire on the part of the Jews to preserve their own existence. He must have been looked upon by his non-Jewish contemporaries as an example of what they considered as the better kind of Jew, the desirable Jew, the Jew against whom they had no prejudice. There must undoubtedly have been in Alexandria other Jews like him who, alienated from the spiritual and intellectual sources of Judaism, came to look upon their heritage as a heap of meaningless customs and beliefs and thus sought to emancipate themselves from Jewish "inhospitality" and "superstition" and "atheism" by learning to relish swine's flesh, to idle on a weekday instead of resting on the Sabbath, and to see piety in the worship of images rather than in the worship of the imageless Jehovah. But, having torn themselves away from Judaism, they were evidently contented to enjoy their newly discovered liberties privately, and did not exhibit themselves to the world as examples of an ideal solution of a vexatious problem. [vol. 2, pp. 404–7]

Such solutions in their twentieth-century garb were subjected to biting satire in the essay called "Escaping Judaism," which Wolfson wrote for the *Menorah Journal* twenty years earlier. The solution found by Philo for his time concludes Wolfson's chapter on political theory. Philo's solution is messianic: with the revival of the promises of the Hebrew prophets the Jewish dispersion will disappear and after the reunion of the exiles there will be a reign of peace between men and men, and men and beasts; the Mosaic constitution will become world law and Judaism a universal religion.

Thus Wolfson culminated his voyage of discovery, which he likened to Darwin's voyage on *H.M.S. Beagle*. He had introduced a theory of the history of philosophy as radical as Darwin's theory of evolution in the history of science. Wolfson called this theory the Philonic philosophy. In this view Philo is regarded not only as a fundamental break with ancient Greek philosophy but also as the founder of medieval philosophy. "Philo," Wolfson says, "is the founder of this new school of philosophy, and from him it directly passes on to the Gospel of St. John and the Church Fathers, from whom it passes on to Muslim and hence also to medieval Jewish philosophy. Philo is the direct or indirect source of this type of philosophy which continues uninterruptedly in its main assertions for well-nigh seventeen centuries when at last it is openly challenged by Spinoza" (vol. 2, p. 457).

In order to communicate the originality of Philo's ideas and their importance to subsequent philosophy and religion, Wolfson employs a literary form as arresting as his ideas are striking. He invents a "synthetic" medieval philosopher who is composed of all the common elements of the Christian, the Muslim, and the Jewish philosophers and in the space of ten pages analyzes and formulates the entire radical revision of Greek philosophy, which is traced back to Philo. The literary form underscores the intellectual drama that unfolds, and the curtain falls on a statement which anticipates and whets the reader's appetite for the volumes to come:

This, then, is the new period in the history of philosophy, ushered in by Philo and ushered out by Spinoza. If we still choose to describe this period as mediaeval, for after all it comes between a philosophy which knew not of Scripture and a philosophy which tries to free itself from Scripture, then mediaeval philosophy is the history of the philosophy of Philo. For well-nigh seventeen centuries this Philonic philosophy dominated European thought. Nothing really new happened in the history of European philosophy during that extended period. The long succession of philosophers during that period, from among whom various figures are selected by various historians for special distinction as innovators, have only tried to expound, each in his own way, the principles laid down by Philo. To the question, then, what is new in Philo? the answer is that it was he who built up that philosophy, just as the answer to the question what is new in Spinoza? is that it was he who pulled it down. [vol. 2, pp. 459–60]

In a work in which Wolfson demonstrates incontrovertibly that the Philonic philosophy is the matrix of all subsequent religious philosophies up to modern times, his sense of the present hovers between the lines and sometimes approaches the threshhold of overt statement. Especially in the introductory chapter, "Hellenistic Judaism and Philo," the implied analogy between ancient Alexandria and modern New York is striking. A couple of quotations from it may serve as examples of his method of projecting the past into the present. Here is part of a description of the uprooted Jewish intellectual:

These uprooted Jewish intellectuals, whether they found it advantageous to themselves to join any of the numerous heathen religious *thiasoi* or not, certainly had no reason to remain within the religious Jewish community. External political and social and economic conditions of the time did not force de-Judaized Jews to cast in their lot, despite themselves, with the Jewish community. Still less did external conditions force them to assume communal or religious leadership. It was comparatively easy at that time for a Jew to escape Judaism. Those at that time who cut themselves off from the body Jewish cut themselves off completely, leaving no dangling shreds of festering dead tissue. They wrote neither books against Jews nor books about Jews. Nor did any of them try to remake Judaism into a sort of inferior heathenism, with Dionysus or Serapis as central figures—if not as deities, then at least as prophets by the side of Moses. Perhaps some of these apostates, either for devious reasons of some practical advantages or for the simple reason that it was easier for them to lose their relish for the God of their fathers than for the cooking of their mothers, had remained within the Jewish part of the city, though without being part of its religious life; and with all their indifference toward Judaism, they could not completely refrain from taunting their fellow Jews, especially the philosophers among them, for maintaining that Scripture was of divine origin and that its stories were something superior to the mythological fables of the Greeks. [vol. 1, pp. 82–83]

And here is a passage on the character of Hellenistic Judaism:

The picture which we have tried to draw of Alexandrian Judaism is that of a community united in its essential beliefs and practices. By the constant attrition and attraction of the environment, every upgrowth of dissent was worn away and carried off; those who remained within did so by choice and out of a sense of unity and loyalty. Whatever differences of opinion existed among them with regard to the interpretation of the Law—whether it should be traditional or allegorical and, if allegorical, to what extent—they all believed in the divine origin of the Law and in its perfection. This belief was their justification to the world at large and to their own selves, for their continued existence as a people apart, which they knew was a source of annoyance to others and which, being only human, they must have occasionally felt also as a burden upon themselves. They all also presented a common attitude toward the religion and culture of the outside world, and this they proclaimed courageously and forthrightly—Greek religion was false; Greek philosophy was an inferior form of Judaism. That courage and forthrightness was caught by early Christianity, when it was only a struggling minority in a pagan world, and, with but one slight change in the wording, it repeated the same proclamation—Greek religion was false; Greek philosophy was an inferior form of Christianity. Indeed, Alexandrian Jews craved good-will, but good-will to them meant to bury the hatchet; it did not mean to bury convictions and cover up differences. They never fawned, they never crawled, they never yielded what they considered to be the truth. [vol. 1, pp. 85–86]

Thirteen years after the publication of *Spinoza,* seven years after Wolfson began to expand his original six chapters on Philo, the two volumes of *Philo: Foundations of Religious Philosophy in Judaism, Christianity, and Islam* appeared. The work was quickly acclaimed in the learned and general press. By the time a third revised edition was brought out in 1962, most of the learned world had echoed Horace M. Kallen's judgment that *Philo* was "an event in intellectual history."

The Alexandrian mystery was now solved. Wolfson had retrieved Philo from the catacombs of scholarship and restored him to a place of honor among the great philosophers.

9
Expedition to the Land of the Fathers

In my beginning is my end.

T.S. Eliot

Wolfson set forth in *Philo* a unifying principle which illuminated as never before the filiation of ideas and the ordered sequence of their development. More and more the word "definitive" came to be used in describing this work. Although he surely was pleased by this judgment, to Wolfson the discovery of a unifying principle was not a palliative but a powerful stimulant to further work. When he pondered over *Philo* and his other writings up to 1947 he could feel that he had at long last reached the beginnings of the harvest. But he was conscious that the history of ideas, like the history of persons, could never be definitively described in the pages of a book. Once the book was written his concern turned to how it could be improved. His copy of *Spinoza* was already interlaced with annotations for a new edition. But his main preoccupation was the manuscripts he had laid aside in order to devote himself (as it turned out for seven years) to *Philo*.

It seemed to him that with *Philo* as the beginning of his theme and *Spinoza* as the end of it he had only to fill in the middle. No sooner had he corrected the page proofs of *Philo* than he took down from his shelf his manuscript on Arab philosophy, particularly on the early rationalist schools centered at Baghdad and Basra, known as the Kalam. From their philosophic speculations he could forge the next link in the chain of the Philonic philosophy. He set to work, and even before the publication of *Philo* three of his papers on technical problems in the Kalam appeared in the *Jewish Quarterly Review*. At the same time he had started on the introduction to the new book. He thought he could finish the entire work in five or six months and thereafter complete the entire series on philosophic systems from Plato to Spinoza by 1960.

However, as he progressed with the introduction to the work on the philosophy of the Kalam, he found himself one day in a situation similar to the one in 1942 when he had put aside the manuscript on Greek philosophy and turned to Philo. But the situation was not identical; he was now working within an historical framework. Certain problems in the Kalam—for example, the creation of the world and the existence and attributes of God—suggested a missing link in the chain of development from Philo to the Kalam. Had nothing happened during the long stretch of eight centuries between Philo and medieval philosophy? During those centuries the Church Fathers had written a library of works. Here of course was the missing link. There was no question in his mind that they had been influenced by Philo and could be treated according to the same plan. As before, then, Wolfson put aside the manuscript on the Kalam and with it the hope of early publication, and he plunged into a study of the original writings of the Church Fathers.

"And so," Wolfson said later in a moment of recollection, "with my own map and compass in one hand and with a Baedecker in the other, I started out on an expedition into that land of the Fathers, which, to students of Church history and Church doctrine, I am sure, was as bright as the brightest spot in Harvard Square but to me, I must confess, in my ignorance and innocence, was as dark as the proverbial darkest Africa."

These words were uttered in the autumn of 1955 at the end of the eight-year journey. His expedition could at that time be regarded as successful, but it had been unexpectedly long and difficult. For the land of the Church Fathers, although at first it appeared to be a land of wide-open fields and green-fledged rivers, soon proved to be full of forests and wastelands where, as he says, he moved about "haltingly and lamely." The compass he used remained in working order throughout, and it resulted in a map that was startlingly new. Let us venture, then, to retrace in a general way his footsteps from the beginning of the journey to the end.

Others had traversed the land of the Church Fathers before Wolfson, but they had seen it with different eyes and they had returned with different maps. A number of Jewish scholars, such as Joseph Klausner, Solomon Zeitlin, and Louis Ginzberg, had studied the patristic literature; but Klausner and Zeitlin had limited themselves to studies of the relations of Judaism and Christianity in the first century, and Louis Ginzberg had used the patristic sources to recover Jewish material. None of them had opened the way for Wolfson. Again, there were Christian scholars who had assiduously studied the vast forest of Jacques Paul Migne's *Patrologiae Cursus Completus* and produced works of importance—for example, Adolf von Harnack's and Joseph Tixeront's histories of Christian dogma, J. F. Bethune-Baker's history of early Christian doctrine, and Jean Danielou's work on Origen. Dealing primarily with theology, homiletics, and Scriptural typology, these scholars can only in a remote sense be called predecessors or forerunners of Wolfson. The Church historian, George H. Williams, goes so far as to say that not only are there "no direct spiritual ancestors or even cousins in the Jewish line of development" but "the only real progenitor of *The Philosophy of the Church Fathers* is Wolfson's own two volumes on Philo."

Philo, then, is Wolfson's point of departure. His first steps were on familiar ground. As early Christianity spread in the wake of Paul's missionary activities on the Mediterranean littoral, and Greek-speaking Jews and non-Jews adopted the new faith, the Scriptures in Greek translation became the Bible of their faith, and the Palestinian apostles of Jewish origin were supplanted by gentile fathers of Hellenistic background. By the middle of the second and through the third century the leading Fathers, like Clement of Alexandria (*c.* 150–215) and Origen (*c.* 186–254), not only lived on the same soil as Philo but also were educated in the same Greek culture and had to cope with the same problems. They derived their faith from the Scriptures and their philosophy from the Greeks, and they derived the method of reconciling faith and reason from Philo. Moreover, they borrowed heavily from Philo's allegory and symbolism. All of this was common knowledge among patristic scholars.

But no patristic scholar had shown step by step, as Wolfson does, the transformation by the Church Fathers of the philosophies of the pagan Greeks into the religious thought of Christianity. It was Philo who set the pattern for this reconciliation of faith and reason. Yet if, like Philo, the Fathers subordinated philosophy to Scripture, reason to faith, they differed from him with regard to the nature of the subordination. Wolfson explains why and how they differed, and this is not the least of his triumphs.

Philo's method was to extract from the literal meaning of the text of Scripture an inner or allegorical meaning. For example, reading the story of Sarah the mistress and Hagar the handmaid, he interpreted Sarah as the symbol of divine wisdom and Hagar as the symbol of human knowledge. In this way, according to Philo, philosophy must be accommodated to Scriptural faith, whose principles can be demonstrated by reason. But what was the nature of that accommodation? To what extent could reason be subordinated to faith? And what of the faith of those who were incapable of the exercise of reason and to whom simple faith was the truth of religion?

Having put the questions to himself, Wolfson found answers to them. Philo believed in the rigidity of the religious and social practices prescribed by Judaism, but he, like the Judaism of his time, was free of any rigidity of thought. As a consequence, individual differences regarding the allegorization of Scripture never led to sectarianism: the allegorists did not condemn the literalists, nor did the literalists condemn the allegorists. "There were renegades," says Wolfson of Alexandrian Judaism, "but no heretics" (*The Philosophy of the Church Fathers,* p. 99). Philo does insist that only those who possess special moral and educational qualifications should engage in philosophical allegorization of Scripture, but he regards these ordinary mortals as an inferior rank of religious believers. He aims his fire at those of his fellow Jews who indulged in the "wrong philosophy." Yet if he recognizes various grades of religious belief, he takes a tolerant attitude toward them all. At the same time he places those who worship God out of love above those who worship God out of fear.

Against this Philonic background Wolfson proceeds with his task of disengaging the strands of the complex web of early Christianity. We are shown how Paul and his apostolic followers completely disavowed the philosophy of the pagan world. However, by the end of the second century Paul's attitude toward philosophy has given way to another and we witness the rise of a philosophized Christianity. Clement illustrates the process. Clement knew Philo, as Paul perhaps did not; thus Clement's commentary on the story of Sarah and Hagar is an echo of Philo's. He applies Philo's allegorical interpretation and even names his source. In the manner of Philo, who had harmonized Judaism and philosophy, Clement does the same thing for Christianity.

What brought about this development in the century between Paul and Clement? Three things chiefly. First, during that century all the Christian thinkers were trained philosophers who had been converted from Greek paganism, and all of them left accounts of how the Old Testament, as they read it through the eyes of Philo, contributed to their conversion. "Thus the Old Testament," Wolfson tells us, "which they learned to know through the tutorage of Philo, was to them a philosophic treatise, like those upon which they were brought up, and so, after the manner of Philo, they continued to read into it whatever philosophy they happened to be acquainted with." Second, the Church Fathers used philosophy as a weapon of defense against the accusations of atheism, cannibalism, infanticide, incest, and treason leveled against them in return for their attacks upon polytheism and idolatry. The line of defense was to present testimonies from the best pagan philosophers in order to show, as one of the Fathers put it, that "the rivals and persecutors of Christian truth from their own authorities [stood convicted] of the crime of at once being untrue to themselves and doing injustice to us."

Third, philosophy was used as an antidote against the wisdom of the Gnostics, who in their pseudophilosophical interpretation of the New Testament, were transforming Christianity "into a mere verbal veneering of paganism" (*Church Fathers*, pp. 12–14).

Within this maelstrom of intellectual controversy, Clement, with the example of Philo before him, devoted himself to harmonizing Scripture with philosophy and at the same time subjecting philosophy to criticism. For one thing, in his struggle against the Gnostics he reclaimed for Christian philosophy the old Scriptural term *gnosis* (knowledge) and called his philosophy the "gnosis of truth" as opposed to the Gnostic's "false gnosis." Faced with the problem of harmonizing the traditional beliefs of the Church with what he considered to be the true principles of philosophy, Clement needed every resource at his command for its solution. On the one hand, Clement believed, there were the teachings of the Scripture, which as being of divine origin were inalterably true without admixture of error; on the other hand, there was philosophy, which as being of human origin contained falsehood as well as truth. Wolfson describes in all its fascinating detail how Clement adapted the Philonic ideas to distinguish between truth and falsehood in philosophy and how he applied them to his conception of Scriptural faith. Far from being as most patristic scholars would have it, Clement is seen by Wolfson as the originator of a new Christian philosophy and a new kind of nonliteral interpretation of the New Testament. Above all, Clement introduced in the course of his battle against heresy a new view of the relation between simple faith untouched by philosophy and Christianized true philosophy. By restating the meaning of faith as scientific or demonstrated knowledge, which was the meaning assigned to it in Greek philosophy; by showing that there is a corresponding view of faith in Scripture, which needs no demonstration; and by showing further that both kinds of faith are of equal merit, Clement, guided by Philo, achieves a high order of originality. He is the creator of what Wolfson calls the "double-faith theory" (*Church Fathers*, chap. 6).

So it is that Clement arrived at the view that the teachings of Scripture are true, whether demonstrated by reason or not, and the simple believer and the philosophic believer are equal before God.

Both kinds of faith, he says, are roads to salvation, the one being the long road and the other the short road. The teachings of Scripture are, in Clement's words, "the shortcut to perfection, viz., that of *salvation through faith*" (*Church Fathers*, p. 129). In other words, there are two roads to true knowledge, that of Scripture, which is direct, and that of philosophy, which is roundabout.

Wolfson might have ended Clement's story with the double-faith theory. Instead, before taking up the other Church Fathers, he inserted a sort of postscript which, because it is buried in a technical paper written in 1942, is worth resurrecting here:

The definition of faith as a voluntary assent which was introduced by Clement of Alexandria in the particular religious discussion of the relation of faith to reason, becomes an established term in the discussion of the problem throughout its history in Christian literature, whether Greek or Latin, both among those who follow Clement of Alexandria's particular double-faith theory and among those who in opposition to him contended for a single-faith theory. . . . The term appears again in modern philosophy under the guise of practical reason, under which Kant includes all speculations about faith. When William James flashed upon the world his phrase "the will to believe," he was merely giving expression to his own understanding of the old definition of belief as a voluntary assent. ["The Double-Faith Theory in Clement, Saadia, Averroes, and St. Thomas, and its Origin in Aristotle and the Stoics," *Jewish Quarterly Review* 32, p. 230]

The problem posed by Plato's theory of ideas loomed as large within Wolfson's historical framework as the problem of faith and reason. Thus he confronted the formidable task of working his way through the chaos of Platonic interpretation, both ancient and modern.

To see how he achieved this, let us follow Wolfson's account in *Church Fathers*, Part Two, of the bearing of Plato's ideas upon the Gospel of John, particularly upon John's statement that "the Logos was God." The operative word of course is "Logos," which harks back to Plato. But the writer of the fourth Gospel uses the word not in Plato's sense but in Philo's. And in Philo the word "Logos," as well as Plato's theory of ideas, has undergone a radical change: the Logos of Plato is redefined as the "place of the intelligible world and the ideas." It is the use and then departure from Philo's conception of the Logos that leads to a new career for the Logos in the development of Christian ideas. In short, the Fathers accepted the Philonic conception of ideas and then turned it to their own account.

Wolfson tells this story as it has never been told before. The author of the Gospel of John in his well-known opening sentence— "In the beginning was the Word [Logos], and the Word was with God, and the Word was God"—is using Philo's Logos to say, in the manner of Paul, that the preexistent Idea, or Logos, of the Father "was made flesh" in the born Christ. Here, and later in more philosophical speculations, the Fathers, while retaining part of Philo's Logos, depart radically from it. Philo never applies the term to God, let alone identifies it with God. The Fathers not only make this identification but try to show that the Logos came into existence with the creation of the world as the Son-Logos. Thus Clement of Alexandria interpreted the verse we have quoted from the fourth Gospel as meaning "in the beginning of the creation of the world the Logos came into being." Subsequently the Holy Spirit enters into the story of the generation of the Logos as the union between Father and Son. Each of the persons—the Father, Logos-Son, and Holy Spirit—is God. We can follow the rest of the story as Wolfson himself told it years later in the *Harvard Divinity School Bulletin* (1955–56):

The discussion of the [Platonic] ideas led to the Logos, a term which with Philo came to be used in the sense of the place of the totality of ideas. The Logos quite naturally led to the Christian doctrine of the Trinity, which included the Logos as one of its three persons; and the Trinity quite naturally led to the Christian doctrine of the Incarnation, for it was the Logos which was made flesh. Strictly speaking, both the Trinity and the Incarnation were outside my original historical framework, and at first I did not plan to deal with either of these doctrines. But having once looked into these two Christian doctrines from the outside and seen them as through a glass darkly, I could not restrain my curiosity to learn more about them. And so I started upon a long and protracted exploration into a terrain of problems entirely new to me. Taking the position of a mere student of the history of philosophy in its impact upon religion and without going into purely theological problems, I presented the results which I arrived at in six chapters, dealing with such topics as: the origin of the trinitarian formula; the various presentations of the Trinity and the Incarnation in the New Testament; the various attempts on the part of the Fathers to harmonize these presentations; the two distinct conceptions, appearing one in succession to the other, with regard to the Logos and the Holy Spirit; and the manner in which the transition from one of these conceptions to the other corresponds to the transition, in the general history of philosophy, from the Philonic interpretation of Plato to the Plotinian interpretation.

Then I noticed that the Fathers describe the doctrines of the Trinity and Incarnation as mysteries; and yet, despite their description of these doctrines as mysteries, they try to explain them; and their explanations, I observed, draw upon certain philosophic terms or philosophic formulas or philosophic analogies. The impression one gets is that, while not trying to solve the mysteries, the Fathers tried to free the conception of a triune God and a biune Christ from the charge of being self-contradictory or meaningless; and this they tried to do by showing how philosophers in various ways sought to justify the common practice of designating the many by the term one. In other words, the Christian problem of the one and the three in the Trinity, as well as the problem of the one and the two in the Incarnation, was treated by them after the manner of the philosophic treatment of the problem of the one and the many, and so in three chapters I tried to show how the various discussions of the Trinity and the Incarnation by the Fathers, however differently stated, are all reducible to certain common philosophic principles.

These philosophic implications and the unity of philosophic thought which I have found in the teachings of the catholic Fathers I have also found, with a single exception, in the teachings of those who were declared heretics. In two chapters, entitled "The Anathematized," I tried to show how all heresies have a philosophic basis and how all of them can be reduced to a certain common philosophic principle. The only exception is Gnosticism. After analyzing the alleged philosophic elements in Gnosticism, I have arrived at the conclusion at which others have already arrived, among them our own Professor Nock, that Gnosticism is not a philosophy; and, in contradistinction to Harnack's famous definition of Gnosticism as "the Hellenizing of Christianity," I suggested the definition that Gnosticism is "the verbal Christianizing of paganism."

And so we have a glimpse of what went on in Wolfson's intellectual workshop during his eight-year expedition into the land of the

Church Fathers. Its upshot was a manuscript of some 1,800 pages, only part of which was published as the first volume, bearing the subtitle *Faith, Trinity, Incarnation*. Wolfson held back the second volume, feeling perhaps that he ought to allow time for digestion of the first and also allow himself an opportunity for further polishing its companion.

The Philosophy of the Church Fathers, while characterized by the same blend of structure and style as *Spinoza* and *Philo*, is written in more austere expository prose. Wolfson found that the nature of the material required a severity of language which precludes the sort of personal identification and revelatory analogies we find in the earlier books. In dealing with so massive and complex a theme, he faced the overriding problem of casting the material into a meaningful structure. Wolfson's staggering apparatus of learning might easily have gotten out of hand, but the literary artist in him molded the material. Each sentence, each paragraph and chapter, is constructed and written so that the reader is never puzzled about its meaning. Such clarity of exposition demands both a mastery of the subject and a power of precise expression. In lesser hands this sort of technical writing would become dry and colorless. But here even the uninitiated reader can follow the movement of the theme as it progresses from chapter to chapter and will find that the author has not entirely suppressed his love of literary form. One example of this quality is found in the preface in a dialogue with an imaginary priest:

A friend on reading these chapters [on the New Testament] commented: "As a Christian who believes in the teachings of the Church as transmitted by tradition, I cannot accept the view that the doctrines of the Trinity and the Incarnation as contained in the New Testament had a human origin and a piecemeal development. However, I am prepared to concede the propriety of such inquiries into these New Testament teachings, provided they are taken not as dealing with the true origin of these teachings but with what may appear to the human mind with regard to their origin from the verbal expressions in which these teachings were made known." To which I answered: "Even in the study of nature, philosophers often wonder whether the laws discovered by science, upon which men ultimately rely for the building of bridges and the flying of airplanes, are based upon a knowledge of nature as it really is or only upon appearances. No historian investigating texts of Scripture, whether of the Jewish or of the Christian Scripture, should therefore object to being considered by theologians as dealing only with appearances." [*Church Fathers,* pp. ix-x]

This is how Wolfson imagines the youthful Paul in his native Cilicia:

". . . Had he [Philo] visited Cilicia during the years in which Jesus was preaching in the synagogues of Galilee, he might have met in its capital city, Tarsus, a youthful student of the Law in whom he would have recognized a kindred spirit. Like Philo, that youthful student of the Law surveyed the gentile world around him and found that it was not wholly filled with the abominations condemned by the prophets. Like Philo, who discovered in Greek philosophy rudimental truths of the teachings of Scripture, he discovered rudimental forms of scriptural beliefs and practices in what happened to have reached him of those occult religions known as mysteries and, like Philo, he came to think that God endowed the gentiles with a capacity to believe and do by nature things contained in the Law. Especially impressed was he by rumors that had reached him from the secret Lore of the mysteries concerning a belief that by the performance of certain rites, such as initiation by baptism in blood or in water and participation in ceremonial meals, one may attain communion with a certain heavenly being who, for the sake of saving men from the fated evils of life and assuring them of a favorable reception in the world of shades, had once come down from heaven into this world of ours and suffered and died and rose again and reascended to heaven. How similar all these are, he thought, to what is explicitly written in Scripture or to what could be inferred from its meaningful words by that midrashic method of interpretation in which he was so expertly trained or to what was already afloat in that accumulation of oral traditions in which he was so deeply steeped. Is not the promised Messiah a heavenly being, created before the creation of the world, who is to appear in the end of days as savior and redeemer? Is not the imagination of the thoughts of man's heart, ever since Adam, only evil and sinful continually? Is not the death of the righteous an atonement for the sin of others? May it not be the promised Messiah of whom the prophets speak as he who hath borne our griefs and was pierced and wounded for our transgressions and for whom the people mourned as one mourneth for his only son? Is not the rising of the dead, as a promise for the future, already an established belief, and have not men in the past ascended to heaven while alive? Is not baptism required for gentiles initiated into Judaism? Does not Scripture teach that by the performance of the commanded rites one cleaves unto God? Is there not a tradition among the Jews of Cilicia, of a source unknown, that they who eat of the sacrifices in the Temple have communion with the altar?

And perhaps Philo would have also learned something of the dreams and visions of that Tarsan youthful student of the Law. Like Jeremiah of old, he fancied himself to have been ordained from birth to become a sort of prophet unto the Gentiles, to teach them the true meaning of those things contained in the Law which they believed and did by nature, so as to hasten the coming of the day when the mountain of the Lord's house shall be exalted above all mountains and all nations shall flow unto it to learn of the ways of the Anointed, the Messiah, the Christ, and to meditate on the Law of the most high God. What the Law will be when all the nations will have come to meditate on it, he sometimes wondered. The Law has an inner meaning which those to whom it was entrusted are empowered to discover in the light of their reason, and often the inner meaning annuls the outer wording; but how much of the outer wording will have been annulled in that end of days? The rites and rituals of the Law were given for the purpose of purifying the heart; but when the heart is purified, are the rites and rituals still to be performed? The Law indeed is eternal and not a jot or tittle of it is to pass away; but, when after it had fulfilled its purpose, should the Law happen to pass away, would it really pass away? Tradition, in which he was so deeply steeped, afforded him no answer to these questions.

These are the thoughts and dreams and visions which Philo would have found to agitate the mind of the youthful student of the Law in Tarsus, the capital city of Cilicia, had he visited it during the years in which Jesus preached in the synagogues of Galilee—and these, in fact, are the things which, under the name of Paul, that Tarsan youthful student of the Law set out to preach publicly when he came to acknowledge the crucified Jesus as the promised Messiah and proclaimed himself "an apostle of the gentiles."[*Church Fathers*, pp. 3–5]

When *The Philosophy of the Church Fathers* came off the press, the Harvard Divinity School held an all-day celebration of the event and

of its author's sixty-eighth birthday on November 2, 1955. Leaders
of the learned and religious worlds came from far and near to pay
their respects to Wolfson. The gathering was genuinely ecumenical
in character, for in addition to the whole academic community, the
diverse religious traditions were represented by members of the
Catholic, Orthodox, Protestant, and Jewish faiths. In addition to the
full faculty of the Divinity School, there were other university scholars of international repute—all of them friends and many of them
former students of Wolfson: Professor Werner Jaeger, the dean of
classical scholars; Professor Paul Tillich, the eminent Protestant
theologian; Professor Robert Pfeiffer, colleague for thirty years in the
Semitics Department and famed biblical scholar; the Reverend J. T.
Clark, the Jesuit scholar of Canisius College in Buffalo; the Reverend Joseph A. Davenny, S. J., the Arabist of Western College;
Professor Robert Ulich, a leading interpreter of the philosophy of
education; Dr. Joshua Bloch of the New York Public Library; Professors Abraham Neuman and Solomon Zeitlin of Dropsie College in
Philadelphia; Professor Jacob Taubes of Princeton; and many other
scholars no less distinguished. The branches of the Christian
churches were represented officially by the Right Reverend Msgr.
Thomas J. Riley, rector of St. John's Seminary; the Reverend Nor-
man B. Nash, Episcopal bishop of Massachusetts; the Reverend
Nicon Patrinacos of the Greek Orthodox Church. William G.
Braude of Providence, Rhode Island, and Joseph S. Shubow of
Boston represented the rabbinate.

Presiding over the ceremony was Dean Douglas Horton of the
Harvard Divinity School. The theme of the proceedings, which were
held in the quiet dignity of Andover Hall, was delicately inaugurated
by the playing of the ancient Hebrew hymn *Yigdal,* which could be
followed in the interdenominational *University Hymnal.* George H.
Williams, professor of Church history, then spoke on the significance of Wolfson's new work. He began by placing it in the context
of Jewish-Christian debate from the apologist Justin Martyr in the
second century to the new era inaugurated by the publication of
George Foot Moore's two volumes on Judaism in 1927. Referring
to Moore, he said:

For the first time a Christian scholar had managed to penetrate the interior of Judaism and present its system in a way illuminating both to Jews and Christians. Harry Wolfson was at first a student and then a younger colleague of George Foot Moore, assisting him at certain points in the publication of Moore's monumental work. Moore's portrait has been temporarily hung above us here to grace our celebration. For now, about a quarter of a century after Moore's study of Judaism, Harry Wolfson is presenting, in the presence of the scholars drawn from four religious traditions, the first of his two volumes on the philosophy of the Church Fathers, which, in the Jewish succession, is the exact counterpart of Moore's two volumes. But in making this comparison, one would not wish to obscure even for a moment the uniqueness of Wolfson's achievement. In the case of George Foot Moore we are able to piece out the prehistory of his great work. Indeed he valuates his own predecessors, notably Gfrörer. . . . But Wolfson's *Philosophy of the Church Fathers* seems to have no direct spiritual ancestors or even cousins in the Jewish line of development!

To this he added many friendly and even affectionate remarks—undoubtedly shared by many of the audience—and one of them revealed a mind of insight as well as distinction: "We are commemorating his birthday because in so doing," he said, turning to Wolfson, "we wish to draw attention to the fact that, in contrast to most birthday celebrations, Professor Wolfson is the *donor* and we of the academic community, representing several major traditions, are the recipients of his gift." Probably little else in the tribute touched Wolfson more deeply, for this was the first time since his childhood that he had attended a birthday party of his own and the first time that he had exposed himself to the embarrassment of public praise.

In response, Wolfson, contrary to his custom, spoke in the first person and gave his report on how he had gone about making the book. His concluding remarks, revealing some of his gratitude and personal conviction, made a profound impression:

Modern scholarship has taught us to treat of religions and heresies, even if it be a religion which we do not profess and even if it be a heresy which is not the particular kind of heresy of which we are accused, not as something to which we are opposed but as something which we try to understand. It is the glory of this University and of this Divinity School that they have fostered and encouraged free inquiry into opinions on which men differ, even if they happen to be the hunted heresies of the time. Ever since President Charles W. Eliot appointed Crawford H. Toy as Hancock Professor of Hebrew and Other Oriental Languages, a year after the latter had been compelled to quit his position in another institution on account of his views on the Bible which happened to be unpopular, every President of the University—Lowell, Conant, and within the last few years President Pusey—had occasion to affirm this principle of free research into the beliefs and opinions of men. On behalf of the Divinity School, this principle was publicly proclaimed by Dean Horton in his convocation address when, speaking of freedom of inquiry in the Divinity School, he said: "Harvard Divinity School is Christian in its history . . . in its scope . . . in its restraints. . . . The school is Christian in its attitude toward non-Christian traditions. It treats them as the beliefs and practices of honored friends." I thought this was a timely explanation of the true meaning of interfaith, of which we hear so much nowadays. . . . And the finest example of objective historical treatment of religion, produced under these conditions of freedom, as all the world now acknowledges, is the work on Judaism written by George Foot Moore of the Divinity School of this University and published by the Press of this University.

And now may I be allowed to say a few words of a personal nature. It is well-nigh half a century since I came to this University as a freshman in the fall of 1908. I have been here continuously throughout these years, as an undergraduate, as a graduate student, and since 1915, as a teacher. I hope that I have not remained altogether unaffected by the spirit of the place. And so, if in my book on Christianity you find some of the merits, merits of objectivity and merits of scholarship, which distinguish Professor Moore's book on Judaism, you may attribute them to the genialness of the intellectual climate of the Harvard community, to the precepts of my teachers, the example of my colleagues, and the stimulus of my students.

Finally, I wish to thank you one and all for coming out here this afternoon to make a celebration of the occasion.

The formal celebration was followed by a dinner at the Harvard Faculty Club attended by some forty colleagues and friends. The food was good and the conversation lighthearted, with the participants recounting humorous anecdotes about Harry Wolfson, which he enjoyed as much as anyone. His mood was elated, which made it possible to seduce him into giving a delightful autobiographical after-dinner talk.

In the course of an interview with a student reporter that winter, Wolfson compared the work of scholarship to the old production system, suggesting the need for greater organization to do the spade work, such as translating and editing, so that the speculative scholar could have more time for creative productivity. Speaking of his own work, he remarked: "I've done the plowing; from now on it will be chiefly the harvesting. . . . It's the plowing and tilling that's hard. The harvest, as in old rural communities, is a time of pleasure."

The publication of *Church Fathers* set into motion a chain of events which constituted a high point in the years of harvesting. For one thing, his mind had been freed of financial concern for the future. Although scheduled for retirement in 1954, he had been invited by the Harvard Corporation to remain on the faculty for an additional four years—a rare honor in Harvard history—and his pension was increased. Then, not long after the appearance of *Church Fathers*, an article in *Holiday* magazine (January 1957), featuring him as a teacher in the great Ivy League tradition, brought him to the fore. At the same time the acclaim that greeted the book both in the professional journals and book review sections of the general press was unprecedented. Harvard awarded him the prize for the best book by a member of the faculty and published by the University Press.

On February 16, at a dinner sponsored by the National Conference of Christians and Jews, Harry Wolfson, together with Senator John F. Kennedy and Robert Cutler, an assistant to President Eisenhower, was honored "for distinguished service in human relations and brotherhood." The dinner, which was held at Boston's Statler Hotel and attended by approximately one thousand people, was featured on the front pages of all the Boston newspapers, with striking photographs of the principals holding hands in a trinitarian grip. Wolfson and Kennedy had never met before, though Joseph Kennedy was a member of Wolfson's class of 1912 at Harvard. Unlike the dynamic campaigner of 1960 who was elected President

Harry Wolfson in his study
in the basement of
Widener Library, May 1956

Talking with students
in front of
Widener Library, May 1956

*Recipients of honorary degrees from Harvard University in
June 1956: seated, from left, Charles Munch, Sinclair Weeks,
Felix Frankfurter, President Nathan M. Pusey, George Magoffin
Humphrey, John Fitzgerald Kennedy, and Herbert Butterfield;
standing, from left, John Franklin Enders, Harry Austryn Wolfson,
John Cowles, John Sloan Dickey, Edward Sagendorph Mason,
David Thompson Watson McCord*

*President Nathan Pusey presenting a citation to Harry Wolfson
in 1957 for* The Philosophy of the Church Fathers, *which was
designated the best book by a member of the Harvard faculty
and published by the Harvard University Press*

Harry Wolfson with Herbert Butterfield (left)
and William M. Pinkerton on Commencement Day 1956

Harry Wolfson, ca. 1960

of the United States, Kennedy was quiet and respectful throughout the evening. He listened intently to Wolfson's speech and appeared to make a mental note of the scholar's sentiment regarding interfaith: "Interfaith is not a sort of super-religion, with a faceless theology, wherein those who have somehow lost their faith may agree upon the verbal usage of certain eviscerated relics of venerated religious phraseology. It is rather the recognition on the part of those who have remained steadfast in their faith that underlying their own particular beliefs there is that common preamble of faith. Interfaith does not mean to bury convictions; it rather means to bury the hatchet. It does not mean to demolish boundaries; it rather means to remove barriers and to establish a sort of intellectual free trade between religions."

When Kennedy followed as speaker, he paid tribute to Wolfson's learning and profundity in words that revealed his enormous admiration for the creative spirit. Departing from his written text, he made one remark which apparently did not impress the reporters but which, in light of his later mobilization of scholars in government, had particular import. "We change slowly in politics, but we are changing," he said. "People are seeing that the times and problems are too serious to be decided by ignorance. As a Harvard teacher put it, 'It is only the profounder minds that are capable of feeling the greatness of the problems of life.'" The reference to Dante was refreshing in a young politician. Afterwards a proper Bostonian in the audience asked prophetically, "Does young Kennedy nourish the ambition to become president of the country or of his alma mater —or perhaps of both?"

Soon afterward Wolfson was selected as one of the ten senior scholars in the United States and given an award by the American Council of Learned Societies of $10,000 for intellectual excellence and distinguished leadership in the field of the humanities.

In April Wolfson was called upon to answer the question that the sergeant at Fort Slocum had put to him in 1918: "What do you think of immortality?" Delivering the Ingersoll Lecture on the Immortality of Man in Andover Chapel, Wolfson treated the theme in the form of a discussion of the ideas of immortality and resurrection in the philosophy of the Church Fathers. The body of the talk was a clear and learned exposition, but his wit surfaced at the beginning and the end—especially at the end, when he employed a literary device to deal with the modern-minded intellectuals in the audience. Concluding his lecture he had this to say about the longing for eternal life so conspicuous among thinkers from Plato to the present day:

This kind of knowledge, I regret to say, I cannot supply. I am the dragoman of the Fathers; I am not their neo-izer. As one who for the past hour has acted the part of pure historian, I should not like to perform before your very eyes a feat of quick-change artistry and of a sudden turn myself into theologian and preacher—and that kind of theologian and preacher, too, who would make the Fathers talk latter-day beliefs and latter-day disbeliefs in the pious language of their own old beliefs. But I think I shall not be stepping out of my character as historian if I let the Fathers speak for themselves.

Let us then imagine that the Fathers are with us here now in body, as I hope they are with us in spirit. Let us further imagine that a bright young man, a student of divinity, came up to tell them how sorry he was that he could not share with them their belief in the resurrection of the body, seeing that modern science is all against its possibility, but how glad he was that he could share with them their belief in the immortality of the soul, seeing that respectable modern philosophers and even respectable modern scientists with a philosophic turn of mind do occasionally give a nod of approval to immortality.

To this, I imagine, the Fathers would answer: "Young man, you are wrong on two counts.

"You are wrong, first, in blaming your unwillingness to believe in resurrection upon modern science. The impossibility of resurrection and the fact of its being contrary to what is known as the laws of nature had already been proclaimed by the outmoded ancient science of our own time; modern science of your present time cannot make it more impossible. If we, despite the science of our time, were willing to believe in resurrection and you, because of the science of your time, are unwilling to believe in it, your unwillingness to believe in it is not to be explained by the opposition of the science of your time. It is to be explained on other grounds, and there are other grounds by which it can be explained.

"You are wrong, second, in distinguishing between immortality and resurrection, by assuming the former to be scientifically possible and the latter scientifically impossible. The kind of immortality in which we believe, immortality by the will of God, and even the kind of immortality in which Plato believed, immortality by nature, is discarded by science—by the modern science of your time—just as is resurrection. The immortality which respectable philosophers and even respectable scientists with a philosophic turn of mind sometimes speak of approvingly is another kind of immortality; it is the Aristotelian conception of immortality, a spurious sort of immortality, an immortality not by the will of God nor by the necessity of nature but by the word of man. And let us tell you the story of Aristotle. He started as a disciple of Plato, with the belief that the soul, or rather one of the souls or one part of the soul, is separable from the body and is immortal. His works still contain reminiscences of this early belief of his, as when, for instance, he says of the intelligent part of the soul *(nous)* that it may survive after death or that it is immortal and eternal. But when later he found himself forced, by reason of his revised conception of soul, to deny the immortality of any part of the human soul, he held out as a consolation the immortality of the human race. Man as individual indeed dies, but the human race, of which the individual man is part, lives on forever."

And here the Fathers would make their final remark: "Dear young man, if you can find consolation in this verbal kind of immortality and if this verbal kind of immortality can serve you as an incentive to do good and shun evil, go and console yourself and sin no more, and mayhap the Lord in His mercy will reward you with true immortality, aye, and with resurrection, too."

And to this, and with this, we say, Amen.

As he spoke these words, the smiling audience burst into applause. Two months later, at Harvard's 305th Commencement, the mood of adulation was expressed in a manner that genuinely touched Wolfson when President Pusey conferred upon him the honorary degree of Litterarum Doctor. He had already received such degrees from other institutions of higher learning and numerous citations from professional and communal associations; but this one, conferred upon him in Harvard Yard in the presence of a throng of almost 15,000 members of the Harvard community—with Justice Felix Frankfurter and again Senator John F. Kennedy sharing the honors—made it appear that he was moving toward the close of his career in a blaze of glory. President Pusey had composed a fitting citation: "From enormous knowledge he graciously illumines the major problems of religious philosophy and their relation to revealed truth." Later, at a gathering for the recipients of honorary degrees in President Pusey's home, Wolfson remarked to a friend that he would not mind if the citation were used as an epitaph.

The series of celebrations was the merest interlude, if that, for Wolfson. No sooner had he read the page proofs for *Church Fathers* than he began to harvest another field that he had plowed long ago: he took down from his shelves the manuscript of the philosophy of the Kalam and set to work on its revision. While the honors were being heaped upon him during 1956, he published three important papers on complex problems in the Kalam and, besides teaching courses and seminars, he devoted a good deal of time to the preparation of a half-dozen volumes of the *Corpus* of Averroes, for which he was serving as general editor and which was being published by the Mediaeval Academy of America, with financial support from the Littauer Foundation.

As his years lengthened—he was then sixty-eight and would retire the following spring—and as he was at least thrice-crowned in a way that rarely comes to a scholar even once in a lifetime, one might have expected him to slacken his pace. On the contrary, he believed that he had only reached the halfway mark, and intensified his activity. He seemed to be able to work harder than ever, and nothing stayed his hand. About that time he had what might have been a serious accident: he slipped in the bathtub and broke two ribs. A doctor strapped up his ribs, and he went directly back to Widener, where he was absorbed in preparing his book on the Kalam.

10
Baghdad in Harvard Yard

Baghdad was in former times an illustrious city,
but it is now crumbling to decay
and its glory has departed.

al-Maqdisi, 985 c.e.

Wolfson's books make it possible for the interested reader to appreciate and savor the traditional thinkers. As a scholar and humanist
he manages to ferret out what is of enduring interest in these thinkers of the past and so makes them as real and significant today as
they were a thousand or two thousand years ago. He sees the past
as closely related to the present and as a means of interpreting
modern ideas and attitudes.

Contemporary readers who know little or nothing about Philo or
the Church Fathers are yet in some way familiar with the tradition
they represent. The case is far different, however, with regard to the
tradition of Islam and the religious thinkers who are the mutakallimun, the protagonists of the Kalam (Word, Logos, Doctrine). The
Arabic culture of which they are a part is hardly known to most
readers, except for the *Arabian Nights* and the Koran. Even among
the scholars who for the past century have been exploring the field

of Arabic culture, few, if any, have mastered the vast printed literature, to say nothing of of the literature that exists only in manuscript. It is precisely in this area that Wolfson excelled, and his labors produced astonishing results.

For many years Arabists from far and near made pilgrimages to Wolfson's study in Widener. An account of one or two of these pilgrimages will be a fitting introduction to this phase of his work.

One day in March 1958 the Office of the Marshal at Harvard received a notice from the State Department regarding the forthcoming visit of an Iranian dignitary. He was Seyyed Hassan Taqizadeh, who had been ambassador to the Court of St. James's, speaker of the Iranian Parliament, and was then professor of Arabic at the University of Teheran. Now the "grand old man" of Iran, he was making a tour of several institutions of higher learning. In connection with the visit to Harvard, the State Department forwarded a dossier regarding Taqizadeh, making suggestions for entertaining him and also underscoring his need for rest. The dossier further said that he was especially interested in meeting Professor Wolfson. A week later the Office of the Marshal called to inform Wolfson that Taqizadeh was in Cambridge and requested him to clear the time for an appointment which would be mutually convenient. When the secretary suggested that Taqizadeh would be glad to come to Wolfson's office, Wolfson said that he would go to the visitor's hotel accompanied by one of his students, an Iranian named Seyyed Hossein Nasr (now a professor at the University of Teheran and engaged in translating Wolfson's work on the Kalam into Parsi). Taqizadeh insisted, however, that he would like to go to Wolfson's study and talk there. Taqizadeh proved to be an excellent scholar, though one without modern technical background, and he was delighted by Wolfson's explanation of philosophic texts and his philological analysis of philosophic terms. Wolfson showed him his works in manuscript, and they discussed problems in the history of Muslim philosophy and theology. On leaving, Taqizadeh invited his host to visit Teheran where, he said, they would spread out a magic carpet for him.

Three weeks later Wolfson was in New York to speak at the annual meeting of the American Oriental Society, of which he was president. He found it hard to decide whether to deliver the conventional sort of survey of the state of Oriental studies or to explore a specific theme. At that meeting the chairman, Professor Franz Rosenthal of Yale University, brought Taqizadeh and his wife to the dais, seated them next to Wolfson, and told the audience something about the Iranian dignitary and his visit to America. Wolfson, with Taqizadeh in mind, decided on a technical topic and spoke on "The Philosophical Implications of the Divine Attributes in the Kalam." It was a heady discourse and, for those whose fields were other than Arabic philosophy, hard to follow. But Taqizadeh kept his eyes glued on the speaker and listened intently. He smiled wisely when in conclusion the speaker remarked, "There are probably more riches in medieval Arab thought than in all the oil of Araby." Afterwards Taqizadeh said that he was surprised to find so much knowledge of Arabic in America. Mrs. Taqizadeh, whose interests were quite down to earth, told Wolfson in the course of conversation that she was fascinated by the ingenuity of American kitchen gadgets and that her favorite dish was ice cream. Immediately Wolfson suggested that she buy an ice cream machine at Macy's, which she said she would do the next day.

Another pilgrimage which became a red-letter event in Cambridge was the visit of three Iranian mullahs, teachers of religious law, from the faculty of Teheran University. They too asked especially to meet Wolfson, and a reception was arranged by the Middle Eastern Center at the Brattle Street home of one of the friends of the Center. There many objects of Islamic art created an Eastern milieu in which some one hundred guests mingled, including scholars from the philosophy, history, religion, and other humanities departments of Harvard and of the Massachusetts Institute of Technology. The three mullahs, in their native dress, were seated on comfortable chairs facing Wolfson at a point in the room where they could be seen and heard by all. Among them also sat Wolfson's Iranian student Nasr, who acted as interpreter. One of the mullahs was a Sunnite (traditionalist) and the other two were Shiites (dissenters), but it was the Shiite who engaged in a colloquium with Wolfson on the Kalam. Both men quoted passages from the Kalam, in tal-mudic style, and Wolfson put the passages in their historical and philosophical context. They discussed the question of the divine qualities and attributes of God and touched upon the Mu'tazilites, Ibn-Rushd, and the cordial relations between Islam and Christianity and Judaism during the Middle Ages. Finally, the mullah made a brief speech in which he said that the discussion reminded him of the great debates in Baghdad during the tenth century.

These exchanges introduce us to the mappemonde which Wolfson created for the background and substance of the debates that ab-sorbed the Muslim thinkers of the early Middle Ages. The cultural upsurge following the Arab conquest of the East and the Mediterra-nean littoral led to a remarkable renascence which flourished from the eighth to the twelfth centuries under the tolerance and patron-age of the caliphs of the Abbasid dynasty. Baghdad was the center of culture, the place where, as the anonymous twelfth-century au-thor of *The Book of Beauties and Antitheses* says, "Wisdom was sought as a man seeks after his stray camels and its judgment of values was accepted by the whole world." It is to the credit of the Abbasids that they encouraged the participation of the "minority" peoples. And so, from the ancestors of Taqizadeh and the mullahs of Teheran, whose mother tongues were Persian and Syriac, there poured into the intellectual marketplace the Hellenized and Chris-tianized traditions of the past, which, by means of translations of their literatures into Arabic, provided the stimulus and patterns for Islamic thought. The result was a great humanist revival in the arts, sciences, literature, and especially philosophy.

It is with the revival of philosophy that Wolfson was concerned, for his problem was to fit Muslim thought into his historical frame-work. The Muslims, like the Christians and Jews, had a Scriptural religion—theirs based on the Koran—and, like Philo and the Church Fathers, they were confronted with the task of harmonizing their Scripture with reason. Moreover, they had to meet the argu-ments of Christians and Jews. In response to these external influ-ences, the Muslim thinkers developed two opposing schools, the

traditionalist, or orthodox, theologians and the liberal Mu'tazilites,*
who vied for supremacy.

The manuscript of the philosophy of the Kalam, which Wolfson
put aside in 1947, presented the ways in which the Muslim thinkers
dealt with the problems of Philo and the Church Fathers; that is to
say, the ways in which the problem of freedom of the will, the
creation of the world, the nature of God, and the like were ordered
from a horizontal viewpoint. The manuscript, he thought, needed
only another six months of revision in order to put it to press. Why,
then, did it take him until 1963 to complete it? It is true, as we shall
see in a later chapter, that he was busy with other matters besides
the Kalam. But the new problems that arose in the course of revision
and his intensive search for their solution are the real reasons for the
delay.

For one thing, the literature of the Kalam consists for the most
part of strands of an extremely complex web. The Kalam writings
are mainly doxographies, digests which compress not only diverse
views but also all shades of opinion. It was from such digests, for
example, that the three mullahs quoted in the colloquium. As then,
although only a few texts were involved, Wolfson had to take a vast,
often undated and unidentified, literature from the earliest centuries, examine the ideas and creeds expressed in the texts, and place
them within their contexts. And again there was the trying problem
of the use and misuse of terms, both in the original and in translations, the study of which often yielded new meanings and interpretations and sometimes even new discoveries. For instance, Shahras-
tani, the author of an Arabic work on religious and philosophical
sects, mentions an unorthodox conception of the Trinity, held by a
sect of Nestorian Christians, which was an enigma to the medievals
as it was to modern scholars. Wolfson's study of this unorthodox
version of a Christian belief led him to the discovery of a splinter

---

*The Mu'tazilites (separatists) adopted the science of Kalam in order to defend their
theories about the unity of God and the inadmissibility of ascribing attributes to God and
the freedom of the human will. They employed Aristotelian logic in their arguments and
opposed blind faith in tradition. They were also opposed to heretics or unbelievers. They
therefore occupied a middle position. Later on the Mu'tazilites (mutakallimun) were opposed
to the Arab Aristotelians, such as Alfarah, Avicenna, and Averroes, and thus became the
conservative wing of Islam.

group of Nestorian Christians whose existence was hitherto unknown. And, to add one more example, in showing the development of Muslim creeds he demonstrated that orthodox creeds were originally heretical.

In the spring of 1962 Wolfson felt again that the revised manuscript was ready for delivery to Harvard University Press and spoke to the director about scheduling the printing of the two volumes. He told himself that it would take only a short time to revise the introduction. Upon rereading it, however, he found that the body of the book as he had revised it now required a somewhat different introduction. Between June 1962 and March 1963 he struggled with the problems of structure and recast the introduction several times until he was completely satisfied with it. From a brief statement of ten pages the introduction grew into an essay of more than a hundred pages. "Writing," he remarked about that time, "is a process of sinning and repenting."

Wolfson presented some of the results of his study of the Kalam in a score or so of technical papers. They are beautiful examples of his sense for the crucial terms of an argument, their history, the shades of thought they express, and the subtle associations of ideas they incorporate. Each paper is a controlled experiment, bringing some fold of Kalamic thought into clear light and establishing its relation to the scholastic doctrines of the Kalam as a whole. Since the papers were intended to be chapters or appendices of the larger work, they provide a sort of scaffolding from which we can glimpse the structure of the Kalam according to Wolfson's blueprint. The Arabic terminology apart, the structure is one that holds no surprise for the reader of *Philo* and *Church Fathers,* for what the advocates of the Kalam say appears to have been filtered through ideas which by that time Wolfson had already made familiar. Whether or not they were aware of it, the religious thinkers of the Kalam were the collateral descendants of Philo and the Church Fathers. Their thought is inseparably linked to the religious thought of Christian and Jewish contemporaries and to the scholastic thought of the medievals.

To illustrate this view, Wolfson's conclusions here may be summarized by way of an example. Among the meanings of "Kalam" is Logos, a meaning which even *Webster's Third International Dictionary* does not give. Wolfson shows that the idea of Logos in the Kalam can be understood only if we see "not only what is within it but also what is behind it." Behind the Kalamic conception of Logos is the Philonic conception, which Wolfson expounds in the chapter of *Philo* called "God, the World of Ideas and the Logos." Philo had revised the Platonic theory of ideas, and in applying it to the nature of God and the creation of the world, he had made the Logos the place of the intelligible world—that is, the mind of the world, created by God as part of the creation of the world—and impacted within it were the archetypal ideas. The Logos is not eternal, as Plato holds; it is not an intermediary or substitute for God but an instrument of God. "In the subsequent history of philosophy," Wolfson writes, "the Logos became separated from the intelligible world and the ideas and came to be treated as something apart from them. As such it entered upon a new career in the history of the Christian doctrine of the Trinity" (*Church Fathers*, pp. 293–94).

This new career is described in Part Two of *The Philosophy of the Church Fathers*, which one scholar has called "one of the truly great essays in intellectual history." As we have already seen, the Logos becomes the second person of the orthodox conception of the Trinity; and, with the rise of the Kalam within Islam, the Logos enters upon still another phase of its career.

Wolfson had set the stage for the drama.

The main parts were played by Scripture and philosophy.

Philo had brought about a meeting of the protagonists in Judaism.

The Church Fathers had united them in Christianity.

The thinkers of the Kalam repeated the performance in Islam.

Such, in briefest outline, is the story.

Wolfson's reconstruction of this development is a feat of scholarly and intellectual acumen. One example is the chapter in his work on the Kalam called "The Muslim Attributes and the Christian Trinity." It illustrates, too, the theme of the Kalam generally. In the early decades of the eighth century there appeared in Islam the belief that certain terms which are attributed to God in the Koran stand for real incorporal beings which exist in God from eternity. Where did this idea originate? Wolfson does not believe that the Koran provides any warrant for it or that it came into being by logical deduction. The explanation, he thinks, is to be found in some external influence—either Greek philosophy or Judaism or Christianity. He eliminates Greek philosophy and Judaism on the grounds of chronology and history, and then examines the assumption that it was Christian influence that accounts for the belief in the reality of divine attributes among Islamic thinkers.

The reports of early followers of the Kalam who opposed the belief in the reality of divine attributes suggest that the origin of this belief may be found in the Christian doctrine of the Trinity. "But," writes Wolfson,

The words of opponents cannot always be taken at their face value, for opponents, especially in matters of religion, are in the habit of accusing one another of things which are not necessarily so. If we are to assume, on the basis of what its opponents said about it, that the Muslim doctrine of attributes had its origin in the Christian doctrine of the Trinity, we shall have to find some external evidence in support of that assumption. We shall especially have to find some logical reason, or at least some psychological motive, to explain how the Muslims, who had started with an outspoken negation of the Christian Trinity on the ground of its incompatibility with the unity of God, happened to substitute for it a doctrine which involved the very same difficulty contained in the doctrine of the Trinity. To say that they did it only as an imitation of the Christian doctrine would not be sufficient. Imitation could be used as an explanation in a case when some peculiarly Christian belief, the like of which existed also in Islam or which at least was not directly rejected by Islam, happened to find its way into Islam. It cannot be used as an explanation in the present case, when nothing resembling the doctrine of the Trinity existed in Islam and, moreover, when that doctrine itself was openly rejected. [*The Philosophy of the Kalam*, pp. 113–14*]

*Although Wolfson's study on the Kalam appeared posthumously, Leo Schwarz apparently had access to the unpublished manuscript and to the proofs, as well as to the published papers which were later incorporated into the work; page references for the published text, which appeared in 1976, are supplied here.—Ed.

In his customary way Wolfson turns to the evidence afforded by terminology for the view that the Kalamic doctrine of attributes originated in the Christian doctrine of the Trinity. It turns out that the fundamental terms in the doctrine of the Trinity—perhaps used haphazardly by Arabic-speaking Christians in their discussions with the Muslims—are traceable to corresponding Greek terms employed in the formulation of the doctrine of the Trinity. It becomes evident, as one follows the steps of the argument, that there is a direct relation between the Muslim belief in the attributes and the Christian belief in the Trinity; and, indeed, two persons of the Trinity, the Son and the Holy Spirit, were transformed into Muslim attributes.

Having established this relation, Wolfson confronts the question of why it was that a Christian doctrine, explicitly rejected in the Koran, should have been formed into a Muslim doctrine. His answer is worth quoting at length:

Let us then reconstruct the logical situation which could have led to the substitution in Muslim theology of divine attributes for the Christian Trinity.

From the passages quoted, as well as from other passages, we may gather some of the main features of the Christian doctrine of the Trinity as it was presented to the Muslims. These main features were four. First, there was the orthodox Christian belief in the equality of the Father and the Son and the Holy Spirit, each of them being God. Second, the Father and the Son and the Holy Spirit are each a hypostasis or person or a thing; Godhood, which is common to all three, is their common essence or substance. Third, the "principle of differentiation" between these three persons or things is that the Father is "goodness" or "essence" or "self-existence" or "existence"; the Son is "life" or "wisdom" or "knowledge" or "power." Fourth, these three sets of terms by which the three persons or things are described are called "properties" or characteristics.

Let us now imagine that when the Christians presented this conception of the Trinity to the Muslims, the latter quoted against it the Koranic verses, "say not Three . . . God is only one God" and "they surely are infidels who say, God is the third of three, for there is no God but one God." Undismayed by this answer, however, the Christians, we imagine, continued to argue that their God is also one God, maintaining that the three "Persons" or "things" are all one in essence, differing only in the peculiarity of their properties or characteristics. In fact, they would say, these three persons are only properties and characteristics of God, though properties and characteristics which have a real existence in God. Where in the Koran, they would challenge the Muslims, do you find a denial of properties or characteristics in God? Moreover, the Christians would argue, these three "persons" or "things" or "properties" or "characteristics" which we call Father and Son and Holy Spirit, are descriptions of God as "existing" or "good" and as "living," "knowing," as "the powerful," and as "the merciful," which means that He is God? And do you not admit that the property or characteristic of "existence" or "goodness," which we attribute to the Father in our Trinity and the Koran attributes to God, stands for something real? Why then should you not admit that the properties or characteristics of "life" and "knowledge" or "power" stand also for things which are real?

The Muslims, we assume, must have felt compelled to admit the cogency of the reasoning. Still they were bound by the Koran to reject the Christian doctrine of the Trinity. Why then was the doctrine rejected in the Koran? they asked themselves. And in order to answer this question, they began to study carefully the verses in the Koran in which the Trinity is rejected. From these verses they gathered that the Trinity was rejected not on the ground that "life" and "knowledge" and "power," which the Christians variously identified with the Son and the Holy Spirit, were conceived of by them, like "existence" (or "goodness"), as being each a real "person" or "thing," but on the ground that "knowledge" and "power" or "life" were conceived of by them as being equal with "existence" in divinity and that, like "existence," they are each called by them God. And so the Muslims finally met the challenge of the Christians. They said: We indeed admit that "life" and "knowledge" or "knowledge" and "power" or "life" and "knowledge" and "power" represent real "things," just as "existence" represents a real "thing." But we do not admit that they are equal with "existence" in divinity and that they are each to be called "God" in the same way as "existence" is called "God." These attributes of "life" and "knowledge" or of "knowledge" and "power" or of "life" and "knowledge" and "power" are indeed to be taken as "things" existing in God from eternity and inseparable from Him, but they are not to be called God. There is no God but one God.

The denial of Godhood is one difference between the attributes of Islam and the second and third persons of the Christian Trinity. Another difference between them is the denial of any causal relation between the attributes and God. In Christianity, where the second person is said to be the Son of God, that very conception establishes a causal relation between them. A similar causal relation is conceived to exist also between the first and third person or between both the first and second persons and the third person, for the Holy Spirit was believed to proceed either from the Father alone or from the Father through the Son or from both the Father and the Son. In Islam, however, there is no causal relation between God and his attributes. What relationship existed between them the attributists never succeeded in explaining in philosophic language. All they could say is that God and the attributes are coeternal; there is a real distinction between them but that distinction is not one between cause and effect but rather between Godhood and non-Godhood.

This, we imagine, was the logical origin of the doctrine of real attributes in Islam. It explains not only how the belief in attributes came into existence, but also why the early controversy was only about the attributes of life, knowledge, and power. These, as we have seen, were the only terms which Christians, to the knowledge of Muslims, used as characteristics of the Son and the Holy Spirit. The omission of the terms "self-existent," "existence," "essence," and "goodness" from the earliest list of attributes, even though these terms occur in the Christian Trinity as characteristics of God the Father, is, as we have seen, not without reason. These terms, in the earliest stages, were considered as characteristics of God himself and were identified with God himself. They were, of course, real in the sense that God himself was a real being; but they were not, like "life" and "knowledge" or "power," distinct from God.

Originally, as we have seen, only these three terms, "life," "knowledge" or "wisdom," and "power," were a subject of controversy between the attributists and the Mu'tazilites as to whether they stood for real beings or not. Later lists containing other terms appear as subject of this controversy, such as a list of four, in which "will" is added to the aforementioned three, and a list of seven, in which the terms "hearing," "seeing," and "speaking" are added to the four in the list of four, and similar other still longer lists. Though the addition of some of the terms in the lists of four and seven may be explained on certain historical or philosophic grounds—and we shall discuss this on another occasion—on the whole the difference in the number of attributes mentioned by the various Muslim theologians who believed in their reality may be explained, as says Maimonides, on the ground of certain Koranic texts which they happened to follow.

Thus the orthodox Muslim belief in the reality of attributes is traceable to the Christian doctrine of the Trinity. [*Kalam,* pp. 128–32]

Needless to say, Wolfson's Arabic philosophical learning was of no ordinary kind. His knowledge of the language dated back to his undergraduate days when he was a student of Jewett, and he put the knowledge to early use when, as a Sheldon Fellow in 1912–14, he was busy trailing manuscripts in connection with his work on Crescas. Both *Crescas' Critique of Aristotle* and *The Philosophy of Spinoza* leave no doubt of his mastery of the philosophic literature in Arabic. It was while he was working with Arabic and Hebrew manuscripts that he became aware of the inaccessibility, sometimes the deterioration, of a vast amount of valuable source material and began to think of ways of making accessible unpublished works dispersed throughout the world and rotting in storerooms of libraries and scriptoria. Thus he wrote in his 1921 article on "The Needs of Jewish Scholarship in America":

When I see, therefore, all these precious treasures rotting away in the obscure holds of European libraries, when I see the waste of time and energy expended by Jewish scholars who are forced to cross the seven seas to verify a reference or to search out a quotation, when I think of the many fields of investigation that these buried treasures would open to the student, I grow indignant at our indifference, callousness, and negligence. I say to myself: Is there no man among us with sufficient national pride to see the shame of it all and with mental vision to see the importance of it all? One lump sum of money, a couple of photographers equipped with photostatic machines, a staff of clerks, and a board of competent scholars—just this, and all these hidden treasures would be made accessible to the wide world . . . these buried treasures are just waiting for us; they are begging and pleading to be freed, like so many prisoners held in captivity. We have the means to free them, to disenchain them, to bring them to light. American Jewry should present the world of Jewish learning with a complete collection of philosophic writings in Hebrew, a veritable *Corpus Scriptorum Philosophicorum Hebraeorum.* [p. 34]

Although his eloquent plea found no response, Wolfson himself indirectly made a start. By the time *Crescas* appeared he had trained two students in the field of medieval philosophy, and they were awarded their doctorates in 1929. These students, Samuel Kurland and Harry Blumberg, became the first native American scholars in the field of medieval Jewish philosophy, and their theses were partly based upon copies of manuscripts in Wolfson's briefcase. At about the same time the Académie Polonaise des Sciences et des Lettres announced a project for the publication of a *Corpus* of medieval texts in Latin and Latin translation, and the Jesuit Arabist Maurice Bouyges announced the preparation of a *Corpus* of medieval Arab scholastic literature. The value of these undertakings was diminished by their being confined to one language, thus truncating the trilingual careers of the authors and their works. Nor did either of these projects take into consideration the Hebrew translations of Arab and Christian authors, translations in which many such works survive, their originals being lost. Soon thereafter the Union Académique Internationale issued a prospectus announcing that the society had taken up the Polish Academy's project of a series of medieval Latin translations of Aristotle.

In the course of these stirrings Wolfson was at work on a project of his own, and in July 1931 his "Plan for the Publication of a *Corpus Commentariorum Averrois in Aristotelem*" was submitted to the Mediaeval Academy of America. After the plan was printed that year in *Speculum* and a reprint of it was circulated, Wolfson discussed the possibilities of cooperation with a representative of the Union Académique. Unfortunately, only the loosest form of cooperation could be agreed upon. As a consequence, the Mediaeval Academy decided independently to launch Wolfson's plan.

The plan is a model of its kind—clear, brief, yet comprehensive. It is based upon Wolfson's conviction that medieval philosophy is one philosophy written in three languages. He confined the project to Averroes for three reasons: first, by means of his commentaries on Aristotle, Averroes had a tremendous influence upon the history of Western philosophy; second, the works of Averroes—as demonstrated in *Crescas*—are of first importance as a key to any attempt at a comparative study of medieval philosophy; and third, Averroes, alone among the major thinkers of medieval philosophy, exerted his influence on European philosophy, not through the language in which he wrote but through Hebrew and Latin, the languages into which his writings were translated. Once, when addressing the Muslim Society at Harvard, Wolfson remarked that a lecturer in one of the thirteenth-fourteenth century universities of Italy or France could speak to the students on the assumption that they were fully acquainted with the works of Averroes in Latin translation. And similar knowledge of the "Commentator" characterized the intensive philosophic activity of the Jews in that century:

Literary material relevant to the study of Averroes' teachings is to be found in almost every Hebrew philosophic text produced since the early part of the thirteenth century. Beginning with Samuel Ibn Tibbon's commentary on the Book of Ecclesiastes, to which a translation of some of Averroes' treatises on the Intellect is appended—and this before the appearance of the first translation of a commentary of Averroes in 1232—there is not a book in Jewish philosophy in which the views of Averroes are not discussed or in which some passage of his writings is not quoted or paraphrased, analyzed, interpreted, and criticized.

One need not go into the details to appreciate the immense scope of Wolfson's plan, which will require about a hundred volumes to carry out and, without adequate financing for staff and the cost of publication, will take half a century or more to complete. It is no surprise that a scholar could conceive a stupendous project of this sort; but it could have been put into effect only by a man with a capacity for organization and administration. Wolfson was stimulated by the challenge. He agreed to serve as editor-in-chief and persuaded his friend Francis H. Fobes to become the Latin editor and David Baneth of the Hebrew University in Jerusalem to become the Arabic editor. Among the first volumes of the *Corpus* to appear were those prepared by his former students Blumberg and Kurland. The funds for the publications were provided by the Lucius Littauer Foundation. By 1956 six volumes had appeared, and the Mediaeval Academy was joined by the Israeli Academy of Arts as a cosponsor of the project.

At the annual meeting of the Fellows of the Mediaeval Academy of America on April 20, 1960, Wolfson gave a talk, "The Twice-Revealed Averroes," which appeared in *Speculum* in 1961. The talk dealt with the peculiar fate of Averroes, showing how his thought was "revealed" to European philosophy first in the thirteenth century through the translation into Latin of his thirty-eight commentaries on Aristotle, and how he was again "revealed" through further translation and printing of his commentaries in the sixteenth century. Wolfson's account of of the circumstances and character of these two events is kaleidoscopic, the entire course of Averroes's influence being placed in a new focus. "The first revelation," he says, "involved translations only. The second revelation involved translations and printing. The third revelation, as projected in the plan, involves three series equipped with three critical apparatuses and a quadrilingual glossary, and, supplementary to all these, a fourth series of translations with commentaries." In order to explain why "this third revelation of Averroes had to take this elaborate form," Wolfson refers to "the brief exegesis of the Latin passage in Averroes which I have acted out before you."

In a more personal vein, Wolfson goes on to say that there must have been a human story behind the first two "revelations":

For we of the Academy know that there is a story, a human story, behind the volumes, so splendidly published in our *Corpus*—the story of scholars who, without the patronage of a Frederick, voluntarily gave up their evenings and weekends, year after year, for the preparation of minute items that make up the elaborate and complicated apparatuses and glossaries of their editions: the story of a provost and a dean of a university who allowed us the use of a certain fund under their care for the publication of certain volumes; the story of the president of a foundation who always came to our assistance when we had to meet the printer's bill; and the story of a mere businessman who at a luncheon, after consulting with one of our editors on a matter on which he needed some advice, said: now that you have done something for me, what can I do for you? And he did. He came just in the nick of time to enable us to publish one of our most expensive volumes. I hope that some future speaker at a future meeting of the Academy, perhaps at the celebration of the completion of the *Corpus* fifty years, or a hundred years, hence, in reporting to the achievement and reception of this third revelation of Averroes, will also tell the story, the human story, behind the achievement.

No doubt, when the historical circumstances of the third revelation are told, reference will be made to the irony of its taking place when the Arab nations and the State of Israel were at war. But perhaps, to show that there are men who can stand above the battle, historians will relate how Arab and Jewish scholars maintained communication and fostered an Arabic-Hebrew renascence in the face of political hostility. And they may add that in reporting the Islamic sessions of the 170th meeting of the American Oriental Society at Yale University in March 1960, an American of Syrian ancestry included in a Voice of America broadcast to the Arab East a summary of Harry Wolfson's paper on the significance of certain terms in the Koran.

11
The Other Half

*All men live by truth and stand in need
of expression. . . . The man is only half himself,
the other half is his expression.*

Ralph Waldo Emerson

On a spring morning in 1958 the classroom came to a hush as
Wolfson entered, quickly walked to the platform and placed a book
on the lectern. Smiling broadly, he looked much younger than his
years. His hair had grayed somewhat, but his eyebrows were black,
and his square, firm jaw, his eyes twinkling behind his glasses, and
his spare, agile body conveyed the impression of a man of energy.
After the first few sentences his personality held sway throughout
the room.

He began with a summary of the ground he had covered in the
course—the ideas in religious philosophy on the subjects of human
freedom, nature and natural law, faith and reason, and so on. In one
lecture, he said, he would attempt to show how Spinoza had tried
to overthrow the underlying philosophy of the Scriptural religions.
He presented the pith of Spinoza's ideas and showed how Spinoza
deposed traditional philosophy by his denial of design and will and

by his conception of God as inseparable from the world. Wolfson read short texts from Spinoza and commented on them. Of Spinoza's conception of Being he said: "Simple language can be used to explain it, but Spinoza used technical language and made things complicated." Of Spinoza's conception of the creation of the world: "Spinoza here discounts the usual formulation with no arguments to support his view, which reveals him more a Christian than a Jewish philosopher" *(laughter)*. Of Spinoza's idea of substance: "He used substance instead of God, as a label pasted on." Of Spinoza's views on church and state: "Spinoza believed that people should be allowed to build churches at their own expense" *(laughter)*. He concluded the lecture by reading—with relish—part of his imaginary sermon delivered by Spinoza in Dr. Cortes's church.

The elements of his teaching art came to the fore in this lecture: a theme logically ordered and pursued from beginning to end; material drawn impartially from Christian, Jewish, and Muslim sources; words aimed directly at the target and behind the words a mixture of the earnest and the ironic; exposition of the most technical matters in language so lucid and pointed that interest never lagged; above all, dissection of the workings of the human mind and a love of the human intellect as man's chief asset. All of this was conveyed to his audience with rapid changes of tone of voice and by walking back and forth as he became excited about his theme. Even though his thick spectacles gave the impression of nearsightedness, he established close contact and spoke directly to his listeners. And to the listeners on that memorable day the intellectual performance became deeply personal, for each profound or witty phrase suggested not only a whole train of ideas but also a long reel of enriching experience. This was expressed in the exuberance of the audience, which was described by a student reporter as follows: "The applause was thunderous and prolonged at the end of the hour. Students flocked about him, reluctant to let him go. Though he will be here completing his scholarly writing, Harvard will miss him on the lecture platform . . . a giant intellect with great love for his work and his teaching."

It was an appropriate and satisfying close to Wolfson's long career as a teacher. The special enzyme of excellence which marked his teaching was recognized in the citation in *Time* magazine that June, when the last annual column of "Goodbye, Messrs. Chipses" appeared. Wolfson could look over his shoulder at this great part of his life and see, probably with startling clarity, the procession of students whose minds he had agitated and delighted. Many of them had achieved distinction as scholars, teachers, judges, doctors, diplomats, writers, and civic leaders. None of them left his lecture hall or seminar room without the feeling that he had been in the presence of a mind intoxicated with learning and a man of wit and imagination. Many of them thought of Wolfson as their friend. Students of great scholars often feel throughout their lives that the master is frowning behind them or breathing down their necks, thus inhibiting their efforts. On the contrary, many former students of Wolfson have the feeling of an encouraging smile before them, turning into an ironic laugh only when they are violating the canons of honesty. He could see them clearly because he watched their careers and often played a role in their lives. He especially liked to see the children and grandchildren of his former students, whom he would charm with stories of their elders. Once the grandson of Ephraim Deinard, who had entered the Harvard Law School, turned up, and Wolfson regaled him with legends of the great book collector's feats. He showed him the Deinard Collection in the stacks, communicating his pride in the invaluable books and their significance to Harvard University. And there were students who enjoyed the same experience in his classes as their parents and grandparents, and consulted him about similar problems.

A style of mind is inseparable from great teaching. It is a style that is vouchsafed to few research scholars whose main preoccupation is in the book stacks rather than in the classroom. "Teaching of ordinary material," Wolfson said in 1958 to a reporter who showed interest in the problems of teaching, "is like selling a commodity You're a retailer of goods manufactured by somebody else. The best kind of teaching is when you give your own conclusions. I think that the purpose of education is to teach students how to dig out material for themselves" *(Harvard Crimson,* 1 March, 1958). Thus speaks a gifted teacher who could make his students share the excitement of his own thoughts, for Wolfson could expound ideas with the gusto of an eager guide. No matter how abstruse or abstract the subject, he disentangled the overgrown brush and if necessary hewed out a new path. And when the landscape was strange to the neophyte, he made it familiar by a deployment of familiar images, symbols, and analogies. In his classes, too, one learned to be on guard against accepting *ex parte* statements at their face value, whether the statements were made by a profound thinker or a canonized interpreter. For example, there was the time-honored notion, associated with the name of Goethe, that Spinoza was a pantheist. But Wolfson refused to treat the *Ethics* as if the work were, as he put it, "an amorphous mass of floating clouds in which one's fancy may cut whatever figures it pleases" *(Spinoza,* vol. 1, p. v). He subjected every word and every line to microscopic scrutiny and then, by comparison and contrast with Spinoza's philosophic forebears and contemporaries, reconstructed the mind of the philosopher. Accepted generalizations fell away like autumn leaves. To support his own view he marshaled all the available evidence from every conceivable source and placed it before the students for analysis and criticism.

One sometimes had the feeling that he was stripping Spinoza bare or, as one critic said of his revolutionary contention that Spinoza's "attributes" were not in God but in our minds, he was making nonsense of a great thinker. The "nonsense," however, as he showed, was "really nothing more than the fact that it presents certain difficulties." As for the specialist on Spinoza who also regarded it as nonsense, Wolfson wrote in 1937: "In his *Way of All Flesh,* Samuel Butler describes the shock which young Mr. Pontifex received when he read in Dean Alford's notes that despite the contradictions in the various accounts of the Resurrection in the Gospels, the whole story should be taken on trust. Such an implicit faith in the integrity of any kind of scripture against the striking evidence of facts has, alas, disappeared from almost every field of learning. It is refreshing to see that it is still alive among students of the scripture of Spinoza." ("Spinoza's Mechanism, Attributes, and Panpsychism," *Philosophical Review* 41, p. 309). Whatever the ultimate view or conviction arrived at, the students were instilled with the habit of free and impartial inquiry, which they were persuaded to apply to everyone, including their teacher. Of his own *Spinoza* he cautioned: "By its mere publication a book does not become to its maker a closed masoretic text in which the right of emendation is to be exercised only by higher and lower criticism" ("Some Guiding Principles in Determining Spinoza's Mediaeval Sources," *Jewish Quarterly Review* 27 [1937], p. 333).

If the varied courses he gave over the years were listed here, they would reveal a progressive exploration of many associated areas of intellectual history. And what he saw fit to retain from the classroom entered into his published works. In each of the courses he used his students as sounding boards for his views as they were formulated in the experimental stages or, in the case of textual studies, as an arena for testing the principle that words, like men, have a parentage —or stepparentage—and suffer the same vagaries. Offered in three departments of which he was a member—Philosophy, Religion, and Semitics—many of these courses were without parallel in other universities. Like an archeologist, Wolfson removed layer after layer of intellectual debris and uncovered treasures of the mind long lost or neglected; the application of his dispassionate inquiry to the troves afforded, like the deciphering of the Rosetta Stone, a suggestive and luminous key to many of the problems in the history of ideas. All this has now become common property through his extensive writings; but to the students who had a preview of one or more reels of the unfolding drama, the actor and the performance were unforgettable.

Each of the courses and seminars evoked an experience valuable for its own sake, and it is worth singling out a few of them for illustration of spheres of Wolfson's interest unmentioned up to now. For many years he gave a course on Hebrew writing and translation, called Semitics 22, for students with an advanced knowledge of the language. Depending upon the background and interests of the students, he varied the subject matter from year to year, ranging from the translation of a medieval text of Maimonides or Halevi to the translation of Emerson and editorials of the *Boston Transcript* into modern Hebrew. The translations presented by students in the classroom at the beginning of the course were in the main awkwardly literal. Wolfson subjected each sentence to analysis and showed how the intention of the original could be accurately and gracefully expressed in English. The transformation of the mistaken literal rendering into literary English was something magical to observe. Sometimes he would also illustrate the changes in the Hebrew language over three thousand years by taking a sentence—say, from an essay of Emerson—and showing how it should be expressed successively in biblical, mishnaic, medieval, and modern Hebrew. One of the singularities was the way in which certain American writers, such as Emerson, Longfellow, and Whitman, read as well in Hebrew as in English.

Wolfson considered translation one of the most difficult of literary tasks. He had of necessity to master it since he was engaged in polylingual work. In *Crescas,* for example, he not only skillfully explicates the writings of the medievals, but he also makes it possible for Crescas to express his own ideas faithfully in English. He makes no wild transposition of the structure of the original, nor is there the slightest modernization of language. Paragraph follows paragraph; the changes demanded by the different structures of the languages are kept within clauses, so that the final rendering is lucid and readable for both the technical and nontechnical reader.

This kind of superior translation can be found in all of Wolfson's books and papers. To linger only on the translations from the Hebrew, we can see in them the validity of his assertion that "every shade of opinion, from extreme adherence to tradition to the most daring adventures into freedom of thought, found expression in Hebrew literature." It is almost as if Wolfson had set himself the task of disproving the remark of the poet Bialik—an excellent translator himself—that reading a translation is "like kissing a girl through a veil." For example, there is Wolfson's translation of a passage from Abraham Ibn Daud's philosophical work *Emunah Ramah,* published in the *Hebrew Union College Jubilee Volume* (1925):

The sciences are many, ranging one above the other, and the aim of all of them is the knowledge of God. Body is to man only a beast of burden, a stepladder, as it were, by which he may ascend to God. But there are some whose sole ambition is to stuff the beast with plenty of fodder—these are the people whose object in life is eating and drinking. There are others whose desire is to adorn the beast with an ornamental saddle, bridle, and blanket—these are the people whose only object in life is to parade in gaudy clothes. Still others waste their entire life in trying to find out what kinds of sickness may befall the beast, how its health may be preserved and how its malady cured, and the nature of herbs and food that are beneficial or hurtful—these are the physicians. I do not mean to say that their art is altogether worthless. Quite the contrary, theirs is an honorable profession, which may do a lot of good in this world now, for through it the worldly life of man may be prolonged so that he may attain perfection and life of a higher kind. This art may also stand its owner in good stead in the world to come, inasmuch as the competent physician may be able to save the lives of God's servants from death and destruction. But I contend that whosoever makes this art the chief aim in life and wastes upon it his entire time does violence to his soul.

There are some who waste their time on something still more worthless, as those who make their chief occupation the art of grammar and of rhetoric, learning it first themselves and then teaching it to others to the end of their days.

Others waste their time in the art of numbers, trying to unravel strange, hypothetical puzzles . . . the like of which will never happen, and think that thereby they may be accounted as distinguished arithmeticians. Similarly, others waste themselves on the subtleties of geometry. Of these sciences only that part is truly necessary which leads to a knowledge of astronomy. ["The Classification of Sciences in Mediaeval Jewish Philosophy," pp. 314–15]

Another irresistable example culled from the same work is the story of a slave who was promised freedom and a kingdom if he went on a pilgrimage to a certain holy place. Instead of hurrying to reach his destination and receive his reward, the slave wasted time and unnecessarily prolonged the journey. According to Wolfson's version, Ibn Daud proceeds:

Like the wasting of too much time on the preparations for the journey is one's excessive devotion to the arts which are mostly of use to the material world, as medicine and law. By this I mean to refer only to a person who wastes his time in the practice of medicine for the sake of picking up fees rather than for the sake of rendering merciful service, or to a person who similarly wastes his time in the practice of law in order to gain a reputation or to amass a fortune or to display his wit. Both of these sciences have something good in common, for both may be useful in alleviating certain evils. Law may do away with some of the unpleasantness that springs up in the mutual relations of men and may establish friendly intercourse among them. By medicine, too, many of the ills resulting from the discordant rheums and from the inclement seasons of the year may be remedied. There is, however, a difference between these two professions. If all men were honest and did no wrong to each other, there would hardly be any need for the legal profession. But without medicine it would never be possible for mankind to get along. . . .

Like the one who prolongs the journey by making too many unnecessary stops and by pacing slowly with lingering steps is the one who is given too much to the purification of the soul in an effort to cleanse it from the cardinal vices and the offshoot thereof.

Like the arrival at the journey's end is one's attainment of perfection in the knowledge of God. [ibid., p. 315]

Sometimes Wolfson's friends, puzzled by a difficult or obscure passage in a text, approached him for help with its translation. One such translation, which he made for Dr. Joshua Bloch, is testimony to the grace in which he clothes a text of worth and beauty. The author is Moses Ibn Ezra, the poet and philosopher who lived in Spain in the eleventh century:

A book is the most delightful companion. If you crave entertainment, its witty sayings will amuse you; if you wish for counsel, its prudent words will gladden you. Within its covers it holds everything: what is first and what is last, what is gone and what still is. A dead thing, yet it talks, discoursing on things both dead and living. A stimulating friend, it brings out your inner gifts. Than it, in all the world, there is no friend more faithful, no companion more compliant, and no teacher more instructive. One friend it is who will cause you no harm and will deny you no favor. If you fall on evil days, it will be a friend in your loneliness, a companion in your exile, a light in darkness, good cheer in your desolation. It will bestow upon you whatever good it can, asking no favor in return. It gives all. It takes nothing. As the Arabic poet says: "A book is the best companion in the world." [From J. Bloch, "The People and the Book," *Bookmen's Holiday*, Notes and Studies Gathered in Tribute to Harry Miller Lydenberg (New York, 1943), p. 311.]

The words are expressive of the personal inclinations of both the writer and the translator.

The same translator, but this time in another style, appeared in Semitics 9—familiarly known among students as "Sem. 9"—a course in post-biblical Jewish history which was a permanent feature of the curriculum. Wolfson originated this course at a time when, except for the bowdlerized English version of Heinrich Graetz's *History of the Jews,* there was no historical literature available in English. Until the 1927 publication of Max Margolis and Alexander Marx's *A History of the Jewish People*—a volume based on sound scholarship but written in outlandish prose and bereft of imagination —students had to resort to the *Jewish Encyclopedia,* Hebrew texts, and works in the modern European tongues. It mattered little, for Wolfson discoursed on the twenty centuries of Jewish historical experience with an imaginative ardor.

I have found one dissenter from this estimate of Wolfson as a vivifier of Jewish history—a woman who attended the class at Radcliffe in 1919 said she was bored because the instructor looked out the window instead of at the girls, and the whole gamut of feminine wiles they employed could not dissolve his shyness—but among the male students in Harvard Yard, he seems to have been deeply appreciated. His treatment of the material was neither diffuse like Graetz's nor monogenetic like Simon Dubnow's. He took into account the infinite variety of expressions of a dispersed, far-flung people united by a culture inseparable from religion, and on this principle he reconstructed the story as a long chapter of Western civilization. The story became vital and fresh because it unfolded as a living component of the culture out of which the twentieth-century American had sprung. Wolfson discussed the temperament and manners of the people in each age and their underlying psychology, and he did not quail at the seamy side of existence; he portrayed rabbi and rapscallion, with oblique references to the Brahmins of

Back Bay and the men of Harvard Square. The sages of the Talmud were lifted out of their scholastic wrappings; there were charming vignettes of the original mind and dazzling physical beauty of Johanan ben Nappaha; of Simeon ben Lakish as a professional athlete; of Simlai disputing points of exegesis with the Church Fathers; of Abbahu, the manufacturer of ladies' veils and expert in Greek; of Samuel, the friend of St. Jerome who studied Hebrew with a rabbi in Tiberias out of a Bible stolen from the local synagogue's free library; and of the clever wives of scholars who influenced their husbands in making political decisions at the academies. And there was the delight of his digressions—humorous sorties that never found their way into his books. Once, after he had examined all the theories proposed to account for the origin of the Jewish community in Arabia and found them wanting, he propounded one of his own. The community in Arabia, he suggested, must have been an ancient one, and for a clue to its origin one should look to the Bible. Are we not told there that the Queen of Sheba came from Arabia and that her beauty took the courtiers of Solomon by storm? Probably some of the adventurous young bucks of Jerusalem could not resist her charms and, accompanying her back to Arabia, they became the founders of the Jewish community which was so influential in Mohammed's time.

Traveling through those twenty centuries of Jewish history with so expert and diverting a guide stimulated in his students an enduring interest in a great historical tradition and the higher intellectual reaches of its ideals. Understandably, those who attended this course waited eagerly for the one-volume work in which Wolfson planned to incorporate the material. For a decade it was at the forefront of his mind, and up to the late twenties he would ask certain students at Harvard and Radcliffe to make full sets of class notes for him; but his subsequent research in philosophy crowded out all other writing plans.

Until the 1950s Wolfson confined himself to lecturing and teaching in Cambridge. Of the numerous requests for lectures, which came to him from universities in the United States and other parts of the world and from public forums, he rejected all except those from student groups on the campus (especially when they presented a challenging topic), learned societies, and those which were held to commemorate or honor friends, such as Louis Ginzberg or Horace M. Kallen. But after the publication of *Philo* and particularly of *Church Fathers,* he seemed to have emerged from his Cantabrigian shell. This relaxation of a stern rule he had imposed upon himself coincided with a sense of solid achievement and the public recognition accorded it. In addition a greater feeling of financial security, derived from an increased salary and an adequate pension, seemed to have loosened his inhibitions. Thus he was able to bring himself to move from his book-cluttered apartment on Prescott Street, where he had lived alone for almost thirty years and where, as a note in *Time* reported, "the scholar once searched unsuccessfully for a book in the refrigerator, thought a moment, and triumphantly fished it out of the unlit oven." The move was to the spacious house of Professor Ben M. Selekman, where he lived until the latter's death in 1961. He then retreated to an apartment at the Ambassador Hotel, only a seven-minute walk from Widener Library. During the fifties and sixties he lectured to academic audiences as far south as Emory University in Atlanta and, in the Midwest, at Ohio State and Wisconsin. To his surprise, he found as much enjoyment in these excursions as the audiences found in hearing him in person.

An account of two of these occasions, divergent in character, will serve to indicate the reasons for the shared excitement.

The annual spring seminar at Dumbarton Oaks is more than a conventional conference of scholars. Once the scene of deliberations for the establishment of the United Nations Organization, the magnificent estate and mansion in Washington, D. C., were deeded to Harvard in 1940 by Mr. and Mrs. Robert Woods Bliss to house a research center in Byzantine art, history, and thought. (The only place to match it in the academic world is I Tatti, Bernard Berenson's beautiful estate on the hills overlooking Florence, which he willed to his alma mater to foster the study of art.) At a typical symposium sponsored by Dumbarton Oaks the staff was joined by about fifty scholars and a special aspect of Byzantine culture was explored. Beginning in 1955, Wolfson was for many years one of the star performers at these three-day symposia, where he obviously enjoyed the atmosphere of the Dumbarton Oaks research "library and collection," with its charming blend of the antique and the modern, its spacious, homelike accommodations, and its little company of first-rate scholars. The well-planned programs left plenty of free time for walks and conversation in the pleasant gardens and on the large veranda where meals were served. Wolfson seemed to feel at home in this oasis where seasoned learning was the price of admission, and the other guests stimulated the best in him, both inside and outside the lecture lounge.

Especially noteworthy is the talk he gave at the April 1955 symposium on "Palestine in the Byzantine Period." Most of the participants were resident scholars at Dumbarton Oaks; they included Glanville Downey, Ernst Kitzinger, and Francis Dvornik. Among the guests were friends like Professor Werner Jaeger, his fellow Aristotelian; Professor Roman Jakobson, the dean of Slavic specialists; and Carl H. Kraeling, of the Oriental Institute at the University of Chicago, who presided over the sessions. Wolfson discussed the "Philosophical Implications of the Theology of Cyril of Jerusalem," a Church Father of the fourth century. As the lecture is included in his volume of essays *Religious Philosophy* (1961), we shall dwell here only on the manner of presentation.

Wolfson, as usual, used no notes. At times, to help clarify subtle distinctions in patristic Greek, he wrote words and phrases on the blackboard. Quotations from Cyril and the whole patristic literature flowed from his lips with profusion and fluency. His literary allusions, pointed and delightful, spiced an otherwise technical discussion. Cyril, he said, "is not counted among those Fathers whom we like to call philosophers. . . . Like the famous unwitting prose-speaking gentleman of Molière's play, [he] speaks philosophy without being aware of it." The demonstration of the thesis was more than an ingenious deployment of texts: the identification of Cyril's language with the philosophical background which it unconsciously reflects was a triumph of deduction. As he built up his case, his speech became rapid, the pitch of his voice grew higher, and his body swayed rhythmically as though it were keeping up with the thoughts running ahead of it.

The process was carried on with the skill of a novelist. The linking of Cyril's conception of faith with that of earlier Church Fathers was achieved by a "spot-the-culprit" method in which some of Cyril's statements appear, so to speak, to be innocent bystanders but then, by a close analysis of the language, are shown to be actually a distillation of a process of reasoning which had gone on for centuries. For example, Cyril says in one of his discourses: "And the Greeks by their smooth tongue draw you aside, 'for honey droppeth from the lips of a strange woman.' " Wolfson has already established that Cyril means by "Greeks" the heathen, among whom he included philosophers. But who is the "strange woman" in the quotation from the Book of Proverbs 5:3? Or, in Wolfson's words, "that mysterious strange woman, who, like the dark lady in [Shakespeare's] Sonnets, turns up occasionally in the pages of the Church Fathers." Evidence is marshaled to show that Cyril is warning his readers against heathen wisdom and specifically Greek philosophy. Yet the evidence does not admit of certainty. "While it may be inferred from his writings," concludes Wolfson, "that he did not recommend philosophy and that he may even have condemned it, it is not certain whether he condemned all philosophy or only the wrong kind of philosophy."

What was impressive was not only the virtuosity of the performance but also the communication of the speaker's own enjoyment of the process to the audience. "It is wonderful to start with an original text, an unstudied text," Wolfson once said, "and to realize that there is nothing between you and this text. You try to find out everything that is implied in every term, every phrase, to get behind the words into the man's mind." And the audience, appreciative of course of the display of erudition, felt his delight in the human mind at work in the solution of problems. As Professor Kraeling afterwards commented to a group: "If only Harry Wolfson had been at the Council of Nicaea, what theological difficulties we would have been saved from!"

Another occasion which lingers in the minds of the Harvard community is his Alfred North Whitehead Lecture, delivered in 1960, on the theme "Descendants of Platonic Ideas." This discourse would have given pleasure to Whitehead, who believed that European philosophy consists of a series of footnotes on Plato. Apart from substantiating—and modifying—the generalization, Wolfson displayed in a little over an hour a historical sweep that made the lecture an engrossing adventure of ideas. Wolfson showed how in antiquity students of Plato made two opposing interpretations of his ideas in relation to God. "According to one interpretation," Wolfson said, "the ideas have a real existence outside of God: they are extradeical. According to another interpretation, which identifies Plato's God with mind, they are thoughts of God: they are intradeical." Then Philo, Wolfson argues, introduced a new method of interpretation: harmonization. Philo brought the contradictions into harmony, so that "all the apparently contradictory statements are made to live in peace." And, Wolfson concludes, from that time on, in the history of philosophy, ideas will be treated either after the manner of Plato or after the manner of Philo. The discourse is philosophy set forth with art, and it should be read aloud. Here, as an example, is the epilogue:

At the beginning of my talk I said that I would trace the history of the two interpretations of Platonic ideas through the successive generations of descendants of these ideas. Let me now, by way of summary, list the generations through which I have tried to trace the continuity of these two interpretations. As there is no better method of showing the continuity of a historical process than that used by the biblical historiographers in those genealogies which begin with the words, Now these are the generations. I shall adopt this literary device and begin:

Now these are the generations of Platonic ideas.

And Plato lived forty years and begat ideas.

And the ideas of Plato lived three hundred years and begat the Logos of Philo.

And the Logos of Philo lived seventy years and begat the Logos of John.

And the Logos of John lived six hundred years and begat the attributes of Islam.

And the attributes of Islam lived five hundred and fifty years and begat the attributes of the Schoolmen.

And the attributes of the Schoolmen lived four hundred years and begat the attributes of Descartes and Spinoza.

And the attributes of Spinoza lived two hundred years and begat among their interpreters sons and daughters who knew not their father.

Among those who attended the Dumbarton Oaks symposia were scholars from various universities who taught courses in medieval history and thought. Many of them were anxious to bring Wolfson to their institutions and sent him repeated invitations to lecture. Some of these he accepted. His engagements at women's colleges—Bryn Mawr, Sacred Heart, and Vassar—were a new experience for him. He made it a point to warn his correspondents that he would give a technical lecture, and to his surprise they invariably responded that this would be a pleasant change from the general lectures usually given by visiting speakers.

The lecture at Vassar, sponsored by the Departments of History, Philosophy, and Religion, took place on Tuesday evening, December 11, 1962. The subject, "How Impious Philosophies Became Religiously Respectable," must have been intriguing, for the large concert hall in the music building was filled. Wolfson occasionally used humorous titles of this sort—such as "Punctures in Aristotle's Universe," "If I Were Lady Magnes," and "Why Not Every Student Be a Philosopher?"—when it fitted his mood and the occasion, and his Vassar discourse was an excellent example of it. Indeed, there must have been a good deal of talk about him on the campus before his arrival, for he was greeted with an ovation.

Wolfson amply fulfilled expectations. In the history of Western religion, he began, there has never been a philosophy insufficiently flexible to be made to fit somehow into orthodox religious thought, and he proposed to show how "philosophies which had been religiously objectionable had been made religiously respectable, often acceptable and sometimes even presentable." Using the opening verse of Genesis, "In the beginning God created the heavens and the earth," as a base of interpretation, he described the ways in which religious thinkers found that their understanding of this statement conflicted with Greek theories of the origin of the world. The verse was taken to imply that the world had a beginning, that God was distinct from the world, that God was beginningless, and that God was the maker of the world. However, they found in their study of the Greek or impious philosophies such theories as the creation from eternity and the creation from necessity and the theory of the eternity of the world, all of which were irreconcilable with their own beliefs. In the course of time the scriptural philosophers, by linguistic gymnastics and intellectual subtlety, harmonized these impious ideas with the religious tenets of Judaism, Christianity, and Islam. His demonstration, peppered with humor, was an absorbing tale of ratiocination and rationalization. The underlying irony of whether Scripture or philosophy underwent more extensive transformation was not lost on the audience.

Toward the close of the lecture he employed his analogical method of projecting the past into the present. How, he asked, would the traditional religious philosophers adapt the impious philosophy of the nineteenth century—Darwinism—to their religious beliefs? He showed how the religious philosophers would have held that the world had a beginning—a fact not contested by Darwin— that God was the cause of evolution, and that evolution was teleological because God was guiding it. He concluded with a sketch of the treatment of the Scopes trial in the film *Inherit the Wind,* suggesting that instead of calling up eminent scientists of the past as witnesses in the trial, it would have been more telling to introduce the great religious philosophers of the past to vindicate the accused.

One could see that throughout almost an hour and a half his listeners shared his involvement with the theme. And a dramatist would have observed the skillful use of suspense, timing, comic relief, and clincher to create a memorable evening. As for the listeners, one of them reported in the *Vassar Miscellany News:* "Professor Wolfson . . . speaking without notes, delivered a lecture remarkable in its erudition and clarity of presentation. He presented his material in a way that was often humorous, particularly in reference to the manipulations in making philosophies respectable. To present this problem humorously, however, was not so difficult as to combine the humor with such knowledge and respect for his subject. Professor Wolfson did just this."

12
Indian Summer

*Blessed art Thou Who givest effort and precision,
control and imagination, sympathy and understanding,
to the mind of the scholar.*

Hebrew blessing on seeing a famous man of learning

At night, almost any night in the early 1960s, one could hear a knock at the door of Room K on the top floor of Widener Library, and then the voice of a library attendant saying, "Almost ten o'clock, Professor." This voluntary chore by a simple man with a pious respect for the lonely scholar working incessantly into the night, without regard for time, became a regular ritual after Wolfson moved into his new study in 1960. He hated to interrupt his work, yet at the same time welcomed the sound of a human voice. Finishing a sentence or paragraph, he arranged his table for picking up in the morning where he left off, turned off the cooler system (in warm weather), walked down the long corridor, stopped and returned to make sure no cigarette or cigar butts were left burning, and then walked through Harvard Yard to his hotel. He was one of the few persons at Harvard who truly regretted leaving the library at night.

We need not wonder at his leaving with regret, but wonder we may that a man full of years continued to labor with undiminished energies, for his way of life had hardly changed since his youth. He was not only the last person to leave the library at night but also the first to arrive there in the morning. Like a machine, it would appear, he turned out prescribed norms of work, oblivious of everything around him, responding only to the hum of his own engines. Yet beneath the steady, machinelike precision of labor coursed a vital life, turbulent with problems and questions, marked by a spirit always alert and intensely present.

Wolfson in his seventies was enjoying the years of his harvest; indeed, inspired by the larger recognition of his work and accomplishment, he appeared to be experiencing an Indian summer of youthfulness.

The ascension from Room 45 in the basement of Widener to his new study in Room K on the sixth floor symbolizes, in a way, certain subtle changes which had occurred in Wolfson's life. In his new quarters he was among other academic dignitaries—his neighbors were Paul Tillich, the theologian; Hamilton A. Gibb, the Arabist; and Samuel Eliot Morison, the historian, who was a denizen of the nearby map room. Wolfson's spacious study, with windows affording a pleasant view of Cambridge and wall-to-ceiling bookcases housing most of his library and records, had the appearance of orderliness. Behind his work table were shelves containing his own collection of all the basic works of medieval philosophy—a library which a famous bibliographer told him would make him rich, were he willing to sell it (he willed it to Harvard University). The briefcase of precious faded manuscripts was nestled snugly in a metal file. Only the long, rectangular work table, which occupied a large part of the room and was stacked with tomes, paper, correspondence, and the impedimenta of the Kalam, was reminiscent of the jumble of the old study. But there was in the room the same atmosphere of unremitting, obsessive concentration.

There Wolfson greeted each day with gusto. As soon as he let himself into his office at eight o'clock in the morning, he entered another world where he immersed himself in assembling his great structure of ideas. What appeared to be the endless rewriting of the Kalam since 1947 seemed to be drawing toward a close in 1963. But the need for clarification of a text or a term often brought him to a halt and led to further research or rethinking of a conclusion reached years before. Such excessive concern with details stemmed from his striving for perfection. A single term in philosophical or theological literature was for him a miniature compendium of thought, embodying a complicated network of primary meanings together with secondary associations; and, armed as he was with an arsenal of philology, Wolfson set to work on such terms like a diamond cutter, dividing a large stone into its recalcitrant carat-grains and transforming each grain into a clear, sparkling entity. The inexhaustible patience and supreme skill that Wolfson brought to bear on his subject resulted in an achievement that approximates the unattainable goal.

During the "Indian summer" of Wolfson's life more than half a century of indefatigable labor rested lightly on his shoulders. The years had neither tempered his zest for work nor quenched his thirst for knowledge. Instead of slowing down, his mind worked with the same, if not greater, rapidity. In his earlier years if he could not recall the exact words of a passage from the Greek, Arabic, or Latin text in the course of writing in the morning, he would use dummy quotations in his manuscript and later in the day would check the books for the texts; the older Wolfson rarely had to resort to this time-consuming task. Yet, as always, he did all his writing by hand and took care of all his own drudgery. He never had a secretary, except for a typist to prepare a copy of a manuscript for the press. In this regard he belonged to a species of scholar which has all but disappeared in the twentieth century.

When Wolfson felt mentally fatigued he would turn from the manuscript in progress and attend to correspondence or write a paper or revise one of his published books. In 1961 he published eight papers and his book of essays, *Religious Philosophy*. In 1962 an equal number of papers appeared or were in press, in addition to a revision of his essay "How the Jews Will Reclaim Jesus" for the valedictory issue of the *Menorah Journal* in 1962, and a revision of

Philo, which the Harvard University Press issued in November of that year.

Happily, Wolfson continued his custom of welcoming visitors, who provided a pleasant diversion from his concentrated routine. Those who ascended the stairs to see him in Room K of Widener did not have the difficulties of those who used to descend the labyrinthian way to Room B45. The marble stairways were bright, and there was an atmosphere of repose in the ample corridor leading to the study. Once inside, the visitor, whether friend, colleague, or newcomer, was invited to sit at the work table, and there he discovered, behind the pallid face and inquisitive eyes, an exuberance that was hard to describe. Reporters always tried to convey this spirit; but even when they managed to extract some autobiographical ore, the picture was usually processed and refined to the point of disguise. Wolfson had a mothlike ambivalence toward publicity, feeling both repelled and attracted by the light of public exposure; but once a reporter showed signs of intelligence, Wolfson's conversation became animated. His strong likes and dislikes, often epigrammatically expressed, made good copy. But when he used the first person singular, it was to express personal conviction and not personal confession. This is in keeping with his reserve and caution, which springs, as he himself shrewdly observed, "not from fear but from an inner sense of decorum which inevitably enforces itself on one in the presence of strangers, especially strangers who are kind." As for friends whom he had not seen for many years, he talked now with less restraint about the past. Such moments of recollection were sometimes only footnotes to a topic of discourse, but frequently, particularly in conjuring up friends who had passed from the scene, he demonstrated a deep capacity for fidelity.

What tales Wolfson would tell, tales of scholars and saints, rabbis and rapscallions, philosophers and philistines! How wonderfully he would strum the chords of his memory when he recalled such men as George Foot Moore, David Gordon Lyon, George Santayana, Reuben Brainin, Louis Ginzberg, Judah Magnes, Stephen Wise, Ralph Marcus, Werner Jaeger, and Joseph Klausner—not to mention living worthies. His generosity in helping other scholars with his special knowledge and great influence has been publicly acknowledged by many scores of his colleagues at Harvard, among them Samuel Eliot Morison, Arthur Darby Nock, Francis H. Fobes, and McGeorge Bundy. One striking example of Wolfson's fidelity can be seen in his relationship with the late Joseph Klausner, historian and Hebraist of the Hebrew University in Jerusalem. Their friendship apparently began in Vienna at the first international gathering of Hebraists in 1913. Klausner was then the editor of *Ha-Shilo'ah* ("The Messenger"), a literary journal of distinction. Wolfson, then a graduate student on a Sheldon Fellowship, was studying medieval manuscripts at the Hofbibliothek; when the meeting of the Hebraists was adjourned they flocked to the nearby sessions of the Eleventh Zionist Congress, where Wolfson was elected secretary of the American Zionist delegation. The following year, while he was sleuthing among the manuscripts in the Bibliothèque Nationale in Paris, he read an article in *Ha-Shilo'ah* on Jewish students in American universities. He wrote a letter to Klausner correcting certain misstatements in the article, and Klausner graciously quoted from it in a note in *Ha-Shilo'ah* with flattering comment about the writer's style. In subsequent decades Klausner's Hebrew writings in history, literature, and religion became well known; his *Jesus of Nazareth* (Jerusalem, 1922), the first study of the life and times of the founder of Christianity written in Hebrew, became a subject of acrid controversy in learned and religious circles in the United States. In 1956 Klausner nominated Zalman Shneour as a candidate for the Nobel prize in literature. At Klausner's request, Wolfson and his colleague Robert H. Pfeiffer seconded the nomination in the following note to the Swedish Academy in Stockholm:

Professor Joseph Klausner, of the Hebrew University in Jerusalem, informs us that he has nominated Dr. Zalman Shneour, of Ramat Gan, State of Israel, as a candidate for the Nobel Prize in Literature. We ardently support this nomination. Dr. Shneour is a poet of the highest distinction, whose work, universal in its appeal, is a superb expression of the life and aspirations of his people. It would be eminently fitting that such an award should be bestowed upon one who is the outstanding living representative of a literature the history of which goes back to the Hebrew Bible.

The prize was awarded to Juan Ramón Jiménez of Brazil. A few years later Wolfson had more success when he sponsored Klausner's election to the American Academy of Arts and Sciences.

In 1957 Klausner wrote an article entitled "Professor Wolfson: Great Historian of Philosophy" in the yearbook of the Israeli newspaper *Davar*. After giving an interesting sketch of Wolfson's academic career and an estimate of his work, Klausner's piece concludes with a touching appeal to him to come to Jerusalem to occupy a chair in Hebrew philosophy, or at least as a visiting professor, so that he may devote himself to translating "one of his four great works into his precise, luminous Hebrew. . . . For who can equal him in the knowledge of medieval philosophic literature . . . and who can match him in rendering his seminal ideas into his distinctive Hebrew?"

Apart from visitors such as those mentioned above, there were the cronies who became Wolfson's companions at meal times. For many years he used to eat at the cafeterias around Harvard Square, where the help got to know him and his culinary preferences so well he hardly needed to articulate his choices. But in later decades he became an habitué of the Harvard Faculty Club on Quincy Street, where he benignly reigned over a large table,* known as "Wolfson's Table," where his friends would assemble. They came from various departments of the University—A. W. Scott and Samuel Thorne of the Law School, Jakob Rosenberg of the Fine Arts Department, Erwin R. Goodenough, formerly of Yale, George H. Williams of the Divinity School, Karl Ulich of the School of Education, and Leo Roberts, an independent scholar who had formerly taught French at Johns Hopkins and philosophy at Harvard. Each of these scholars constituted a province and principality in his own right, and at the table their conversation was compensation for the unimaginative cuisine. Wolfson generally listened while eating, often appearing to be turned inward as though fixed on a mental image; but between the courses and after the meal he would rally and his comments were always pointed.

*The *stammtisch* antedates this table by some years. Its composition kept changing, but there was a nucleus of the faithful, such as L. Brillouin (mathematics), Sydney Freedberg (art), P. E. Le Corbeiller (physics), and Leo Roberts (philosophy).

Wolfson was an easy talker, often punctuating what he had to say with ironic humor. One day a guest gave a detailed report of a lecture by Wolfson's old friend David Levy on animal psychology in relation to psychiatry, in which the psychiatrist demonstrated the existence in dogs of neuroses found in human beings. The guest described in detail Levy's observations of clinical cases of neurotic behavior in dogs: as one example, one of Levy's dogs, up to his sixth or seventh year of life, would bite at a bush when Levy would refuse to throw a ball for him to fetch, thus expressing its frustration through release of aggression just as in human beings; in the familiar example of a dog's mourning for his departed master, Levy observed the same type of depressive response to the loss of a loved object as is observed at the human level: in the case of a pet dog and a new baby, the dog barked more than usual, growled at the baby though he never attacked it, tugged at his mistress's skirts when she fondled the baby, and after six weeks "accepted" the situation. Levy was reported to have concluded that the clinical observation of regressive behavior in dogs (and in other animals) appeared to be identical with that observed in human patients. "That proves simply," Wolfson said, "that man is a dog."

Complimenting him on a sermon he had delivered earlier at Appleton Chapel, Williams asked whether Wolfson had written it out for publication. "No," he replied. "That would deprive me of the pleasure of embellishing it later on." At the end of one table discussion regarding certain philosophers who forsake the responsibility of their discipline for popularization, Wolfson said, "They are intellectual bootleggers who run speakeasies of scholarship." To a teacher of English who complained of the difficulty of finding appropriate topics for graduate theses he suggested, "Why not have one of your students write a thesis on the role of 'Sixthly' in the sermons of the seventeenth century?" But when conversation turned to the sport of dissecting a man's character, he would keep mum, though occasionally beaming encouragement at a shrewd thrust.

Wolfson was particularly engaging when a topic interested him enough to evoke extended comment. A leading sociologist once joined his table and commented on the changes taking place in Harvard Square. Wolfson pounced upon the theme and gave an account of the sociology of the Square since 1908—booksellers, rapacious coal dealers, the rise and decline of tutorial schools, usurious secondhand-clothing dealers, and Greek hash-slingers all passed in review. His observations on food there and the kind of people who cooked and served it were detailed. He dilated on the transformation of restaurants and he described with relish their changing fashions in food, showing special finesse on such details as the way to detect the difference between pumpkin pie and squash pie. He deplored the gradual disappearance of real Yankee food (even at Patten's restaurant in Boston, where it had been a specialty for generations) such as Indian pudding, pettijohns, coffee jelly, and gingerbread, which he called "the French pastry of Boston." He went on to talk about changes in real estate, transportation, stores, apparel, recreation, and manners. "How in the world," asked the sociologist, "can a person like you who is buried in Widener all the time know so much about what is happening outside?" Employing a figure from an ancient midrash, he replied, "I live in a room with convex windows on the inside and concave on the outside." On another occasion, the talk taking a sanguinary turn, Wolfson was asked if he had ever heard of Daniel Mendoza, the Anglo-Jewish boxer. It was like asking him if he had ever heard of Spinoza; his knowledge of Mendoza's feats in the ring would have done credit to a professional sports writer.

Inasmuch as the "regulars" used to eat at home in the evenings, Wolfson made a habit of inviting out-of-town visitors to have dinner with him at the Faculty Club. Among them were many former students and parents of students. These were pleasurable occasions —he always appeared to be in an affable, cheerful mood—and sometimes they also had surprising consequences. One evening his guest was a student's father who was the owner of a famous grape-juice corporation. Soon after the visit a huge case of the product arrived at the Faculty Club as a gift. It was stored in a cool section of the cellar, and for the following year or so all his guests were plied with tumblers of the juice. During this period he forewent his usual bottle of beer at dinner.

Besides the enjoyment afforded by the amenities of the Faculty Club, the reading lounge was also the mise-en-scène for many interesting encounters. One pleasant day in April 1953, just after Passover, Wolfson went into the lounge, took a magazine from a table, and sat down on a comfortable chair in a corner. But he could not

read. Saddened by the death of his mother, whose funeral he had
attended in New York a week earlier, he was pensive. She had been
one of those remarkable women whose ninety-four years were full of
struggle and pain but whose fine intellect and bouyancy overcame
the vicissitudes of her life. The mainstay of her family, she never lost
her sparkle or dignity or faith, and her conversation was spiced with
native wisdom and enriched by an inexhaustible store of parables
and fables. Her pride in her oldest son was deep, especially as he had
made his mark as a man of learning; and although he only saw her
periodically, Wolfson's love for her was strong. He admired the rich
humor with which she put her children and friends in their due place
and the literary talent which effortlessly came through in her Hebrew letters to him. Had she been born and educated in America,
he thought, and freed of the common toils of a poor family, she
would doubtless have become a writer . . .

Suddenly, in the midst of this reverie, a voice exclaimed, "Professor Wolfson, *pozdrowienie z Ostriny,* greetings from Ostryna"—the
sound of his birthplace and the Polish pronunciation of it was like
a distant echo of his thoughts. Looking up, he saw a priest smiling
broadly. The man introduced himself as Father Michael Urbanowich, a native of Mashevka, a farming village just outside Ostrin. Wolfson was always delighted to see anyone from his birthplace, and at that moment the priest was doubly welcome. The men
scrutinized each other's faces. They were about the same age. Had
they met in Ostrin as boys? They could not remember but agreed
that they probably had passed each other occasionally in the marketplace. Soon they found that they knew one Ostriner in common, a
Jewish woman named Tsinka who came to the priest's father's farm
each morning to buy milk and sell it to the housewives in Ostrin.
Hence they had both drunk milk from the same cow. And the
starosta of the church? No, the priest did not know him, for, being
a Roman Catholic, he attended mass in another town. And Kiva-
Kiva, the nickname for Akiva, a wealthy grain merchant in Ostrin,
was another link. Wolfson remembered him as an official of the
synagogue, and Urbanowitch recalled his visits to the farm where
Kiva bought grain and fruit from his father. . . . And so on, for several
hours.

"And how did you find me?" inquired Wolfson. Urbanowich said it was by sheer luck. In January he had read a paper at a conference of the American Association of Slavic and East European Languages at the University of Kentucky. One of the members of the Hebrew and Yiddish section of the conference asked him afterward where he was born. When he replied "Ostrin," the Hebraist asked him whether he knew Professor Wolfson of Harvard, who was a native of Ostrin and often spoke about the town. As soon as he arrived in Cambridge he telephoned Roman Jakobson, the eminent Slavic scholar, who suggested that Wolfson would probably be at the Faculty Club at midday.

Urbanowich added that while meeting Wolfson was mere chance, he had been searching for Ostriners ever since his arrival in America in 1923. Wolfson supplied him with a list of names of Ostriners and their children: Mirka's daughter, the wife of a rabbi in Providence, Rhode Island; the undertaker of Ostrin, who lived in New York and had made burial arrangements for Wolfson's grandparents and parents. During the ensuing decade the priest looked up these people and kept Wolfson abreast of his findings.

Wolfson's own feelings about Ostrin were never detached. To begin with, he was interested in the town because he had been cradled in it. There, in his boyhood, he drank the elixir of tradition and his imagination dreamed its richest dreams. Across the years and the seas the outline of things no longer real and persons no longer alive pierced his intensely logical mind, touched his controlled emotions, and filled him with rapture. With only a slight stretch of his memory he could release a jet of recollection that flowed as from a natural spring and refreshed his spirit with scenes of that distant and happy past. The scenes were peopled with family, friends, and neighbors who are never time-worn, who are always interesting, and whose lives are as full of deeds and ideas as a pomegranate is full of seeds. That world was gone and past; indeed, it was expunged in the wake of the Hitlerian evil. Yet the Ostriners who survived in America and Israel were like leaves fallen from a tree to make a fertilizing compost. Not the least among them were members of Wolfson's own family: there was the son of his Uncle Bernard, Erwin Wolfson, who achieved fame as a builder of skyscrapers, including the Pan American Building in New York, completed just before his death in 1962, and who endowed the Harry A. Wolfson Chair in Philosophy at Brandeis University; and there is Bernard Davis, an eminent immunologist at the Harvard Medical School and the grandson of the uncle who provided Wolfson with lodging during his freshman year.

Wolfson's manner of life changed somewhat as a result of his move from Professor Ben Selekman's comfortable house on Francis Avenue to a four-room apartment in the Ambassador Hotel. Situated on the sixth floor, with windows affording a fine view of part of Cambridge, the apartment was more spacious and orderly than his old one on Prescott Street. Except for framed awards and citations stacked in boxes in a closet, all of his possessions had been removed to Widener K, making it easy for the maid to keep the apartment in order. After the interlude of several years of "family life," he seemed at home again in his bachelor quarters and occasionally joshed about his middle-class (*balebatish*) status.

Wolfson's movie-going, in the past his chief form of relaxation, slackened during his later years; instead, upon his return from the library at night he watched television. Political broadcasts interested him, but mostly he viewed Westerns and mysteries. He would turn them off when the commercials came on, generally doze off for a while, and then wake up in time to check the outcome against what he had anticipated. The Westerns seemed to keep him awake longer, and he would make comments on what the players should do in critical situations and forecast what the directors would make them do. Of the "whodunits" he was fond of those that centered on court, especially if they were presented in a realistic manner; but the hokum of the Westerns amused him most. He did not like educational programs but, as he once remarked, "hokum makes a pleasant change." Until falling off to sleep about 1:30 A.M., he would read detective stories in magazines—he preferred the short, fast-moving tales to long drawn-out ones in books.

When he was living at the Ambassador Hotel, Wolfson used to rise, as always, a little before 7:00 A.M. and prepare his own breakfast. The menu varied little: a glass of orange juice, dry cereal in the summer and minute oats in the winter, and two cups of coffee with sugar and milk. (He shopped once a week at a nearby supermarket where he occasionally also got a fifth of Bourbon.) On one visit to Boston I joined him for breakfast and observed his morning regimen. He set the table in the kitchen, passed to me two large boxes of dry cereal, one of large wheat flakes and the other of small balls of a rice mixture, and invited me to help myself. I poured some of the small rice cereal into a dish, but he immediately stopped me, saying, "No, no. First the flakes and then the balls. That's the only way." I poured the balls back into the box and he gave me specific instructions on how to proceed, explaining that this procedure was the result of considerable experimentation with dry cereals. There were, he said, two reasons for it: an esthetic and a practical one. He explained at length, as though he were analyzing a text, why the balls with the background of the wavy flakes had a more artistic appearance; and then, how the milk filtered through the little balls better than through the flakes, when the flakes were on top. After breakfast he methodically washed the dishes and returned everything to its place in the cupboard and refrigerator.

For sixty years New York was alternately Wolfson's home, refuge, and workshop. Yet he never considered himself, nor was he considered by others, a New Yorker. The old landmarks on the Lower East Side had disappeared in the rebuilding of the city—the Rabbi Isaac Elhanan Yeshiva on Henry Street, his parental home on Canal Street, the cafés, the synagogues, the theaters and the restaurants— and with them had gone the older generation of family and friends. Still his impromptu visits continued: one saw him from time to time at the Jewish Room of the New York Public Library, talking with members of the staff or with E. R. Malachi (whom he called "the Steinschneider of modern Hebrew literature"); at Columbia in the company of Moses Hadas, Horace M. Kallen, and Salo W. Baron; and at the Jewish Theological Seminary, conferring with Louis Finkelstein and Saul Lieberman. Occasionally he would drop into the office of his cousin, who managed a midtown dress business where Wolfson's sister Bessie worked, or meet his brother Nathaniel, a practicing dentist on the East Side.

When Wolfson was in New York he rarely stayed at the Harvard Club, which in its Victorian dignity was for him too reminiscent of the Faculty Club in Cambridge. For many years he made his headquarters at the Edison, a commercial hotel in the heart of the Broadway theater district where crowds and bright lights, like the movies and tabloids, afforded a pleasant escape. He was diverted by the noise and liveliness of the crowds in search of pleasure, intrigued by the flamboyance of the barkers and hucksters, and fascinated by the peculiar species of people who survive in little stores submerged in the basements of antiquated buildings. He would often walk alone, enjoying the stir in the streets, or sometimes, accompanied by a friend, walk up and down Broadway conversing animatedly about his work. In his later years, as the demands upon him by academic societies steadily increased, he met his friends at the Edison and, undisturbed by the chatter of salesmen and convention delegates, sat in conference in the corner of the lobby unraveling problems in connection with the publication of the Averroes *Corpus* or like enterprises. Afterward he would return and relish the streets, the color and variety of the crowds to which he was drawn.

In the sixties, after the death of his friend Pearson Neaman, he began to stay at Neaman's plush apartment on upper Fifth Avenue with a beautiful view of Central Park, and there he could enjoy, as his mood dictated, either privacy or company. A loyal, admiring friend since the early twenties, Annabelle Neaman was tolerant of his eccentricities and catered to his whims. She and her two grown children listened avidly to reports of his doings since the last visit, and he discussed freely their problems and plans. And, as had been customary in the past, she corralled some of the "Doc" circle for dinner and conviviality.

Looking backwards, one may say that to Wolfson New York was a systole compared to the diastole of Cambridge.

At rare moments intimations have emerged from this portrait, as through doors left unexpectedly ajar, of a trait of character known perhaps only to Wolfson's closer friends. Through the years he preserved a childlike delight in the simple things that are taken for granted by most sophisticated mortals: a new suit, a new gadget, an encomium. During a visit at the home of the historian Salo W. Baron, his wife and collaborator Jeanette, who had been reared in Ossining and whose grandfather Wolfson had met on his arrival there in 1903, showed him their first child in a bassinet, and Wolfson remarked, "She has the eyes of a philosopher" (he was wrong). What they found truly surprising however was his intense interest in the household novelties. When Baron showed him a new type of chair constructed to be used for reading or relaxation, Wolfson enthusiastically tried it out in every possible position, radiating a childlike exuberance. He left with the feeling that the ordinary chair had become as extinct as the bustle.

One afternoon in the thirties James and Dorothy Feibleman and several of their friends took Wolfson to Revere Beach. As they stopped at each of the amusements, Wolfson compared them with their counterparts at Coney Island and tried, without success, to persuade his hosts to ride, paddle, swing, and fly. When they came to the trick mirrors, Wolfson was held there inexhaustibly: he took steps backward, forward, and sideways, laughing uproariously at the distorted variations of himself in the reflections. His disportments and uninhibited enjoyment of so boyish a diversion charmed and fascinated his friends.

As worthy of note as these moments of childlike exuberance is Wolfson's discovery in his sixties that a man's birthday could be something more than a vital statistic. His birthday had never been celebrated, so that when he found himself at his first birthday party, he found the experience overwhelming. The event took place at the home of the Goulds. Sophie had remained an admirer and friend since her childhood, and as a matron she had inherited the charm and efficiency of her remarkable mother. Having lived all her life in a scholarly milieu, she managed learned visitors with understanding and poise. Of the houses Wolfson visited in Boston and New England, he felt thoroughly at home only at the Rabs (formerly Rabinovitzes) in Swampscott and the Goulds in Brookline; and, after the death of Sophie's father, Louis Ginzberg, in 1953, Wolfson's visits to her home became frequent. One day in 1955, when Wolfson came to dinner, the Gould family sang "Happy Birthday" and presented him with an elaborate birthday cake. The rituals of blowing out the candles and serving the cake afforded Wolfson moments of exquisite delight; he was like a boy with his first bicycle. He expressed his pleasure and reexpressed it throughout the evening without restraint.

There is a sequel to this story. To celebrate his seventy-fifth birthday in 1962, the New Century Club of Boston tendered a dinner in Wolfson's honor at the Faculty Club of the Massachusetts Institute of Technology. In his remarks to hundreds of friends and admirers that evening, he commented on the phenomenon of birthday celebrations substantially as follows:

All of us who are now accustomed to celebrating birthdays, in addition to bar mitzvahs, should be indebted to the pioneers of Jewish scholarship. The celebration of birthdays is not an old Jewish custom. Jews never celebrated birthdays; we commemorated days of death in the form of *yahrzeits*. Not that there is a law against it; we simply did not celebrate them. In the Bible, as you may remember, there is a reference to the celebration of a birthday for Pharaoh, king of Egypt, but there is no reference to any birthday celebration of an Israelite or Jew. In the Talmud, there are references to the celebration of the birthdays of gentile kings; and according to some interpretations of some passages, perhaps also the birthdays of Gentiles in general. There are also references in Josephus and the New Testament to the Herodian kings who, under the influence of non-Jews, did celebrate birthdays. But there is no reference in ancient or medieval literature to the celebration of a birthday by a Jew.

The first public celebration of a birthday occurred when Jewish scholars celebrated the birthday of Leopold Zunz. Thus, when we are all here tonight celebrating a birthday, we owe it to these Jewish scholars who established that custom. But there is something else. Zunz had to wait until he was ninety years old before people thought of celebrating his birthday. You have anticipated this celebration by fifteen years, and that is something for which I ought to be grateful. To the president of the New Century Club, to the members of the Arrangements Committee, and to all of you, I wish to thank you, one and all, for coming here tonight to make a celebration of this occasion.

In another special commemoration of this milestone in Wolfson's life, President John F. Kennedy (with whom he had received the Brotherhood Award of the National Conference of Christians and

Jews in 1956 and Harvard's honorary doctorate that same year) sent him a presidential citation for his "extraordinary personal influence, not only on your students at Harvard, but on all those engaged in reflective learning and research. You have broadened the horizons of human thought and have given an example of personal devotion and humility for which we are all grateful."

Apart from these necessities and pleasantries, Wolfson's preoccupation remained the completion of his lifework. Anticipating the publication of the two volumes of *The Philosophy of Kalam* in 1964, he planned to proceed with the second volume of *The Philosophy of the Church Fathers;* a volume to be entitled *Greek Philosophy,* dealing with problems in Greek philosophy as they evolved in the development of philosophy to Spinoza and including a prolegomenon to the methodology of the study of the history of philosophy; a volume to be called *The Muslim Philosophers,* examining Muslim philosophy from Alfarabi to Averroes; a volume on *The Philosophy of Halevi and Maimonides,* explicating the major systems of medieval Jewish philosophy with reference to all the other Jewish philosophers within that framework; and finally a volume on *Latin Philosophy from St. Thomas Aquinas to Descartes,* dealing with the systems and principles of the Scholastic Christian philosophers and their descendants. Thus he projected the completion of his twelve-volume series on the Structure and Growth of Philosophic Systems from Plato to Spinoza, following which he planned a definitive revision of *Spinoza,* with cross-references to all the previous books of the series.*

Wolfson's devotion to the weighty scholarly projects he set on his own agenda did not limit his participation in other academic undertakings. He vigorously pursued the publication of volumes in the Averroes *Corpus* and even helped to secure financial support for them. He continued to serve actively as a trustee of several foundations instrumental in the advancement of learning, including the Lucius Littauer Foundation and the Alexander Kohut Foundation.

*See "Bibliography: The Principal Writings of Harry A. Wolfson," p.260, for a listing of the publications that Wolfson completed, including those published posthumously.—Ed.

Nor did he diminish his interest in undertakings that he helped bring into being, such as the Yale Judaica Series. He also served as the Honorary Curator of the Hebrew Collection in Harvard College. For all these he had a protective instinct that was almost motherly.

This attitude characterized his relations with his friends as well. Wolfson was avid to hear of their doings, delighted in their triumphs, and always was glad to participate in honoring them. The feeling was reciprocal. In January 1961 a dinner was given to honor his classmate Oscar Hauserman at the Union Club in Boston, at which he was presented with autographed copies of all Wolfson's works, including *Crescas*—an "Oscar" to Oscar. To grace the occasion, General William J. Blake of the class of 1913, an old friend of Wolfson's since College House days, composed an ode that praised the constellation of worthies of the class of 1912. It concludes with the following stanzas:

But the "tops" is Harry Wolfson, coming here from Poland's plains,
To dazzle old John Harvard with his magnitude of brains.
He worked, researched, and lectured in this land where all are free,
Got a "Sheldon," a Doctorate, and a Phi Beta Kappa Key.

Our Harry's one pursuit in life has been religion's place
From days of Zeus, down to the coming of dear old Daddy Grace.
He's so thorough he will shun not the gods of the lowest peon,
And we Romans sometimes wonder what he thinks of Fulton Sheen.

He's a scholar, too, in all the works of that great man Aristotle
And can tell you why old Islam stays away from that old bottle.
He has studied and has written of Spinoza, plus and minus,
And can quote to you verbatim from Theologian Aquinas.

Our Oscar will be proud to get these treasured volumes five
By one of our great historians, who's still very much alive.
He'll think of this fine classmate when this meeting comes to an end
And say, "God love you, Harry—you're my old and precious friend."

Over the years his classmates, though widely dispersed and variously engaged, have felt pride in Wolfson's achievements. Among them was Clarence Randall, a friend from Scranton days, and chairman of the Inland Steel Company. Wolfson had hoped to see him in Chicago when, on December 24, 1953, he was awarded an honorary degree of Doctor of Humane Letters from the University of Chicago with the following citation: "Singularly endowed with the ability to make crystal clear the profound and involved speculations of ancient and medieval thinkers."

On February 14 Randall wrote as follows:

Dear Harry:

My life has been chaos for the past six months because, as you may know, I have been active in Washington as Chairman of the Commission on Foreign Economic Policy.

When the report was filed my wife and I fled to Arizona for a brief vacation. I am back at my desk for two days, and then return to Washington for further service.

I find, however, that my beloved University of Chicago, where I have been a trustee for many, many years, awarded you an honorary degree, and I want to join with your many friends in extending my congratulations for this richly deserved honor.

It seems only yesterday that we met in Scranton, and I have followed with the deepest interest through the years your very distinguished career.

With kindest regards, I remain

Clarence

And Wolfson replied:

Dear Clarence:

Many thanks for your very kind congratulatory note. I missed you in Chicago, but I was proud that you were away on such a highly important mission abroad. Members of our class, it seems, are now entering upon the harvest season in their various fields. Your mention of Scranton, where we took the college entrance examinations together, brings home to me how immensely indebted we all are to that great institution which is Harvard.

With every good wish for the success of your work in Washington, I am

Sincerely,
Harry

*At a dinner given by the New Century Club of Boston
in May 1962 to commemorate Harry Wolfson's seventy-fifth
birthday: standing, from left, Harry Walker, Dr. Harry A. Savitz,
Dr. Jacob Cushner; seated, from left, Samuel A. Goldblith,
Leo W. Schwarz, Harry Wolfson, Bernard Gould*

*Douglas W. Bryant, Harvard University Librarian, presenting
Harry Wolfson with the first catalogue of Hebrew books
published by Widener Library, 23 October 1968*

Harvard University Gazette

May 1, 1970
Volume LXV

The occasion is the traditional wine toasting at "the Wolfson table" at the Faculty Club, celebrated whenever a table regular publishes a book. This time the author is Professor Harry Wolfson (Hebrew Literature and Philosophy), *Emeritus*, himself (above right). His book is *The Kalam*, a systematic exposition of Muslim philosophy out of the Koran and tradition comparable to scholasticism in Christian history. Mr. Wolfson had just delivered the manuscript of volume II to the Harvard University Press when the *Gazette* photographer took this picture last Monday. Professor George H. Williams (Divinity), a member of the Wolfson table (foreground), describes *The Kalam* as "a world event in intellectual history and interfaith relations. It is perhaps Mr. Wolfson's most important achievement and remarkable undertaking." Others at the table: Professors Richard R. Baxter, Eduard F. Sekler, and Morton G. White.

left: *Harry Wolfson chatting with Lewis Weinstein at a reception marking the publication of the first Judaica catalogue for Widener Library, 23 October 1968*

Harry Wolfson in his study on the top floor of
Widener Library, December 1965

Among his younger friends—mostly former students and their families—Wolfson was always ready, if called upon, to help solve problems, whether professional or personal, and, as always, he shared the riches of his intellect with those who devote themselves to the pursuit of learning. Evidence of his largesse can be found in literally hundreds of acknowledgments in books. As a consequence, many of his students have a devotion to him that few scholars elicit.

Thus, while wholeheartedly dedicated to learning, Wolfson also was inspired by a strong sense of duty and loyalty toward his family and friends. He lived through three periods in his own life: until his twenties he knew poverty; during the following thirty years he was able to live modestly but under the shadow of insecurity regarding the future; for the last decades of his life he was able to live without thought of money. So he shared his modest income and the windfalls from prizes with his family; in cases of individual hardship he applied his principle of the "double tithe," contributing more than what was asked of him provided that no public mention would be made of these acts. One small example of his personal kindness: for more than thirty years up to the time of his retirement, at each June commencement he had lent his academic gown to a student who could not afford the rental. The immigrant boy was the psychological father of the man.

The goal of the hero, the general, or the scholar, however single-minded it may be, is never achieved in a straight line—on a single plane, so to speak; the struggle on the way is double-minded—it is combat between two natures, two minds within the man. In Wolfson they are Henricus the scholar and Harry the poet, and our portrait, if it be true to the man, shows the scholar vanquishing the poet. But if the scholar was the victor, he did not succeed in obliterating his opponent. The defeated poet in Wolfson remained alive but submerged. Our pursuit of the man behind the books would be incomplete without some attempt to appreciate this fact.

The group of essays published in *Religious Philosophy* may serve as our text. Here are ten essays, altogether an intimate and rich tapestry of ideas, displaying on almost every page scholarship spiced with wit. Thoughts swarm through the pages like crowding, living bees. In the first essay, for example, Wolfson defines a recognizable species of philosopher: "For nowadays, as we all know, to be called philosopher one must be ordained and one must be hired to teach philosophy and one must also learn to discuss certain hoary problems as if they were plucked but yesterday out of the air" (p. 1). Speaking of certain Spinoza interpreters, he says: "With their bare wit they try to extract some rootless meaning out of his mnemonic phrases and, if sometimes they happen to summon aid from without, they make him split hairs with Descartes or share honors with Berkeley" (p. 67). Showing in the essay on "Spinoza and Religion" that for all his daring Spinoza introduces no novelty, he wryly sums up the philosopher's view of man: "The singularity of man consisted in the fact that he had a special soul of special origin. Spinoza himself, in his book called *Cogitata Metaphysica*, which is really not a book but a scrapbook, alludes to the three theories of the origin of the human soul held by various religious philosophers. In technical language they are known as the theories of creation, preexistence, and traducianism. In plain English they may be described, respectively, as the theory of custom-made souls, the theory of ready-made souls, and the theory of second-hand souls" (p. 257). And at the end of an analysis of the problem of causality and freedom from Greek philosophy to the present, he gives this clinching statement: "If we cut through the jungle of words which so often obscures the discussion of this problem, we shall always find the two old roads, the Philonic and the Epicurean, modernized, perhaps, broadened, lengthened, straightened out, smoothed out, macadamized, and heavily academized—but still the same old roads. Not all who traveled these roads, however, were equipped with good road maps, and so occasionally some of them lost their way and got to the wrong place" (p. 216).

These literary sallies, delightful and illuminating as they are, bear something more than the mark of a master of prose. It should be kept in mind that they are detached from a work of technical scholarship, which was composed with infinite labor and skill and written with reserve and restraint. Why, then, should the author have from time to time been impelled to season a style of classic distinction with the condiments of irony and wit? The answer lies in part in a mind richly endowed with diverse talents. As a youth Wolfson began to write fiction and poetry, literary and social criticism, and finally philosophic prose. He might have become a laughing philosopher in the manner of Montaigne or a philosophic litterateur in the manner of his teacher, Santayana. But somewhere along the way he chose to become a philosopher's philosopher and embody the substance of his study and thought in technical works. In making this choice and sticking to it, the freedom and gust of more personal expression were perforce suppressed. However, these happy faculties survived in the clever repartee and the sardonic humor of his conversation. And, on occasion, they forced their way to the surface and found expression in the literary sallies imbedded in his learned tomes.

While the scholarly masterpieces which comprise Wolfson's projected twelve-volume series on the Structure and Growth of Philosophic Systems from Plato to Spinoza reveal a range of learning, mastery of original sources, and an interpretive faculty rare in studies of the history of ideas, they in the main conceal the man behind the ideas. Yet the literary forays tell us something about him. The personality revealed in them possesses a humane mind and a sensitive spirit blessed with innate distinction and natural wit. Sometimes his witticisms have an undertone of disdain, but this cudgel is reserved for those who confuse the latest fashion with the last word. He is contemptuous of the scholar who wraps his ideas in bales of wool and substitutes effusion for logic. But his sense of decorum prevents him from roaring down his critics. His mind, like his style, is always under control; if his polemics are devastating, it is their honed-edge logic that makes them so. Above all, the literary sallies reveal a mind which, although it dwelled in intellectual solitude, remained alive and fresh.

For Wolfson, irony was the spice of life. To him humor, like work, was the great solvent of life—and the sharp edge of the knife of criticism.

But there is another aspect of the struggle between Henricus and Harry that needs examination. There is no doubt that Henricus lived in the past and revered it. Up to the early twenties Harry had his day: the essays discoursing on contemporary problems expressed the thoughts of Harry in the words of Henricus. From that time on, however, Henricus triumphed, and so the impression was fostered that Wolfson was, in mind if not in emotion, entirely absorbed in the past. Undoubtedly he gave his best energies to exploring and rehabilitating the thinkers of past epochs. When a friend once asked him how far along he had come, he replied, "Well, I'm in the tenth century, but I'll reach the twentieth one of these years." As a matter of fact, a careful reading of his books, and especially some of the essays in *Religious Philosophy*, suggests that the contemporary world was always in his consciousness. Every now and then he seriously considered writing an article or a book on a current issue, but he always kept himself on his chosen course.

Nevertheless, he did not always suppress these "wayward" thoughts, and thus they come to the surface in oblique references here and there, even in his most intensely scholarly writing. Surely he is drawing on his own knowledge of twentieth-century New York when in *Philo* he describes the alienated Jewish intellectuals of first-century Alexandria. Spinoza, on page after page, is a foil for such contemporary allusions. Wolfson calls Spinoza's practical remedies for diseases of the mind and the passions "a metaphysic for bilious souls" in the text of *Spinoza*, but there is also an index reference that reads "Psychotherapy, Spinoza's principles of." To be sure, the word "psychotherapy" (*refuat ha-nefesh*, literally "healing of the soul") was already in use in medieval Hebrew, but he cannot refrain from alluding to the modern practitioners of the healing art. Consider also his remark in *Philo:* "It is only recently that Philonic philosophy . . . began to gain vogue and currency in quarters where it is not an inherited tradition, but that is due only to the breakdown of philosophy as a learned discipline, from which some inquiring minds try to seek escape in scholasticism as a substitute for scholarship" (vol. 2, p. 458). Is it not clear here that he is speaking of a certain school of Neo-Thomists of the University of Chicago variety?

Nor is this all. In some of the essays in *Religious Philosophy* and elsewhere, Wolfson deals directly with philosophers of the modern epoch. He shows how the same problems and terms of the traditional philosophers, both Greek and Philonic, reemerge in Liebniz, Hume, Locke; and with telling logic and irony he suggests that these thinkers are perhaps only espousing "philosophies of labels." To those who think that philosophy begins with Kierkegaard or Wittgenstein, Wolfson's view may seem to be nothing more than caricature. But, in truth, it cuts deeper: the implication of his assault on modern philosophy is that if one rejects the age-old solutions of traditional philosophy only science can replace it.

Wolfson's creative method of research surely will continue to exercise a strong influence among historians of ideas. The beginnings already were visible in a book that appeared in Israel on the medieval Jewish philosopher Arama, expounding his thought "in the framework of Philonic philosophy." In Germany, too, a scholar published in 1960 a work in philosophy "according to Wolfsonian principles." In the sixties there already were signs of Wolfson's influence on scholars in the humanities, both here and abroad, among whom he was considered both pioneer and exemplar. As one instance, Professor Edwin E. Calverley's essay on "Arabic Religious Literature," which appears in the *Ignace Goldziher Memorial Volume* (Budapest, 1948), refers to the way in which Professor Osman Amin of Cairo is revising his studies in Arab philosophy on the basis of Wolfson's papers in that field. One little story I happened to hear is also a straw in the wind. In 1960, while staying at a hotel in Salisbury, Rhodesia, I met a Nigerian teacher who said it was his dream to study at Harvard. He had an interest in comparative religion which had been stimulated by things he heard from a Nigerian friend who was a professor at the University of Lagos. He asked me many questions about Harvard. His friend had been a student of Wolfson's and a great admirer; he had apparently endowed Wolfson with a *personalité africaine,* and had said of him, "That Wolfson is Ngwazi." "Ngwazi," a Bantu expression usually reserved for political leaders, means "greatest of the great."

But the bold thesis of the Philonic philosophy has critics as well as friends. Both have their unofficial camps, and the battle lines are being drawn. "One thing is clear," Leo Roberts wrote in *Isis* (40:200

[1949]), "as even his less friendly critics are obliged to admit: Wolfson knows his subject through and through. Not all the evidence is in yet, so that anything like a definitive appraisal is out of the question. But it may be said at once that Wolfson's thesis, even in its present, only partially implemented form, is set forth with so much art and supported by so much learning that it must induce, except in the most obdurate, a willing suspension of disbelief."

In the autumn of his life, Harry Wolfson—honorary curator of the Hebrew Collection in Harvard College, past president of the American Oriental Society, and of the American Academy for Jewish Research, and fellow of the American Academy of Arts and Sciences and of the Mediaeval Academy of America—could graciously and deservedly have rested on his accomplishments. Most of the honors which can be bestowed by scholars and academies had been proffered to him. But he preferred to sit in the saddle and ride out his chosen course.

Far from being a hermit, he was nonetheless a solitary man, and his books are the offspring of his solitude. Endowed with tremendous energy and rich talents, he had a strain of self-absorption; and the resulting inner struggle fostered his scholarly art and shaped his multi-faceted character. In practical affairs he was a man of decision who jumped in where the hard-boiled businessman fears to tread; he was an adviser who never turned away an inquirer empty-handed; he was a lecturer who wondrously spun a web of ideas. As a scholar he was priest of his craft, delighting in the human intellect as man's proudest possession, resolute and dedicated in his work, prepared to spend himself prodigally in his study to attain his lofty goals. And there, for more than half a century, Harry Wolfson fashioned his magisterial contribution to philosophic literature, unique in our time.

Epilogue
Bibliography
The Principal Writings of Harry A. Wolfson
Index

Epilogue:
The Last Decade
LEWIS H. WEINSTEIN

As a long-time friend of both Harry Austryn Wolfson and Leo W. Schwarz, it is a privilege for me to set forth here the details of the last decade of Wolfson's extraordinary life, the years that Leo Schwarz did not live to recount.

On November 2, 1965, Harry Wolfson, ripe with achievements and laden with honors, celebrated his seventy-eighth birthday. There was a special gift for Wolfson that year, the presentation of a three-volume *Festschrift*, prepared by the American Academy for Jewish Research (of which Wolfson had been a founder and a president), containing a tribute of articles, in Hebrew and English, by a galaxy of scholars. The editorial committee for this work was headed by Saul Lieberman of the Jewish Theological Seminary of America, and the contributors included the following distinguished individuals:

Alexander Altmann, Milton V. Anastos, Salo W. Baron, Samuel
Belkin, Israel Efros, Louis Finkelstein, Judah Goldin, Abraham S.
Halkin, Abraham J. Heschel, Saul Lieberman, Abraham A. Neuman, Moshe Perlmann, Gershom Scholem, Shalom Spiegel, Isadore
Twersky, Meyer Waxman, George H. Williams, and Solomon Zeitlin. Leo Schwarz provided the introduction, which was a forty-six
page paper entitled "A Bibliographical Essay." The *Festschrift* had
originally been intended as a seventieth-birthday tribute, but the
scholarly contributions could not be assembled in time. Now the
three jubilee volumes were to be presented to Wolfson on his seventy-eighth birthday in honor of his seventy-fifth—*nunc pro tunc*, as
the lawyers might put it.

Another public tribute that year was proferred by the Jewish
Theological Seminary which, to mark Wolfson's seventy-eighth
birthday as well as its own eightieth year, presented him with its
Special Anniversary Medal. The accompanying scroll recalled all of
Wolfson's major scholarly works, cited his unique contribution to
Jewish scholarship, and noted especially his capacity both "to inves-
tigate the parts and to conceive a vision of the whole of Western
religious thought."

Further honors followed. In September 1969, at the first annual
meeting of the Association for Jewish Studies, held at Brandeis
University, Wolfson was named the organization's first honorary
member in recognition of his "pioneering efforts in establishing
chairs of Jewish studies in American universities and colleges." The
Association now has some nine hundred members, more than half
of whom are full-time teachers of Jewish studies in American and
Canadian institutions of higher learning; the remainder are librarians, teaching fellows, and graduate students engaged in part-time
teaching. A half century earlier Harry Wolfson had been the sole
occupant of a chair in Jewish studies at any American university.
Now, as he noted the proliferation of colleagues, he took special
satisfaction in the fact that so many of the current teachers of Jewish
studies were former students and, in some cases, even children of
former students.

Prior to 1970 Wolfson had received eight honorary degrees, including the one which he cherished the most, his citation from

Harvard in 1956. In early June 1970, Wolfson traveled to New York to receive an honorary doctorate from Columbia University. Over seven thousand degrees were to have been conferred, but many of the recipients-to-be stayed away in protest against the U.S. involvement in Vietnam. A "counter-commencement" attracted almost a thousand students and their friends, and some five hundred more rose and left the auditorium as President Andrew Cordier began to speak. Wolfson remained calmly in his place throughout all the excitement. Three years later Wolfson was present at another academic convocation to receive yet another honorary degree, this time from Stonehill College, a Jesuit school in North Easton, Massachusetts. With the Bishop of Fall River presiding, he was cited as "a man whose life has already merged with legend because of a reputation for prodigious scholarship and a genius for expression."

As honors continued to come his way, Wolfson was becoming the object of some journalistic attention, and newspapers in Boston and New York carried accounts of "Harvard's resident sage." He was photographed so frequently—sitting at his overflowing desk in his office at Widener Library, strolling across the Harvard Yard with a green book bag slung over his shoulder—that he quipped that he was Harvard's newest "pin-up professor."

Throughout this period, Wolfson's abiding scholarly concern remained the preparation for publication of his masterwork on the Kalam, his far-ranging investigation of Islamic thought, a task to which he devoted many years of intense labor. For almost a decade now—he had begun his study of the Kalam literature in 1955— Wolfson had been at work on this massive project which was to occupy the rest of his life, gradually feeding portions of the manuscript to Harvard University Press and correcting galleys and page proofs. He continued making revisions until just before his death, unable or unwilling to surrender the finished work for release to the world. Wolfson himself was acutely aware of his procrastination and —these being the years of the U.S. agony in Southeast Asia—he often referred to the Kalam as his private Vietnam.

Wolfson had considered his work on the Kalam by and large

completed in 1964; nevertheless, he could not refrain from the seemingly endless task of revision, employing what he called, in Benjamin Cardozo's phrase, "tonsorial and agglutinative methods" —cutting and pasting, inserting and deleting, editing and transposing. Never satisfied with the results, he worked away unceasingly in the time that remained, all the while complaining to close friends that the Kalam had taken too many years of his life, years that he might better have devoted to finishing up his study of Greek philosophy or his proposed work on Judah Halevi and Maimonides.

The Philosophy of the Kalam, the first of the contemplated two volumes on the Kalam, finally appeared in 1976, two years after Wolfson's death. Wolfson had been working on the page proofs almost to the end, completing the preface only five months before his death. Isadore Twersky, who succeeded Wolfson as Nathan Littauer Professor of Hebrew Literature and Philosophy at Harvard, undertook to see the volume through press. Mrs. Eleanor Kewer completed the index and the bibliography. The second volume, *Kalam Repercussions in Jewish Philosophy*, is yet to be published.

In May 1970, when Wolfson delivered the remainder of his Kalam manuscript to Harvard University Press, the occasion was suitably recorded with a front-page story and photograph in the *Harvard Gazette* and was marked by the traditional wine-toasting at the "Wolfson Table" in the Harvard Faculty Club, attended by a joyous group of colleagues. The *Gazette* quoted one of the celebrants, George H. Williams, Hollis Professor of Divinity at Harvard, as noting that publication of Wolfson's Kalam studies would constitute "a world event in intellectual history and interfaith relations. It is perhaps Mr. Wolfson's most important achievement and remarkable undertaking." Shortly after Wolfson's death, Professor Williams again paid tribute to his friend's achievement in a profile published by the Harvard Divinity School:

The *Kalam* is the greatest of Wolfson's achievements. Only one who had learned Hebrew as a boy, mastered the classical languages and Greek philosophy, written authoritatively on Philo and on the philosophy of the Church Fathers, could have done this intricately difficult task of setting forth this first phase of systematic Muslim thought, as once again, another revealed religion, that of the Koran, had to be brought into relation with traditional philosophical categories both in their Christianized and in their original form. The *Kalam* is that lofty peak of Wolfsonian scholarship that crowns the long range of studies from monographs on Greek philosophy as foothills to the abrupt end of the chain of scriptural philosophy represented by the two-volume *Spinoza*.

Wolfson's intimate knowledge of Arabic, Islamic texts, and Muslim philosophers, as well as his many published papers on Islamic philosophy predating his work on the Kalam, had created important associations with Arabic and Islamic theologians in various parts of the world. In April 1971 the Department of Near Eastern Languages and Literatures at Harvard convoked a three-day "Conference on Early Islamic Thought in Honor of Harry A. Wolfson," in the expectation that the publication of the *Kalam* opus was imminent. A distinguished group of Arabists and scholars of Islamic thought assembled for the occasion. While the greatest number of participants were from Harvard, two journeyed from Oxford, two from Cairo, and others from Jerusalem, Beirut, Benghazi, Paris, Toulouse, Teheran, and Tübingen. Harvard had ten formal participants, Yale two, Chicago two, and there was one from each of the following universities and colleges: Brandeis, Columbia, Princeton, Toronto, Weston, Iowa, UCLA, SUNY-Buffalo, Yeshiva, Dropsie, and SUNY-Brighthaven.

The conference included twenty-one formal papers, in addition to three luncheon and two dinner sessions, each with its own talks. Serving as hosts for these occasions were various Harvard divisions, the Divinity School, the Center for Middle Eastern Studies, the Department of the History of Science, the Press, in addition to the official sponsor, the Department of Near Eastern Languages and Literatures. Wolfson was the last to speak and he talked on "Stages in the History of Kalam," a preview of the second chapter of *The Philosophy of the Kalam.* The applause that followed was like a crashing burst of thunder.

The final dinner was hosted by Harvard University Press. There were more than forty conference participants; invited guests included some twenty-five other Harvard representatives, as well as three special guests—Dr. Harry Austryn Savitz (Wolfson's cousin, physician, and closest friend), Professor Bernard Gould of the Massachussets Institute of Technology (at whose home Wolfson was a frequent visitor), and myself. The keynote address was delivered in French by Professor Ibrahim Madkour, chairman of the Arab Academy in Cairo. Madkour concluded his tribute thus:

Knowledge has no boundaries, religious, racial, or national. Philosophy, intellectual problems have no limits or borders. . . . Whenever I have a difficult problem that I can articulate in a letter, I write to Professor Wolfson and he gives me clear and irrefutable answers. When I need to talk it out with him, I telephone; and I always receive wise and thorough responses. When communication by letter or telephone is inadequate, I come to see him. He talks, I listen. He talks more, I listen more. Everything becomes clear. My problems are solved; my doubts are removed; my hesitations are gone. He is truly our master. *(Il est vraiment notre maître.)*

Not long thereafter there was to be a farewell dinner for Benjamin Mazar, the noted archeologist and then president of the Hebrew University, who had been serving as a visiting professor at Harvard and was about to return to Jerusalem. The invited guests included presidents and delegates from nearby institutions of higher learning. Wolfson, a long-time friend of Mazar's, attended as the representative of the Harvard faculty, bringing greetings in Latin from Harvard to the Hebrew University. With due courtesy to the guest of honor and his university, Wolfson also delivered a speech in elegant Hebrew. Needless to say, he spoke in both languages without notes.

Wolfson not only maintained close ties with Jewish scholars throughout the United States, Europe, and Israel, but he also enjoyed warm friendships with many Christian theological and philosophical scholars. Father Joseph A. Davenny of the Society of Jesus, who taught philosophy at Weston College and was one of Wolfson's most intimate friends, took Wolfson for an automobile ride at least once a week so that they could "talk philosophy" and any other subject that crossed their minds.

As Wolfson's eightieth birthday approached—November 2, 1967—
he agreed that my wife and I could plan a party for him. However,
about a week before the event he announced that he had to go to
New York—in all likelihood a ruse to avoid having to face the
festivities marking the attainment of his four-score years. We
thought it useless to protest or to persist. But happily, as it turned
out, the milestone birthday was not to go unnoted. A day or two
later, Bernard and Sophie Gould called to invite us to their home
the night of Wolfson's birthday. Wolfson had agreed to be present
with a few friends, but he was insistent that there was to be "no
birthday party." Nevertheless, the Goulds requested that I "write
something" in honor of the occasion.

After dinner—which finished with a huge birthday cake, to Wolfson's obvious delight—Alexander Altmann, Lown Professor of Jewish Philosophy at Brandeis, read an ode addressed to the guest of
honor, composed in Hebrew. Professor Altmann later provided his
own translation:

> How good is Wisdom's quest
> When firmly rooted in Tradition!
> Yaphet's splendor dwelling in the Tents of Shem!
> Thou hast achieved that splendor,
> Abiding in the very midst of thy people,
> A glorious citizen of two worlds.
>
> In a lofty place of teaching
> Didst thou reveal thy powers,
> On the summit of that Har-Moriah
> Which is known as Har-Vard,
> The flower-decked mountain of learning,
> That is America's pride.
>
> Thou didst open the gates of understanding
> The hidden depths of metaphysical systems,
> And where the texts were silent
> And meaning unexpressed in words,

Thou didst unravel the secret thought—
"Even though there was no word in my tongue,
Lo, thou knowest it all"—
By the hypothetico-deductive method.

The teachings of Philo of Alexandria
Thou didst search and interpret
In their consistency and loveliness
As the beginning of the ways,
As the archetypal pattern
Of all religious philosophies,
Of the true one and those that err in faith,
Yet all one in following the path
Of Faith and Reason, Philo's footsteps in the
   sands of Time.

The words of Hasdai Crescas
Thou didst explain, illumine,
With eyes wide open, with counsel from afar,
Sifting each term, defining every concept
Of Aristotle's *Physics*,
Making it shine in the "Light of the Lord"
—Even as it lies shattered by Hasdai's critique.

With the lamp of subtle analysis
Thou didst examine the innermost chambers
Of Spinoza's rebellious mind,
And behold, Maimonides's face appeared as in a mirror,
And Crescas's and all the hosts of the pure heavens,
Substance and attributes, yet strangely twisted
By logic inexorable behind the geometrical method.
Bereft of grace, forsaking Philo,
Yet wrestling more rabbinico!

The Church Fathers too thou didst investigate,
Even as Joseph's steward searched the brethren's sacks
And found the goblet,
Yet was the wine in it of varied vintage,
Mixed of pagan myth, rabbinic lore,

Aristotelian notions.
The trinitarian dogma:
A "threefold cord"
Easily to be broken!

Like Jacob for Rachel,
Thou didst serve seven years,
Watching daily at Kalam's gates
Without calamity,
And the years of labor
Seemed unto thee but as few days
For the love thou hast for clarifying every word.

Who can count the mighty troupes of thine essays,
All perfect in scholarship,
Delightful to the ear,
Each one in shining armor,
And each a harp
Resounding with the melody of soul,
Revealing the poet behind the scholar.

Life in abundance, may it stay with thee,
Now that thou enterest into thy strength,
In wisdom ripe, with vision clear,
With childhood images undimmed.
This we pray for,
Who revere thee,
Who seek thy good and relish
The radiance of they presence,
Who have no words to thank thee
For all the gifts received.

Wolfson beamed and embraced the author of this poetic tribute. There followed toasts, stories, and reminiscences, after which I recited my offering, prompting Wolfson to break into a broad grin, punctuated by outbursts of laughter:

Four score years ago in Austryn
Zvi Hirsh ben Mendel's life did begin.

In the arms of his mother Soreh Dvereh,
He learned to face life without any *mereh.*
Shmuel Leib's *einikel* was an obvious *iluy,*
At Slobodka yeshiva, he was *generis sui,*
The youngest in years, but the first in his class,
In Talmud, no one his skill could surpass.
His talents were many, he wrote poems galore,
Drew sketches of heroes—Herzl, Montefiore—
'Til the Statue of Liberty from over the sea
Beckoned; and he came in Nineteen-o-three.

To New York he sailed to become American
With the help of Yeshiva Yitzhak Elhanan.
His self-sufficiency was a need adamantine,
Soon he was a teacher of Hebrew in Scranton.
Mornings at high school he studied with zeal,
In his lexicon no such word as "difficile."
Three years elapsed, a cynosure of all eyes,
A scholarship to Harvard, his graduation prize.
His class year was twelve; his degree was eleven,
And his three college years were his nearest to heaven;
His brilliance brought him a Sheldon award,
And all Europe's book shelves with care he explored.

Back in Cambridge, his Ph.D.
Was ticket of admission to the faculty,
Instructor in Hebrew Lit., his rank,
'Til the Army called: "We need you, Yank!"
So off to battle, off to war
Marched Harry Wolfson, bachelor;
His potato-peeling licked the Hun,
His scrubbing floors the victory won.
The world now safe for democracy,
Back to ivy halls with glee,
Then progress upward, with steady grip,
Assistant, associate, full professorship.

His teaching skill brought widespread fame,
His literary style won him acclaim,

In Jewish studies, the man of the hour,
Occupant of the chair, endowed by Littauer.
Head of Bible exegesis, he had his own thesis,
He wrote how the Jews would reclaim Rabbi Jesus,
Not as a God, nor God's prophet or son,
But Galilean sage, with sermons homespun.
For Harvard he assembled with fulsome measure,
Rare Hebrew books, a bibliophile's treasure;
And his Sunday teas brought much romance,
But not to Wolfson, not a chance!

Hypothetico-deductive, his Crescas Hasdai,
Illuminated the work called *Or Adonai,*
His critique of the *Physics* of Aristotle
Shattered clichés, stand-patism did throttle;
Historico-critical, he analyzed Spinoza,
Elliptical ethics were his *amorosa;*
He separated Baruch from his twin Benedictus,
And cleared away cobwebs of thought that afflict us;
A warehouse of learning, of scholarship a silo,
His analysis of philosophy of Alexandrian Philo,
A link in the chain back to classics of Plato's—
This was the sweep of our peeler of potatoes.

Years of study and careful research
Went into his Fathers of the Church;
He played the theme with variation
On Faith, Trinity, and Incarnation.
Priests, bishops, even the Pope,
Scrutinized his work with a microscope—
Rumor hath it that in Rome
Wolfson was offered a permanent home.
But Islam cast its potent spell,
The Kalam, the work of this infidel,
Will *imyirtzeshem* sing his philosophic song,
With footnotes often chapters long.

The psalmist's non-believing fool
In Wolfson's hand becomes the tool

To fashion sense from ideas obscure,
Write philosophy as literature.
Manifold manuscripts fill all his files,
Bundles of writings lie heaped in piles.
First into Widener, last to leave,
He drives himself without reprieve;
Tireless in his quest for truth,
He studies the text like a mystery sleuth,
But sit for a portrait? *Chas vechalilah,*
Until he succumbs to a modern Delilah.

With delicate midrashic style,
Scholar, linguist versatile,
Disdainful of ideas absurd,
Genius of the written word,
Profound in *pilpul,* razor sharp,
Lyric as King David's harp;
We admire the brain, we cherish the man,
We pray for the gift of a long life-span
To permit the children of his mind
To enrich the thought of all mankind.
Your friends bring you all their love,
They wish you their fondest *Mazel Tov,*
We ask you to accept this rhyme,
With our wishes for health, for joy, *l'chayim!*

Five more years elapsed before there was to be another birthday gala. For Wolfson's eighty-fifth birthday, in 1972, a group of friends, led by George Williams and Charles Berlin, bibliographer in Judaica at the Harvard Library, collected an endowment of $85,000 for a book fund in honor of Wolfson, who had founded the Harvard Judaica collection and served as honorary curator. The celebration took place in Widener Library, where the books assembled in Wolfson's name would repose. Professor Williams, in presenting the gift to Harvard, addressed his remarks to Wolfson: "In this effort to increase Hebraica and Judaica at the very heart of the Harvard College Library, we who are Jews and we who belong to the general community are saying, in honoring you this day, that we acknowledge the centrality of the Jewish religious, moral, and scholarly tradition in any great library dedicated to the preservation of the whole human endeavor."

The principal address on this occasion was delivered by Milton V. Anastos, professor of classics at the University of California in Los Angeles and a former colleague of Wolfson's. His tribute noted the particular aptness of the endowment:

As we look back now upon Professor Wolfson's many momentous discoveries and the library of books he has written, we realize that any single one of them would have won an international reputation for its author. Never before has there been a scholar who has taken over the entire history of philosophy as his domain and impressed his own original stamp upon the whole, treating each successive author and problem with the knowledge and acumen of the specialist. In a real sense, he is the greatest and the best. . . . It is particularly fitting that the books collected to honor him should be shelved in Widener Library which he has adorned by his presence night and day seven days a week, as the first to arrive in the morning at seven A.M., or earlier, and the last to leave at night, year after year, in countless hours of unceasing and selfless toil for sixty years. This constitutes a record of self-denial and devotion that has no equal. No Harvard man, indeed no American, has done more for the humanities than he. In these ambiguous days, when his kind of ecumenical scholarship is disappearing from the earth, and the vast panoply of esoteric languages upon which his researches are based becomes rarer and rarer, we give thanks for Professor Wolfson.

Although Wolfson was now showing signs of frailty, he virtually skipped forward from his seat to acknowledge the plaudits. Reminiscing with great wit—and precision—he recalled how specific books and collections of books in the Judaica section had been acquired.

Following ceremonies at Widener, Wolfson and some thirty friends came to our home for the evening. Harry Starr, president of the Lucius Littauer Foundation and a friend of Wolfson's for over half a century (ever since Starr's days as an undergraduate, when he had served as president of the Harvard Menorah Society), proposed a toast to the honoree, expressing the hope that he live to reach Moses' age of one hundred and twenty. The evening continued with lively conversation and much lighthearted reminiscence. Wolfson chuckled, and even exploded into laughter, at the retelling of stories concerning various incidents in his life. Later, as he was being driven home, he remarked: "This was an evening to treasure."

Parties were not the only occasions where Wolfson was able to relax with old friends. Friday nights and holidays were often spent in the company of Bernard and Sophie Gould and their family, or at the home of Harry and Beatrice (Bea) Savitz. Wolfson enjoyed the gaiety and intimacy, but above all the total Jewishness, of these households. When Mrs. Adele Ginzberg would come up from New York to visit her daughter Sophie Gould, it was warming for Wolfson to sit and chat with the widow of one of his dearest friends and her family. As for the Savitzes, Harry Savitz was not only Wolfson's first cousin but also had been his physician ever since graduating from Harvard Medical School. He had changed his middle name to Austryn when Wolfson did so, and the two Harry Austryns also shared a passion for Hebrew word games. Other friends included Rabbi Israel Kazis and his wife "Sis," Burton and Raya Dreben, Philip and Sally Lown, and my wife Selma and me. Our homes were further places of refuge for Wolfson. He basked in the domestic atmosphere and savored the home cooking. Above all, he was pleased to be in friendly surroundings where, at least for a while, he could rest from his Harvard activities of writing and research. He was particularly fond of young children and, like any doting grandfather, would check up on their schoolwork, question them about their aspirations, and help them solve problems.

One day in early 1974, Wolfson was with us at our home, from about ten in the morning until six in the evening. It was a day I shall always cherish and Wolfson's conversation still echoes—almost verbatim— in my memory.

Most of the morning, Wolfson reminisced about Lithuania and his early education, about his family, and about what had happened to them and to his fellow townspeople. He described his Uncle Yitzhak, Harry Savitz's father and Wolfson's mother's brother, as a man of great "learning and nobility" who had many of the qualities of Yitzhak's sister, Wolfson's mother. When it was decided that Wolfson would apply for admittance to the Slobodka yeshiva, it was Uncle Yitzhak who took him there. "I was very fond of Harry's father," Wolfson mused. "I wrote the epitaph for his tombstone. We prepared a lot of epitaphs, Harry and I, until I decided I didn't want to be known as a *matzevah kratzer* (gravestone scratcher)."

Did we know that a book had been published about Ostrin and other nearby towns in Lithuania and that he had helped the editors with material? He reminded us that the villages in question included Arany (Varenna), Meretz, and Radin, all places where my family hailed from, as well as Baltremantz, home of my wife's family. He also recalled that I was a great-great-nephew of the sage known as the Hofetz Hayim, and told stories about him, which in turn led to talk of other great scholars and rabbis, masters of *musar* (ethics) and *drush* (homiletics). He summoned up his high-school days in Scranton, his Harvard years, his Sheldon fellowship, the latter account replete with colorful details of his European travels, not as a tourist but (after the first few months) as a cataloguer of books. The notes he took and the copies he made during those two years stood him in good stead all of his life. Reminiscing along, he recounted his work as a consultant on Judaism for the 1947 edition of the *American College Dictionary.* He had taken basic terms like "rabbi," "Torah," "Talmud," and "synagogue," and, as he put it, had made their definitions "more nearly accurate."

Wolfson then began to discuss the origin and development of several of his books and articles, and before long Selma and I were being called upon to read aloud from his work, a request which always gave us pleasure. Spelling each other, we read selections from his *Menorah Journal* articles (Wolfson particularly liked to have me read, "with expression," the last paragraphs of "How the Jews Will Reclaim Jesus," "Escaping Judaism," and "Jewish Books at Harvard"), from his *Crescas* preface, and from *Spinoza, Philo,* and *Church Fathers.*

All through lunch the talk continued. Wolfson spoke about his hypothetico-deductive method, about the search for the words and the phrases to warrant his inferences. As he was stimulated by the hunt, so was he overjoyed by the solution, by the discovery. "Listen," he said, "do you know where this comes from?"—and he began to quote (the same passage that is also cited by Leo Schwarz in his preface to this volume)—" 'There is sleuthing in scholarship as there is in crime, and it is as full of mystery, danger, intrigue, suspense, and thrills—if only the story were told.' "

We guessed correctly. It was indeed a sentence from one of his books, from *Crescas,* from the preface.

"That wasn't a fair exam," he laughed. "You'll find those words repeated by me in one form or another in other places in my works. The sleuthing goes on. It has been particularly difficult for the Kalam. Some of the texts were incomplete, truly fragments, but the method is still sound."

The conversation took a more sober turn as Wolfson remembered departed friends whom he sorely missed: Ralph Marcus, Pearson Neaman, Leo Schwarz, Leo's classmate Wolf Winer, Rabbi Joseph Shubow, Horace Kallen, Henry Hurwitz. He also spoke of his disappointment in no longer being able to go to New York to see his brother and sister and other members of the family, as well as such old friends as Annabelle Neaman, Harry and Cecile Starr, and Peter Solomon.

Wolfson talked on, of the dead and the living. "Where can I find people who are as understanding and as devoted as those right here in Boston? Selma was the best Radcliffe student I ever had in my Sem. 9 course. Do you remember, Lew, in the middle 1920s, you formed a Menorah dramatic group? Leo Schwarz, Fay Goell, and a few others were the first performers. You put on a play by Z. Levin called *Poetry and Prose.* Fay was the prosaic housewife and Leo Huberman was the poet. But the poet turned out prosaic and had his mind on only one thing. The housewife had a poetic soul. At the end of the play there was the poet stretched out, lying on the sofa, drawing the woman to him, when the curtain fell. Do you remember what I asked you after the performance? 'What would have happened if the curtain hadn't fallen?' You answered, 'The embrace would have taken a little longer.' "

Wolfson then recalled his Sunday afternoon teas, where Selma and the other ladies of his circle had been pressed into service as hostesses. Returning to the general theme of his Boston friends, he reflected: "My closest friends have been those with happy marriages and with Jewish homes. Of course, Father Davenny and Professor Williams and most of the other faculty friends don't meet the second standard, and the Father doesn't meet either, but they've been very good to me all of these years and have given me wise counsel. My life would have been empty without them. Sophie Gould has all of the good qualities of both her parents, Louis and Adele Ginzberg. She's a true *beryeh* and very dear to me, and Bernie is a gem. My cousin Harry Savitz has no equal: it's a *mechayeh* to go to their house. Bea is like a daughter to me. Pesach and Hanukkah and breaking the fast at the end of Yom Kippur—these are the times when being in a Jewish home with my family renews my conviction that Judaism will survive, not only through books but through people."

Wolfson continued in the same vein: "My friendship of more than sixty years with Rab [Isidor Rabinovitz] has survived the obstacles of time and space. When I see him I'm renewed. But I don't see him often since he moved to Florida. . . . And then there are my dear friends at Harvard, especially George Williams and Isadore Twersky, and the members of the 'Wolfson Table.' I've been blessed with friends. I owe them much more than I can ever repay."

Regarding his public activities, Wolfson then observed: "I've cut down considerably on lectures, talks, acceptances of honors. And I'm following the advice of an old friend, a retired philosophy professor: Don't act like some of those elder statesmen who try to run the ship of state from their various drylands. Don't advise, don't preach, don't deplore. Reminisce, simply reminisce. And so, at every postprandial occasion, I reminisce."

By now the sun had set and we turned on the lights. Wolfson suddenly became silent. We suggested that he stay for dinner and that we then bring him back to Cambridge. "No, no. I have work on those galleys." He sat still for a moment, and then, in an urgent tone, said: "Selma and Lew, listen. I've made three mistakes in my life. I should have married early. I should have written my works in Hebrew, or a least published one article a year in Hebrew. And I've spent too much time on the Kalam. It's my Vietnam. I could have finished all the dozen works in my series and now it looks as though I won't even finish my Halevi and Maimonides."

We protested as best we could and for a moment or so he seemed to regain his cheerful self. But again he declined to stay for dinner and throughout the drive home he remained silent. As he got out of the car, his only words were, "Thank you, call me soon."

During the 1970s, problems of everyday living came to the fore. Wolfson's mandatory move from his residence in the Ambassador Hotel to 20 Prescott Street was like jumping from the frying pan into the fire. The new apartment was tiny; with more than two persons in the room it became crowded. A search for a new apartment by the "Wolfson Ladies' Aid Society"—Sophie Gould, Bea Savitz, "Sis" Kazis, Raya Dreben, and Selma Weinstein—resulted in countless inspections and consultations but turned up no suitable alternative. There was at least one advantage to 20 Prescott: living there meant crossing only two short, quiet streets to get to the Harvard Library, and only one street to the Faculty Club. This was no small consideration. In his last years Wolfson required the help of a cane for walking and for that reason sought, wherever possible, to avoid crossing in heavy traffic. From Prescott Street he could walk to his two prime destinations with relative ease, and there he remained for as long as he could.

In 1971 Professor Ephraim Isaac, then of Harvard's Department of Afro-American Studies, had suggested that Wolfson settle in Adams House, one of the Harvard residences developed under former President Abbott Lowell. Wolfson was willing, the Adams residents were agreeable, the house master delighted. However, it turned out that Wolfson, as a retired professor, did not fall within the definition of permissible house residents. Wolfson's plight spurred the Harvard Faculty of Arts and Sciences to consider the particular problem, and in due course a special committee issued a report. Although the committee recommended that "some flexibility and variety should be given the Houses to use what resources they have to exploit the immense reservoir of gifted talent that *Emeriti* . . . can provide," it also noted that, for one reason or another, the Harvard houses were not quite satisfactory as residences for retirees. At any rate, for all the concern, there was little that Harvard was ready to do about Wolfson's housing problem.

Changes in the culinary geography of Harvard Square caused additional difficulties for Wolfson. Many of the old restaurants that he had frequented were gone; new eating places were not open on Sundays, when the Faculty Club was also closed. Fortunately, he acquired the assistance of several graduate students and friends who volunteered to help prepare meals, perform minor household duties, even sleep over when necessary. Joel Isaac Braude, a doctoral candidate at Harvard whose father, Rabbi William G. Braude of Providence, had once been a student of Wolfson's, was particularly devoted and frequently acted as cook, chauffeur, valet, messenger, and sounding board.

In April 1972 Wolfson developed a cataract in his left eye; he was unable to read or find his way about. Harry Savitz brought him, almost in a panic, to Dr. Sumner Liebman, an ophthalmologist who calmed Wolfson down and told him that his impaired vision was only a temporary matter. The cataract was removed and Wolfson went into a convalescent home to recuperate. Before long his vision was pronounced excellent. A few months later Wolfson again appeared in Dr. Liebman's office complaining that he could not see. Vision was restored when Dr. Liebman discovered that his patient had been using his long-distance glasses for reading and his reading glasses for distance.

Wolfson's general health now began to deteriorate. He found it progressively difficult and painful to walk, even with the aid of a cane. The problem was diagnosed as a form of arthritis but the prescribed treatment afforded little relief. Even more serious was the increasing discomfort he began to experience in the gastrointestinal tract. He was constantly tired. He continued to work, of course, but his fatigue was evident. Moreover, he was anxious about the possibility of a fall with resultant disabling injuries (his previous falls had left a few scratches but no wounds). He was also worried, if not actually frightened, at being left alone at night when he might not be able to reach the telephone in time to call for help. It had been his practice, when an emergency arose, to call Harry Savitz. Savitz's own illnesses, however, now made it impossible for him to respond to a middle-of-the-night emergency, and Isadore Twersky assumed the particular duty.

It became obvious that Wolfson would have to go into a nursing home. He visited several in Cambridge but they all seemed unsuitable. He finally settled upon the Hebrew Rehabilitation Center for the Aged in Roslindale, familiarly known as the Rehab Center, whose warm and comfortable atmosphere proved to his liking. (Harry Savitz had once served as the Center's medical director and was now director emeritus.) Savitz and I were to arrange for the application and the move. As the application was proceeding through channels, Wolfson, with Father Davenny at the wheel, clocked the odometer from Widener to the Rehab Center to determine distance and time, for Wolfson declared that he expected to go to Widener every day except possibly Saturday or Sunday, have lunch at the Faculty Club, and return to the Center.

However, Wolfson's admission to the Rehab Center was delayed for several months because of his poor health. He began to experience increased pain and the diagnosis disclosed that, in addition to anemia and intestinal obstructions, he suffered from a spreading malignancy that necessitated the removal of portions of his intestines. An earlier report of the Harvard Health Services had revealed Wolfson to be suffering from congestive heart failure "associated with streptococcal cellulitis of his left leg." Because of internal bleeding, Wolfson was brought to Peter Bent Brigham Hospital. Dr. John Brooks performed surgery, but while he excised a great deal of the malignancy, it could not all be removed. Chemotherapy was prescribed. Wolfson remained serene throughout the ordeal.

On April 25, 1974, Wolfson was at last able to come to the Center. He was brought there by his graduate-student friend Joel Braude, and they were joined by Harry Savitz. After arranging for the payment of his bills, Wolfson told Susan Roberts, a social worker, that he knew he would like the Center very much. He was pleased with his private room and took special delight in his desk. He announced that he would not be spending too much time at the Center, since he expected to resume work in his study at Widener as soon as he felt physically stronger. When Wolfson was left alone with Savitz he remarked: "This is the last station"—the shouted call of the train man, long familiar to them both, as the subway cars pulled into Harvard Square from Boston. Savitz assured Wolfson that he would undoubtedly outlive most of the residents at the Center.

Wolfson soon made friends. We introduced him to a fellow-resident, Samuel Maude, my wife's uncle, a man in his nineties. Maude's education had been limited, but he was bright and sharp, and he immediately undertook to help Wolfson become adjusted. Maude would present himself at Wolfson's room before meals, and arm in arm they would go down to the dining room, where Wolfson, who had always been a severe critic of food, found the cooking to his satisfaction. Maude, who laughed at Wolfson's jokes, was impressed by his friend's intellect and learning, and Wolfson appreciated Maude's common sense and devotion.

For all his resolve, Wolfson was able to negotiate the trip to Widener only a very few times. He always hurried back to the Center. The nurses and the staff adored him, and his room was often filled with students, colleagues, and friends. He worked every day on his galleys and manuscripts and carried on far-flung communications by telephone and letter. His condition, however, continued to grow weaker. Once, during one of Harry Savitz's visits, Wolfson asked him, in Hebrew: "Harry, what's the most important verse in the Bible?" Savitz, echoing Rabbi Hillel, promptly replied, also in Hebrew: " 'Love your neighbor as yourself,' Leviticus, chapter 19, verse 18." "No," said Wolfson. " 'It is not good for man to be alone,' Genesis, chapter 2, verse 18." Savitz bantered, "Since it's between Hillel and Wolfson, I'll take Wolfson."

On September 9, 1974, I paid a visit to Wolfson at the Center. Selma and I were to leave for Europe the next day, and I had come to say goodbye. I did not know that this was to be our last time together. Wolfson was resting in bed from an extended stint at his desk. He had slipped down far under the cover and asked me to move him up toward the headpost. I was shocked at how little he weighed. He was extremely tired but mentally as alert as ever. He said to me: "We'll get you a job as a male nurse. Special lesson: It usually takes three steps for me to get from bed to desk. To get that down to two steps, just turn the desk chair slightly to the left. That should save a third of the time in and out of the desk chair. In a month that should be enough time to write an article for a *Festschrift* or a letter answering a critic."

He praised the Center and the doctors who visited him. He was particularly grateful to Mary Handlin, his devoted nurse. He spoke of unfinished business: "The *Kalam* is practically done. The indexes are moving along. My nurse has warned me that I ought not to have so many visitors. I told her it was better to be adored than ignored." I told him that our trip would be brief and that I would look in on him immediately upon our return. *"Nesiah tovah.* Have a good trip," he proferred in Hebrew. I wished him *refuah shlemah,* a complete recovery. He put out his arms, we embraced, and I took my leave.

When Harry Savitz visited later that same day, Wolfson said to him: "I've been carrying my *Kalam* as a heavy burden. I'm like a pregnant woman whose child is overdue. When the child is finally delivered, the mother, exhausted by her labors, dies. I know that I have very little time left. I'm not being morbid, just realistic." Protestations were of no avail.

On September 10, following a severe drop in weight and extreme pain, Wolfson entered Harvard's Stillman Infirmary. The doctors discovered that his cancer had spread further and blood was emanating from his gastrointestinal tract. To their distress, they realized that nothing could be done to save him. Wolfson's life was drawing to a close.

While still at the Rehab Center he had signed a "living will" requesting that "no extraordinary treatment be administered" that would needlessly prolong the inevitable course of his death. His wishes were respected. On September 17, from his hospital bed, Wolfson signed another "living will," prepared for him by his old friend George Williams and witnessed by Williams and Joel Braude:

To my relations, friends, colleagues, and my lawyer,

To my several friendly and caring physicians, who have ministered to me faithfully,

To all also who may in the future have responsibility for me in my frailty,

I NOW, of sound mind, still thinking through aspects of my academic tasks, preparing for the second volume of my collected works, and awaiting the publication of the Kalam,

HOLDING that death is a part of life and wishing to maintain its dignity to the end,

DO HEREBY, with witnesses testifying thereto,

DECLARE it to be my desire

THAT the vitalities of my mind and body be allowed to run their natural course

WITHOUT the interposition of any extraordinary means that would interrupt the ebb.

AND IF toward the end, when there is absolutely no possibility of medically reversing the natural processes set in motion by aging or disease,

AND if the pain should ever become manifestly unbearable,

I SOLEMNLY REQUEST THAT those in attendance consider it my well deliberated wish

THAT they administer such medicine as will best relieve me in that time of suffering,

EVEN if that same medicine might also have the indirect consequence of shortening the process of my departure from you.

ALL of you who have loved and admired me and thought well of my life's work,

ALL of you who, as doctors or nurses, dedicated your lives to the healing skills

WILL, I trust, be the most resolute in carrying out my final wishes,

To the formulation of which I hereby affix my signature.

Two days later, on Thursday, September 19, 1974, at several minutes past 10 o'clock in the evening, with his closest friends and relatives nearby, Harry Austryn Wolfson breathed his last. With the Sabbath approaching, the funeral was delayed until Sunday. The crowded services were conducted by Isadore Twersky and Israel Kazis, both graduates of the Hebrew College of Boston which Wolfson had helped found, as well as graduates of Harvard College and holders of Ph.D. degrees from Harvard obtained under Wolfson's guidance. For Wolfson of Harvard it was a fitting farewell.

The next day Harry Wolfson was laid to rest in the Mount Zion Cemetery in Maspeth, Long Island, in the plot reserved for "Ostriner," alongside his parents. On the following June 22, a monument erected to his memory was unveiled. Inscribed on the stone are words from the citation of the honorary degree confered on him by Harvard in 1956: "From enormous knowledge he illumines the major problems of religious philosophy." There is also a Hebrew verse, with English translation, composed by Harry Savitz: "Preeminent scholar of his generation,/Students flocked to him for inspiration."

Wolfson's will, dated May 4, 1973, left to Harvard his "collection of books of medieval Jewish philosophy, together with books of Arabic philosophy and other philosophic books related to them (all of which I have kept together and listed in a brief card catalogue), such books to be kept together as a collection of Jewish philosophy and not to be dispersed among other collections." After making bequests to his brother Nathaniel and his sister Bessie and to eight other close relatives, he left the residue of his entire estate to Harvard, the income and principal to be used "in the discretion of the then Littauer Professor of Hebrew Literature and Philosophy." Wolfson's legacy to scholarship is of course incalculable.

In a memorial tribute to Wolfson, Bernard Gould observed: "Harvard was his home, the study in Widener his sanctuary, Harvard Square . . . his domain." It was therefore only proper that when, in the fall of 1975, Harvard announced a program with a goal of $15 million to establish a Center of Jewish Studies, the announcement spoke of the proposed Center as "fitting recognition of Harry Wolfson's unequaled scholarly achievements." As Harvard President Derek C. Bok noted: "At Harvard we have a special tradition to uphold in Jewish studies—the tradition exemplified by the teaching and scholarship of the late Harry Wolfson."

Exhibit of honorary degree hoods received by Harry A. Wolfson, along with 1965 photographs by Irene Shwachman, on the occasion of a memorial service in his honor at Boston Hebrew College, 15 December 1974

Bibliography

The Principal Writings of Harry A. Wolfson
(From 1912 through January 1963)
Prepared by Leo W. Schwarz

I wish to record my gratitude to E. R. Malachi of New York and Dr. Eisig Silberschlag of Boston for their help in locating several of the references in the early Hebrew periodicals, to Arthur Mark Wolman of Boston for checking a newspaper reference in the cellar of the Boston Public Library, and to Dr. Abraham Berger and his staff in the Jewish Room of the New York Public Library for many courtesies. —L. W. S.

1912

Bibliography of C. H. Toy, *Studies in the History of Religions Presented to C. H. Toy.* New York, 1912, pp. 367–73.

"Maimonides and Halevi: A Study in Typical Attitudes towards Greek Philosophy in the Middle Ages." *Jewish Quarterly Review*, n. s. 2 (1912):-297–339.

1915

"Jewish Students in European Universities." *Menorah Journal* 1, 1 (January 1915):26–32; 1,2 (April 1915):106–10.

"The Arch of Titus." *Menorah Journal* 1, 4 (October 1915):201. Poem translated from the Hebrew by H. M. Kallen. Reprinted in *The Standard Book of Jewish Verse,* edited by J. Friedlander and G. A. Kohut, pp. 153–54, 517, 539 (New York: Dodd, Mead, 1917). Also reprinted in the *Anthology of Jewish Poetry,* edited by Philip Raskin, pp. 179–81 (New York: Behrman's Jewish Book Shop, 1927).

1916

"Crescas on the Problem of Divine Attributes." *Jewish Quarterly Review,* n. s. 72 (1916):1–44, 175–221.

Review of *Jewish Mysticism* by J. Abelson. *Harvard Theological Review* 9 (1916):332–34.

1918

"Pomegranates." *Menorah Journal,* 1st ser. 4, 1 (February 1918):-16–26; 2d ser. 4, 3 (June 1918): 162–70. Pseud. "El. Lycidas."

1919

"Note on Crescas' Definition of Time." *Jewish Quarterly Review,* n. s. 10 (1919):1–17.

1921

"Spinoza's Definition of Substance and Mode." *Chronicon Spinozanum* 1 (1921):101–2.

"The Needs of Jewish Scholarship in America." *Menorah Journal* 7, 1 (February 1921):28–35.

"Dr. H. A. Wolfson Considers the Jewish Problem." *Harvard Crimson,* 3 May 1921, p. 2.

"Escaping Judaism." *Menorah Journal* 7, 2 (June 1921):71–83; 7, 3 (August 1921):155–68. Reprinted as a Menorah Pamphlet, no. 2, 54 pp. (New York: Menorah Press, 1923).

1922

"Spinoza on the Unity of Substance." *Chronicon Spinozanum* 2 (1922):92–117.

1923

"Spinoza on the Simplicity of Substance." *Chronicon Spinozanum* 3 (1923):142–78.

Review of Hilaire Belloc's *The Jews,* under the heading "A Roman Catholic Talks about the Jews." *Harvard Crimson,* 23 March 1923, pp. 4, 5.

1924

"Notes on the Proofs of the Existence of God in Jewish Philosophy." *Hebrew Union College Annual* 1 (1924):575–96.

Comment on *The Old Testament: A New Translation* by James Moffatt. *Boston Sunday Post,* 14 December 1924, p. 3.

1925

"How the Jews Will Reclaim Jesus." Introductory Essay in *Jesus as Others Saw Him,* by Joseph Jacobs, 2d ed. New York: Bernard G. Richards, 1925. Revised and reprinted in the *Menorah Journal* 49, 1, 2 (Autumn–Winter 1962):25–31.

Review of *Spinoza* by Leon Roth. *Philosophical Review* 34 (1925):-303–6.

"The Classification of Sciences in Mediaeval Jewish Philosophy." *Hebrew Union College Jubilee Volume,* 1925, pp. 263–315.

1926

"Spinoza on the Infinity of the Corporeal Substance." *Chronicum Spinozanum* 4 (1926):79–103.

"Towards an Accurate Understanding of Spinoza." *Journal of Philosophy* 23 (1926):268–73.

Letter in *Twenty-Fifth Anniversary of the Jewish Encyclopedia.* New York and London, 1926, p. 9.

"The Problem of the Origin of Matter in Mediaeval Jewish Philosophy and Its Analogy to the Modern Problem of the Origin of Life." *Proceedings of the Sixth International Congress of Philosophy,* 1926, pp. 603–8.

"Additional Notes to the Classification of Sciences." *Hebrew Union College Annual* 3 (1926):371–75.

1927

"Solomon Pappenheim on Time and Space and His Relation to Locke and Kant." *Israel Abrahams Memorial Volume,* 1927, pp. 426–40.

1929

Crescas' Critique of Aristotle: Problems of Aristotle's Physics *in Jewish and Arabic Philosophy.* Harvard Semitic Series, Vol. 6. Cambridge, Mass.: Harvard University Press, 1929.

"Isaac Ibn Shem-Tob's Unknown Commentaries on Aristotle's *Physics* and His Other Unknown Works." *Freidus Memorial Volume,* 1929, pp. 279–90.

1931

Plan for the Publication of a *Corpus Commentariorum Averrois in Aristotelem. Speculum* 6 (1931):412–27. Thoroughly revised in *Speculum* 38,1 (January, 1963):88–104.

1932

"Hebrew Books in Harvard." *Harvard Alumni Bulletin* (29 April 1932). Reprinted in *The Brandeis Avukah Annual* of 1932, edited by J.S. Shubow, pp. 651–64, and translated into Hebrew by Noah Stern in הספר העברי בין העמים. גליונות, תל־אביב 4, 7–8(1436):77–84.

1933

"Spinoza e le Prove dell' Esistenza di Dio, *Richerche Religiose."* 9 (1933):193–236.

1934

"Studies in Crescas." *Proceedings of the American Academy for Jewish Research* 5 (1934):155–75.

The Philosophy of Spinoza: Unfolding the Latent Processes of His Reasoning, 2 vols. Cambridge, Mass.: Harvard University Press, 1934. One volume ed. 1948. Also paperback edition in one volume, New York: Meridian Books, 1958. The Index of References is omitted.

Judah Monis, *Dictionary of American Biography.* Vol. 13, pp. 86–87. New York: Scribner, 1934.

1935

Letter, *New Republic* 81, 1051 (23 Jan. 1935):306–7.

"The Internal Senses in Latin, Arabic, and Hebrew Philosophic Texts." *Harvard Theological Review* 28 (1935):69–133.

"Maimonides on the Internal Senses," *Jewish Quarterly Review*, n.s., 25 (1935):441–67.

Addendum to "The Internal Senses in Latin, Arabic, and Philosophic Texts." *Jewish Quarterly Review*, n.s. 26 (1935):97.

"Isaac Israeli on the Internal Senses." *Jewish Studies in Memory of George Alexander Kohut*, 1935, pp. 583–98.

"Stephen Sewall." *Dictionary of American Biography*, vol. 16, p. 612. New York: Scribner, 1935.

1936

Note on Maimonides' Classification of the Sciences, *Jewish Quarterly Review*, n.s. 26 (1936), 369–77.

עדותו של קלמנס מאלכסנדריה על מנהג בלתי ידוע בעבודת יום הכפורים בבית המקדש. New York, 3 (1935), 90–92. Published first in different form in R.P. Casey's edition of *The Excerpta ex Theodoto of Clement of Alexandria*, 1934, 122–24.

1937

"Some Guiding Principles in Determining Spinoza's Mediaeval Sources." *Jewish Quarterly Review*, n.s. 27 (1937):333–48.

"Spinoza's Mechanism, Attributes, and Panpsychism." *The Philosophical Review* 41 (1937):307–14.

1938

"The Aristotelian Predictables and Maimonides' Division of Attributes." *Essays and Studies in Memory of Linda R. Miller*, 1938, pp. 201–34.

"The Amphibolous Terms in Aristotle, Arabic Philosophy, and Maimonides." *Harvard Theological Review* 31 (1938):151–73.

1940

"A Case Study in Philosophic Research and Spinoza." *The New Scholasticism* 14 (1940):268–94.

Review of Madaleine Frances's *Spinoza dans les pays Neerlandais de la seconde moitié du* xviie *Siècle. The Philosophical Review* 49 (1940): 466–67.

"The Kosher Code." Review together with Frederic T. Lewis. *Science* 92 (1940):173–75.

1941

"Goichon's Three Books on Avicenna's Philosophy." *The Moslem World* 31 (1941):29–38.

"Halevi and Maimonides on Design, Chance, and Necessity." *Proceedings of the American Academy for Jewish Research* 11 (1941):105–63.

1942

"Philo on Free Will." *Harvard Theological Review* 35 (1942):345–70; 33 (1942):49–82.

"The Double-Faith Theory in Clement, Saadia, Averroes, and St. Thomas, and Its Origin in Aristotle and the Stoics." *Jewish Quarterly Review*, n.s. 32 (1942):213–64.

"Halevi and Maimonides on Prophecy." *Jewish Quarterly Review*, n.s., 32 (1942):345–70; 33 (1942), 49–82.

"The Platonic, Aristotelian, and Stoic Theories of Creation in Halevi and Maimonides." *Essays in Honour of the Very Rev. Dr. J.H. Hertz, Chief Rabbi of Great Britain*, 1942, pp. 427–42.

1943

"The Terms Tasawwur and Tasdīq in Arabic Philosophy and Their Greek, Latin, and Hebrew Equivalents." *The Moslem World* 33 (1943):-114–28.

"The Kalam Arguments for Creation in Saadia, Averroes, and St. Thomas." *The Saadia Anniversary Volume of the American Academy for Jewish Research*, 1943, pp. 197–245.

1944

"Philo on Jewish Citizenship in Alexandria." *Journal of Biblical Literature* 63 (1944):165–68.

1945

"Maimonides on Negative Attributes," *Louis Ginzberg Jubilee Volume*, 1945, pp. 411–46.

"Colcodea," *Jewish Quarterly Review*, n.s. 36 (1945):179–82.

1946

"Synedrion in Greek Jewish Literature and Philo." *Jewish Quarterly Review*, n.s. 36 (1946):303–6.

"The Kalam Problem of Nonexistence and Saadia's Second Theory of Creation." *Jewish Quarterly Review*, n.s. 36 (1946):371–91.

"Notes on Proverbs 22:10 and Psalms of Solomon 17:48." *Jewish Quarterly Review*, n.s. 37 (1946):87.

"Atomism in Saadia." *Jewish Quarterly Review*, n.s. 37 (1946): 107–24.

"Our Survival in the Modern World," *Hebrew Union College Monthly* 34 (1946):11, 20–21.

1947

"Arabic and Hebrew Terms for Matter and Element with Especial Reference to Saadia." *Jewish Quarterly Review*, n.s. 38 (1947):47–61.

"On the Septuagint Use of *TO HAGION* for the Temple," *Jewish Quarterly Review*, n.s. 38 (1947):109–10.

"Causality and Freedom in Descartes, Leibnitz, and Hume." *Freedom and Experience: Essays Presented to H.M. Kallen*, 1947, pp. 97–114.

"Infinite and Privative Judgments in Aristotle, Averroes, and Kant." *Philosophy and Phenomenological Research* 8 (1947):173–87.

"The Knowability and Describability of God in Plato and Aristotle." *Harvard Studies in Classical Philology*, 56–57 (1947):233–49.

Philo: Foundations of Religious Philosophy in Judaism, Christianity, and Islam, 2 vols. Cambridge, Mass.: Harvard University Press, 1947. Chapter "What is New in Philo" translated into Spanish, *Davar*, 17 (1948):7–24, and into Yiddish, *Davke* 7, 27–28 (1956):144–58.

1948

"'Unsur and Te'ālāh." *Jewish Quarterly Review*, n.s. 38 (1948): 481–82.

"The Meaning of *Ex Nihilo* in the Church Fathers, Arabic and Hebrew Philosophy, and St. Thomas." *Mediaeval Studies in Honor of Jeremiah Denis Matthias Ford*, 1948, pp. 355–67.

1950

Spinoza and Religion. Issued by the New School for Social Research, New York, 1950, 26 pp. Reprinted in the *Menorah Journal*, 38, 2 (Autumn 1950):146–67. Translated into Spanish, *Davar* 45 (1953):32–59.

"The Veracity of Scripture in Philo, Halevi, Maimonides, and

Spinoza." *Alexander Marx Jubilee Volume*, 1950, pp. 603–30. Translated into Yiddish, *Davke* 6, 22–23 (1955):2–26.

1951

"Averroes' Lost Treatise on the Prime Mover." *Hebrew Union College Annual* 23, 1 (1950–51), 683–710.

"Clement of Alexandria on the Generation of the Logos." *Church History*, 20 (1951):72–81.

1952

"Albinus and Plotinus on Divine Attributes." *Harvard Theological Review* 45 (1952):115–30.

1953

"Maimonides and Gersonides on Divine Attributes as Ambiguous Terms." *Mordecai M. Kaplan Jubilee Volume*, 1953, pp. 515–30.

אצילות ויש מאין אצל קרשקש, ס' אסף.   Jerusalem, 1953, pp. 230–36.

1954–1955

"Morning Chapel Talk." *Harvard Divinity School Bulletin* 20 (1954–55):69–70.

1955–1956

"Reply by Professor Harry A. Wolfson" (to an address of Professor George H. Williams on "The Place of Professor Wolfson's Philosophy of the Fathers"). *Harvard Divinity School Bulletin* 21 (1955–56), 95–100.

1956

"The Meaning of Interfaith." *Congress Weekly* 23, 11 (12 March 1956):7, 8.

The Philosophy of the Church Fathers, vol. 1: "Faith, Trinity, Incarnation." Cambridge, Mass.: Harvard University Press, 1956.

"Notes on 'An Old Russian Treatise on the Divine and Human Word.' " *St. Vladimir's Seminary Quarterly* (1956):49–50.

"The Muslim Attributes and the Christian Trinity." *Harvard Theological Review* 49 (1956):1–18.

"Avicenna, Algazali, and Averroes on Divine Attributes." *Homenaje a Millás-Vallicrosa*, vol. 2, 1956, pp. 545–71.

"Immortality and Resurrection in the Philosophy of the Church Fathers." *Harvard Divinity School Bulletin* 22 (1956–57):5–40.

1957

"Philosophical Implications of the Theology of Cyril of Jerusalem." *Dumbarton Oaks Papers* 11 (1957):1–19.

"Negative Attributes in the Church Fathers and the Gnostic Basilades." *Harvard Theological Review* 50 (1957):145–56. Also in *Ricerche di Storia Religiosa*, Studi in onere di Giorgio La Piana 1 (1957):269–78.

1958

"Philosophical Implications of Arianism and Apollinarianism." *Dumbarton Oaks Papers* 12 (1958):5–28.

"The Plurality of Immovable Movers in Aristotle and Averroes." *Harvard Studies in Classical Philology* (volume dedicated to Professor Jaeger in honor of his seventieth birthday) 63 (1958):233–53.

"Logos." *A Handbook of Christian Theology*, pp. 214–16. New York: Meridian Books, 1958.

1959

"Philosophical Implications of the Problem of Divine Attributes in the Kalam." *Journal of the American Oriental Society* 79 (1959):73–80.

"Philosophical Implications of the Pelagian Controversy." *Proceedings of the American Philosophical Society* 103, 4 (August 1959):554–62.

"St. Thomas on Divine Attributes." *Mélanges Offerts à Etienne Gilson.* Paris, 1959, pp. 673–700.

"Ibn Khaldūn on Attributes and Predestination." *Speculum* 34 (1959):585–96.

"The Meaning of *Ex Nihilo* in Isaac Israeli." *Jewish Quarterly Review*, n. s. 50 (1959):1–12.

A sermon based on Psalm 14:1 under the title "A Fool Hath Said," delivered in Appleton Chapel, Harvard University on 17 March 1955 and printed in *Jewish Affairs* (Johannesburg) 14, 4 (April 1959):42–43.

1960

"The Philonic God of Revelation and His Latter-Day Deniers." *Harvard Theological Review* 53 (1960):101–24.

"The Preexistent Angel of the Magharians and Al-Nahāwandī." *Jewish Quarterly Review*, n.s. 51 (1960):89–106.

"An Unknown Splinter Group of Nestorians," *Revue des Etudes Augustiniennes* (Paris) 6 (1960):249–53.

"Bible Teaching About Nations." *The Churchman* 174, 6 (June 1960):12.

"The Terms Muḥdatti and Hadatti as Applied to the Koran." *The Joshua Bloch Memorial Volume*, 1960, pp. 92–100.

1961

"Extradeical and Intradeical Interpretations of Platonic Ideas." *Journal of the History of Ideas* 22, 1 (1961):3–32.

"Notes on Isaac Israeli's Internal Senses." *Jewish Quarterly Review*, n.s. 51 (1961):275–87.

"The Twice Revealed Averroes." *Speculum* 36, 3 (July 1961):373–92.

Religious Philosophy: A Group of Essays. Cambridge, Mass.: Harvard University Press, 1961. Paperback edition, New York: Atheneum, 1965.

1962

"Saadia on the Trinity and Incarnation." *Studies and Essays in Honor of Abraham A. Neuman*, 1962, pp. 547–68.

"An Unknown Pseudo-Democritean Fragment and the Muslim Unextended Atoms." *Festgabe für Eric Voegelin*, 1962, pp. 591–606.

"The Problem of the Souls of the Spheres from the Byzantine Commentaries on Aristotle through the Arabs and St. Thomas to Kepler." *The Dumbarton Oaks Papers* 16 (1962):67–93.

1963

"Was There a Hebrew Translation from the Arabic of Averroes' *Long De Anima?*" *Speculum* 38, 1 (January 1963):98–100.

"The Identity of the Hebrew Translator from the Latin of Averroes' *Long De Anima.*" *Speculum* 38, 1 (January 1963):100–4.

Books Published since 1963

Studies in the History of Philosophy and Religion, vol. 1. Isadore Twersky and George H. Williams, eds. Cambridge, Mass.: Harvard University Press, 1973.

The Philosophy of the Kalam. Cambridge, Mass.: Harvard University Press, 1976.

Studies in the History of Philosophy and Religion, vol. 2. Isadore Twersky, ed. Cambridge, Mass.: Harvard University Press, 1977.

From Philo to Spinoza: Two Studies in Religious Philosophy. Paperback. New York, N.Y.: Behrman House, 1977.

Kalam Repercussions in Jewish Philosophy. Cambridge, Mass.: Harvard University Press, forthcoming.

Index